Theological and Halakhic Reflections on the Holocaust

edited by

Bernhard H. Rosenberg

co-edited by

Fred Heuman

Ktav Publishing House, Inc.
Hoboken, NJ

Rabbinical Council of America
New York, NY

5752/1992

UNIVERSITY OF WINCHESTER
LIBRARY

Copyright © 1992
Rabbinical Council of America

Library of Congress Cataloging-in-Publication Data

Theological and halakhic reflections on the Holocaust / edited by
Bernhard H. Rosenberg, co-edited by Fred Heuman.
    p.   cm.
  ISBN 0-88125-375-8
  1. Holocaust (Jewish theology) 2. Holocaust, Jewish (1939-1945)-
-Infuence. I. Rosenberg, Bernhard H.   II. Heuman, Fred S.
BM645.H6T44 1991
296.3'11--dc20   90-28304
                                                          CIP

Manufactured in the United States of America

Table of Contents

Some Lessons

Survivors Recall

The Sephardic Experience

Resource Materials

Acknowledgement

*This book was made possible
through the generous donation of*
Riverside
Memorial Chapel

David A. Alpert,
Senior Vice Pres. for Public Relations

Preface

Every Rabbinical Council of America administration for the past several years has appointed a Holocaust Committee. More often than not the Holocaust Committee contented itself with urging members of the Rabbinical Council to observe Yom ha-Shoah, and sometimes it produced program materials for such observances. It is to the credit of the Holocaust Committee of the present administration that it undertook the major task of producing a volume on the Holocaust.

It is interesting to note that the Holocaust was almost ignored for the first two decades after World War II. The task of rescuing the survivors and rebuilding their lives had to take precedence over reflecting on the tragedy. Perhaps also the enormity of the tragedy prevented serious study of what had happened. In the course of time, however, the Holocaust has become an important area of study, for it is one of the watershed events of Jewish history of the twentieth century. In recent years there has even been an urgency about remembering the Holocaust, since the generation of survivors is passing from the scene.

Hopefully this volume will represent an important contribution to Hololcaust studies. It brings together for the first time some of the sermons that members of the Rabbinical Council of America preached during and after World War II in which they referred to the Holocaust. It also includes reflections by members of the Rabbinical Council of America who served those liberated in the concentration camps and worked with the survivors. In addition, some of our survivor members, or members who are children of survivors, lend us their insights, and valuable bibliographical and program material is presented in order to stimulate Yom ha-Shoah programming. Finally, this volume includes more recent material by veitchik, the preeminent scholar of our generation, and Rabbi Dr. Norman Lamm, the distinguished President of Yeshiva University.

The entire project was conceived by the Chairman of the Holocaust Committee, Rabbi Bernhard H. Rosenberg. He was ably assisted by a committee that included, among others, Rabbis Fred Heuman, Bertram Leff, and Binyamin Walfish. We are grateful to them for their diligent efforts in seeing this important volume to its publication.

Rabbi Milton H. Polin, President
Rabbinical Council of America

In Memoriam

Rabbi Ephraim Zimand

אָבִינוּ מַלְכֵּנוּ אֵל אֱלֹהֵי הָרוּחוֹת לְכָל בָּשָׂר, תֵּן מְנוּחָה נְכוֹנָה עַל כַּנְפֵי הַשְּׁכִינָה.
בְּמַעֲלוֹת קְדוֹשִׁים וּטְהוֹרִים כְּזֹהַר הָרָקִיעַ מַזְהִירִים אֶת נִשְׁמוֹתֵיהֶם שֶׁל שֵׁשׁ מֵאוֹת
רִבְבוֹת אַלְפֵי יִשְׂרָאֵל, אֲנָשִׁים וְנָשִׁים יְלָדִים וִילָדוֹת, שֶׁנֶּהֶרְגוּ וְשֶׁנִּשְׂרְפוּ וְשֶׁנִּטְבְּחוּ
וְשֶׁנֶּחְנְקוּ חַיִּים בִּידֵי מִפְלְצוֹת הַצוֹרְרִים בְּגָלוּת אֵירוֹפָּה. כֻּלָּם קְדוֹשִׁים טְהוֹרִים,
בָּהֶם גְּאוֹנִים וְצַדִּיקִים, אַרְזֵי הַלְּבָנוֹן וְאַדִּירֵי הַתּוֹרָה. בְּגַן עֵדֶן תְּהֵא מְנוּחָתָם, בַּעַל
הָרַחֲמִים יִצְרֹר בִּצְרוֹר הַחַיִּים אֶת נִשְׁמָתָם, יְיָ הוּא נַחֲלָתָם, וְיִזְכֹּר לָנוּ עֲקֵדָתָם,
וְתַעֲמֹד לָנוּ וּלְכָל יִשְׂרָאֵל זְכוּתָם, אֶרֶץ אַל תְּכַסִּי דָמָם וְאַל יְהִי מָקוֹם לְזַעֲקָתָם
בִּזְכוּתָם נִדְחֵי יִשְׂרָאֵל יָשׁוּבוּ לַאֲחֻזָתָם, וְהַקְּדוֹשִׁים לְזִכָּרוֹן תָּמִיד נֶגֶד עֵינֶיךָ צִדְקָתָם,
יָבוֹאוּ שָׁלוֹם וְיָנוּחוּ עַל מִשְׁכְּבוֹתָם וְנֹאמַר אָמֵן.

Our Father, Our King: Lord of the souls of all flesh.

Grant perfect rest unto the six million souls of all the martyred children of Israel who gave their lives for the sanctification of Thy Name, the men, women and children who were brutally and tortuously murdered by the legions of oppressors and tormentors in the European Holocaust. They were holy and pure; amongst them were great men in scholarship and piety, veritable giants of Torah and saintliness.

Master of Compassion! May they find quietude and repose under the wings of Thy Divine Presence in Paradise, amongst the holy and pure who shine as the brightness of the Heavenly Spheres. Bind their souls with eternal life, with Thee as their eternal heritage. May the merit of their martyrdom be a source of strength and inspiration to us. Let the earth not cover their blood and cries!

May the merit of their great sacrifice intercede in behalf of all the

xi

scattered and oppressed of Israel, that they may be enabled to return to the lamd of ancestors. As for the martyrs, may their righteousnes ever be before Thee, in peace and eternal rest.

Let us say Amen.

Introductory

Mourning and Consolation

RABBI ISAAC L. SWIFT

There is no experience that we are called upon to undergo, whether individually or as a people, concerning which the rabbis of old fail to help us express our sentiments; alike in *Halakhah* and *Aggadah,* they enable us to formulate our thoughts, in prosperity as in adversity.

How shall we express our anguish as we ponder the worst adversity of all time, the most unspeakable instance in recorded history of man's inhumanity to man? How indeed recall the unforgettable in terms commensurate with the catastrophe which we call the Holocaust?

The rabbis do not fail us.

Among the halakhot governing bereavement is the somber requirement to rend the garments as an outward mark of grief. There are some circumstances in which the rent garment may be resewn after a prescribed period. But there are others when the garment may never be resewn because of the profundity of the grief it represents. These circumstances are spelled out in a baraita:

> These are the rents that are not to be sewn up: One who rends [his garments] for his father or his mother; for his teacher who taught him Torah; for the prince—the people's leader; for the head of the rabbinic court; on hearing evil tidings; on hearing God's Name blasphemed; on the burning of a Sefer Torah; on beholding the ruins of the cities of Judea; on seeing the ruins of the Temple; on beholding the ruins of Jerusalem.[1]

The Holocaust wrought for us all these ten categories.

"For his father or his mother": Among the six million martyrs

3

were parents of families, cherished by children and grandchildren, whose descendants—those who survived—grieve to this day "for the touch of a vanished hand and the sound of a voice that is still." They were fathers and mothers, not to their own children alone; they were exemplars of what Jewish parentage is, and of what it involves in precept and example for us all. Torn from their children and their people, they must be mourned by us all today as we mourned them then. The garment must remain rent; the loss dare never be forgotten.

"For his teacher who taught him Torah": The victims who were slaughtered included those who taught their generation Torah and forged new links in the unbreakable chain of Jewish knowledge. They were renowned *roshei yeshivah,* celebrated heads of schools and seminaries, and "mute inglorious Miltons"—the less-known but equally dedicated teachers in Talmud Torahs and hedarim. They taught not only those who came under the immediate impact of their benign influence—they taught us all, for they provided noble examples of what commitment to the propagation of Torah has ever meant in Jewish life. We must continue to mourn their cruel end; we must leave the garment of grief unsewn.

"For the prince—the people's leader": European Jewry boasted down the ages men—and women—of light and leadership, who guided communities great and small in all the vicissitudes of European Jewish history. The generation of the Shoah was no exception. In the cities and towns and townships, the leaders showed the way amid peril and destruction, as they had in the years before. They were an example not to their communities alone, but to us all who know of the guidance they gave and venerate them for their place in our people's story. Their memory must live on, and our loss in their annihilation must remain with us. The garment of grief must remain unstitched.

"For the head of the rabbinic court": Not the least grievous of the incalculable losses that we suffered was the slaughter of great luminaries of Torah, each a fount of halakhah, each fit to be an *av bet din.* They were renowned rabbis and *posekim,* carrying with them to their unmarked graves the vast scholarship with which they had enriched our Jewish world: "The cedars of Lebanon. The noble of the Law, great champions in Mishnah and in Talmud, mighty in strength who toiled (at their books) in purity."[2]

The cutting down of these "cedars of Lebanon" left their generation and ours impoverished and orphaned. They dare never be forgotten—the rent garment of our mourning them may never be resewn.

"On hearing evil tidings": Were there ever in our people's troubled story tidings more evil than those which reached us during the Holocaust, those which were excruciatingly confirmed when the enemy was defeated? The memory of those tidings dare never be obliterated; we must continue to wear the unsewn garment of our mourning.

"On hearing God's Name blasphemed": The Name of God was blasphemed by the obscenities of the Holocaust as never before. Six million such blasphemies were perpetrated: young and old, each made in the divine image, each endowed with the potential to make God's word and will known and revered among men, all callously and mockingly made into sacrifices on the altars of gods of evil and of the lust for blood. Can that ever be forgotten? Can that rent in the garment of the Jewish people ever be repaired?

"On the burning of a Sefer Torah": Not only Sifrei Torah were desecrated and burned, but great libraries enshrining the most sacred of our texts were reduced to ashes. Jewish literary treasures went up in flames that made the medieval burning of the Talmud in Paris and elsewhere pale to flickering pyres by comparison. If Meir of Rothenburg could lament the fires which he witnessed, and in mournful dirge grieve over what he saw, what shall we say whose generation witnessed a funeral pyre of books that burns in our hearts to this day? "O Sinai, was it for this that God chose you and shone on your heights?"[3] With what anguish do we echo those words today, we who learned of sacred scrolls defiled by monstrous hands and used for untold squalid purposes!

"On beholding the ruins of the cities of Judea": Warsaw, Cracow, Grodno, Lodz, and the scores of towns and villages and hamlets that were the "cities of Judea" in Europe—they were laid waste as surely and as completely as were the ancient cities of the Holy Land at the hands of the Romans. These too we mourn with a grief so profound that we can never forget them. The rent garment may not be resewn.

"On seeing the ruins of the Temple": Hundreds of sanctuaries were destroyed, from the most ornate of Europe's synagogues to the humblest of its conventicles. If for the Beth ha-Mikdash we mourn without the right to forget, we must assuredly continue to mourn for these sanctuaries which adorned and animated European Jewish life through long centuries of preserving the Jewish spirit. Our garment must remain unsewn.

"On beholding the ruins of Jerusalem": As the holy city of old was the nerve-center of Jewish life and purpose, so was the "Jerusalem of Lithuania"—Vilna, the holy city of the Diaspora—a vibrant center of Jewish thought and ideals until it was laid waste, its shrines in ashes and ruins, its sons and daughters butchered and wiped out. Not Vilna only, but Kovno and Panavez, Lublin and Belz, and scores of cities like them, centers of Torah and centers of Hasidism, each hallowed by the pious worship and devout obedience to mitzvot on the part of generations of Jews who lived by their faith—all were destroyed; as their fathers had sanctified the Name of God in their lives, so did the Nazis' victims sanctify His Name in their deaths. As the halakhah requires us to leave unsewn the garment rent for Jerusalem, so does it require us to leave unstitched the garment rent for the holy cities of European Jewry.

All ten categories of grief and agony listed in the baraita are reflected in the Holocaust calamity. "What shall I liken to thee, what shall I equal to thee that I may comfort thee? For thy breach is great like the sea; who can heal thee?" (Lamentations 2:13). Who indeed shall heal the wounds? How, while we remember, shall we find solace?

Once again the rabbis of the Talmud help us with the answer: "He who sees the houses of Israel rebuilt and inhabited should say: Blessed be He who restores the border of the widow. He who sees the houses of Israel destroyed and uninhabited should say: Blessed be the righteous Judge."[4]

When we look back and remember—as we dare not fail to remember—the destroyed "houses of Israel"—the enormity of the Holocaust, we declare *Barukh dayyan ha-emet:* We acknowledge the righteous Judge whose inscrutable decree meant so unparalleled a catastrophe. Ours not to question, though we fail to comprehend. Ours to accept, with grief indeed and with agony, with a *cri de coeur* which may not be silenced, but to accept the divine will.

But when we see Jewish life rebuilt, our people restored to Zion and Zion restored to our people, then is the time for *barukh maẓiv gevul almanah,* the berakhah thanking God for establishing anew the borders of "the widow," as Jeremiah called Jerusalem in her downfall.

"The people that walked in darkness have seen a great light; they that dwelt in the land of the shadow of death, upon them hath the light shined" (Isaiah 9:1). History has surely never manifested so complete a transformation of a people's lot as was wrought while the Holocaust was still raw in Jewish memory, while the wounds were still bleeding. Here was a people brought to its very knees by the annihilation of its greatest centers of vitality, by the massacre of the flower of its manhood and womanhood. And here, but three years later, was the same people rising from the ashes to the greatest achievement in post-exilic history: the renewal of its sovereignty in the land of its birth in the land of its destiny! For such transformation we utter the berakhah *barukh maẓiv gevul almanah.*

The halakhah continues to guide us: in the midst of mourning we receive consolation; in the midst of our continued grief over the immeasurable cost of the Holocaust in priceless life and precious treasure, we receive consolation in the renewal of our sovereignty. We proclaim, for all the world to hear, and not least for ourselves and our children to be gladdened: Blessed be that righteous Judge who in His mercy has directed that the widow shed her weeds, gather her sons and daughters to her side, and advance with them to her destiny in justice, in majesty, and in peace.

Notes

1. Mo'ed Katan 26a.
2. Abraham Rosenfeld, trans., *Authorized Kinot for the Ninth of Av* (London, 1965) no. 23.
3. Ibid., no. 43.
4. Berakhot 58b.

First Reactions

Ohab Zedek's Rabbi's Bulletins

1. One Thousand Jewish Children

Rabbi Dr. Jacob Hoffman

Among the victims of the Nazi barbarians in all Nazi-influenced countries the children are the most unfortunate. First there are the countless orphans whose parents have been slain or have perished by starvation. Then there are the children whose parents have been sent away to concentration camps and labor camps. And lastly there are those children, and especially the Jewish children, whose parents have been sent to ghettos in Poland and Russia, while the children were left behind. The last is the case of the children in unoccupied France.

Because of this situation, a committee in the United States for helping these unfortunate children has been formed. I refer to the U.S. Committee for the Care of European Children. As a branch of this general committee there is the German Jewish Children's Aid Committee, formed for the purpose of aiding Jewish children.

The government of the United States has granted 1,000 visas for the immigration of Jewish children from unoccupied France on the condition that a responsible Jewish Committee take care of these children and on condition that these children be placed in responsible private homes, once they get here. It is understood that these homes must be in a position to take adequate care of these children both physically and morally.

Canada and Bolivia have granted similar visas for the immigration of Jewish children of France into those two countries respectively.

Among the 1,000 Jewish children who are supposed to immigrate to this country there are 275 children of Orthodox parentage who must be placed in Orthodox homes. A special sub-committee is in charge of providing suitable homes for these children.

11

I would like to call the attention of members of our congregation and readers of this bulletin to this fact, asking them to see what they can do in this matter. It is needless to say how important and how sacred this work is, namely—the providing of homes for unfortunate homeless children. There are some who may not be in a position to take a child into their own homes, but who are in a position to pay for the upkeep of a child. In such a case the child could be placed in a proper home and maintained by a benefactor.

Those who are willing to do their share in this holy work, may get in touch with the office of our congregation or with me personally. To be sure, the work of the immigration of these children will take time, nevertheless it is necessary to secure homes for them in advance.

> "Distribute your bread to the hungry; bring the afflicted poor into your house; when you see the naked, clothe him; and do not hide yourself from your own flesh."
>
> (Isaiah 58,7.)
>
> —October 30, 1942 (Vol. 14, no.5, p.1)

2. A Duty of the American Jew

One need not travel to Nazi Germany today in order to be confronted with the unprecedented catastrophe of the German Jews. Nor need one travel to Czechoslovakia or Hungary, countries which from day to day are drawn deeper and deeper into the bane of Nazi influence, in order to witness the gloomy shadow of Hitler's rampage and the results of his inhumanly wanton work of destruction. In the democracies of Western Europe, too, where one meets the Jewish refugees from Germany and from Austria, the picture of the horrible state of these tortured and exploited Jews is revealed. And with this is revealed the tremendously difficult problem of the immigration of these Jewish masses who have become homeless.

I had first-hand contact with the misery of refugees on my European trip of a few weeks ago in England, Belgium, and cursorily, in France. Intelligent, capable and industrious people—academicians, merchants, artisans, industrial workers, technicians—are compelled to pass their days idly, to watch the precious hours slip by in thoughts of despair and self-censure because to them every avenue to gainful occupation of the possibility of earning a living is closed. And since the vast majority of refugees must leave their homes penniless—even personal belongings of some intrinsic value are taken from them at the border—they are compelled to eke out a pitiful existence from the meager allowances which the Jewish immigrant aid societies are able to place at their disposal.

In Belgium, and in Antwerp particularly, there are many hundreds of refugee-families who entered that country "illegally." Legal entry into Belgium is possible only in very rare instances. The Belgian government quite evidently takes cognizance of the anti-Semitic sentiments and the anti-Semitic tendencies which there, too, are quite evident in certain circles and political units. But the government is humane enough not to cause difficulties for those Jews who succeeded in entering illegally, and to countenance their temporary sojourn in the country. What is "illegal entry"? It means trudging on foot, generally during the night, for many, many weary hours, exposed to grave danger and inhuman hardships. And there are "Aryans" on both sides of the border who, in return for money and kind words—more frequently the former, of course—offer their services as guides. At times, very small children cross the border without their parents. The unhappy parents, driven back from the border, want at least to gain a semblance of safety and some Jewish care for their little ones. Because of their numbers, increasing daily, the refugees there had to be housed in barracks. And even the modest care they can there be given strains the resources of the Jewish aid societies.

Nothing speaks more eloquently of the horrible state of Jews in Greater Nazi Germany than that hundreds of thousands of them would *gladly become refugees.* They *envy* the sad and hard fate of the Refugee. They are consumed by one thought: to flee the Nazi hell as soon as possible, to escape as soon as possible the daily—yes, hourly—calumny, fear, threat, and danger to which they are exposed.

The object of their longing, next to Palestine, is emigration to the U.S.A. An *affidavit* is a treasure, a life-belt, a hope to them. To be sure, it by no means guarantees the possibility of their coming here. One great barrier stands in their way: the *quota*. They must wait and wait. And many affidavits expire before they can be used. And still, every affidavit is a *tremendous boon*. The most difficult fate becomes easier to bear, the most hopeless life seems worthwhile again, if one sees, no matter how far away, a goal, a shimmering light of hope and salvation. In addition, the affidavit offers a certain protection against the terror and other excesses in Nazi Germany. The holder of an affidavit is frequently released from a concentration camp.

It is therefore the sacred duty of every American Jew, if he finds it at all possible, to help, by means of affidavits, his threatened and tortured brothers and sisters abroad. It is a duty inherent in Jewish solidarity, in Jewish *gemilut hesed*. It is a duty that means the saving and maintenance of life itself. No one may withdraw from such a duty. Everyone ought to do whatever lies in his power in his field. Everyone ought to keep in mind the motto: *haverim kol yisrael*.

Every incoming boat brings to me letters from deserving, worthy Jewish people asking and begging for affidavits. How happy would I be if I could be the connecting link between these people who so sorely need help and those members of our congregation and those readers of these lines who want to do their share.

—October 30, 1942 (vol. 14, no. 5, p.2)

3. The Meeting at Madison Square Garden

The meeting on Monday evening, March 1st, justified all expectations. It was an impressive and stirring demonstration. More than 20,000 people, from all walks of life, filled the Garden. Not one seat remained vacant. And tens of thousands filled the surrounding streets, listening to the addresses by means of amplifiers.

The meeting started with Hebrew prayers in memory of the dead, the two million innocent victims of the Nazi barbarians. Deeply moved and stirred, the audience wept aloud.

Many important addresses were delivered. Besides noted Jewish speakers such as Dr. Chaim Weizmann, Rabbi Meir Berlin, and others, there were also many well-known statesmen, heads of large church organizations, labor leaders and scientists who addressed the gathering. Important messages, also from Europe, were read by the chairman, Dr. Stephen S. Wise.

The aims of the gathering, as expressed in most of the addresses, were protest and demands. Protest not against Hitler and his hordes. You cannot protest against savage beasts. And you cannot protest against human beings who have lost all traces of humanity and mercy. The protest was turned against the apathy of the civilized world and above all against the indifference and inactivity of the United Nations in the face of the greatest crime in recorded history, in the face of the cold-blooded systematic extermination of millions of Jews.

When Hitler first started his atrocities against the Jews, the democratic nations still had the power to put a stop to it. But they remained indifferent because the victims were only Jews. And even now the United Nations are not entirely powerless. They still have ways and means of saving and rescuing at least a part of the threatened Jews. But this cannot be done by declarations and condemnations only. What is necessary is immediate and effective action.

A resolution, adopted by this gathering, formulates a comprehensive program of action, to be submitted to the President and the government of the United States and through them to the United Nations and the neutral states. The main demands are the following:

Neutral states and agencies be asked to serve as intermediaries with Germany and nations under Hitler's domination for the release and emigration of their Jewish victims. To designate and establish a number of sanctuaries in Allied or neutral states to serve as havens of refuge for those Jews whose release from captivity may be arranged for, or who may find their way to freedom through efforts of their own.

England should be asked to open the doors of Palestine—the Jewish homeland—for Jewish immigration on a large scale. To organize through neutral agencies for the feeding of the unfortunate Jewish men, women, and children who are doomed to linger under Nazi oppression.

Now we expect immediate and effective action on the part of the United States, Great Britain, and all the Allied and neutral nations.

—March 5, 1943 (vol. 14, no. 14)

4. The Conference of the Big Three

According to press reports, preliminary arrangements have been made for the meeting of President Roosevelt, Prime Minister Churchill, and Marshal Stalin, to be held somewhere in Europe.

This meeting will have to handle the world political problems. First of all, it will have to work out a united plan for bringing this world war, which has taken a favorable turn for the Allies, to an early victorious conclusion. Secondly, it will have to draw up the final peace terms. And thirdly, it will have to iron out the differences which have arisen among the three most important nations. In other words, this meeting will have to create a united war front as well as a united peace front. And so this meeting will be of momentous importance in shaping the future of the world.

We Jews are greatly interested in the outcome of this conference not only as Americans but also as Jews. And this because it is to be expected that the various aspects of the Jewish problem will also be dealt with at this great conference.

There is the plight of some half a million Jews who are still in Nazi-occupied Europe and who are threatened with destruction by the Nazi beasts. Many of these Jews can be saved if proper and energetic action is taken by the United Nations in agreement with certain neutral states.

There is furthermore the problem of the Jewish remnants in the liberated territories. These people, broken in body and soul, are left without any means of existence and are facing an uncertain future. It will be up to this conference to see that these people are rehabilitated and resettled as soon as possible.

And last but not least, there is the question of Palestine, which is the only possibility for hundreds of thousands of homeless Jews to live in security and safety, in freedom and dignity.

The Palestine question was already under consideration at the Quebec meeting last spring, but no decision was taken at that time. We expect this forthcoming conference will settle this question once and for all. We expect that the United Nations will repay the debt of humanity to the Jewish people, who suffered more than any other people in this cruel war, by opening the doors of Palestine for Jewish immigration and by making Palestime a Jewish Commonwealth.

We particularly put our trust in President Roosevelt, who in his message of October 15, 1944, to the Zionist Organization of America said among other things: "I know how long and ardently the Jewish people have worked and prayed for the establishment of Palestine as a free and democratic Jewish Commonwealth. I am convinced that the American people give their support to this aim and if re-elected I shall help to bring about its realization."

We expect President Roosevelt to live up to his solemn promise. And we hope that he will also use his influence with Prime Minister Churchill in this matter. The Jewish people the world over expect from this conference the final solution of the problem of Palestine. They expect Palestine to become a Jewish Commonwealth.

—January 26, 1945 (vol. 16, no. 10)

5. The War Criminals

The war in Europe is still going on. We don't know when it will come to an end. We don't know when the fatally wounded beast will finally expire. We should not be over-optimistic and over-confident.

However, with the Russian armies deep in East Prussia, Silesia,

Pomerania, and Brandenburg, and with the American and British armies on German soil, preparing a large-scale offensive into Central Germany, we may say that the handwriting on the wall is visible to everybody who is not completely blind. "Mene mene, tekel, upharsin" (Daniel 5:26). The desperate struggle of the beaten and panic-stricken Germany may be continued for weeks or months, but its fate is sealed.

This being so, the question of the punishment of the German war criminals has become an actual one.

The question? Is this a question at all? Up until recently the matter of punishment for all crimes committed by the Axis leaders and their henchmen seemed to be beyond all question. It seemed to be a certainty. In the last few weeks, however, it has become apparent that this matter is still questionable. As proof of this, we have the resignation of Mr. Herbert C. Pell, the American representative to the War Crimes Commission in London. It has been brought to light that this resignation was caused by the attitude of certain reactionary officials in our State Department who are opposed to the opinion of Mr. Pell, who advocated severe punishment of all war criminals, regardless of rank and governmental position, and who also demanded the punishment of crimes committed even within the borders of Germany against religious and racial minorities, including the Jews. It has become obvious that there are certain officials in Washington and in London who put technical legalistic considerations above the sense of justice and above human feeling.

Needless to say, we Jews are particularly interested in the severe punishment of all war crimes, because we are the main victims of unheard-of atrocities and bestialities. Therefore, we demand, together with all democratically minded people, that Hitler, Himmler, Goebbels, Goering, and all others responsible for atrocities and cruelties, whether they ordered them or had them carried out, be called to the bar of justice and be punished accordingly. The murder camps of Dachau, Maidanek, Oswiecim, Treblinka, and many others, the millions of innocent lives of men, women, and children, should not remain unavenged.

What we demand is not vengeance in the ordinary sense. It is the prosecution of justice and morality. The hard-won peace could never be permanent and lasting; the new world, to be built up upon the ruins of the old, would lack stability, if the war criminals, the big or the small, would go unpunished.

Speaking of the punishment of the wicked, the Torah says the following: "And the people shall hear, and be afraid, and not act presumptuously anymore" (Deut. 17:13). Severe punishment for the guilty is necessary as an example set before the whole world to prevent similar crimes to be committed in the future.

—February 9, 1945 (vol. 16, no.11)

Ninety Percent

Rabbi Dr. Osher Kahn

An ordinary night, an ordinary subway, ordinary people. I had barely seated myself when the train began its mad race toward its next stop. Since I was a little fatigued, I reclined in my seat, stretched my legs as far as I could, and wearily closed my eyes. I knew that there was a long ride ahead of me, and I was determined not to waste it completely. I was going to relax, perhaps even catch up on some long-needed sleep.

But as I was in the process of making myself comfortable, I felt something crumpled behind me on the seat. My hand quickly reached for it, intent upon removing even this minor cause of disturbance. While bringing the "crumpled something" forward, I glanced at it nonchalantly with my eyes already half closed, but immediately the blood rushed to my face and I nearly jumped from my seat. The word "Jew" in bold white letters on a black background was staring me straight in the face. Inwardly I thought that this must be just another one of those rabble-rousing, anti-Semitic pamphlets planted by young hoodlums on subways and in other public places. I nevertheles swiftly smoothed the crumpled paper and to my surprise found it to be something entirely different from what I had expected. In reality it was a small booklet entitled *Jewish Affairs*. On the cover was a picture that made me shudder: A coffin with a *magen-david* on it, sunken into a gaping, black grave which in turn was superimposed upon a map of Central Europe. Printed below were the words "Balance Sheet of Extermination." It was not a pretty picture!

My mind was now devoid of everything but this grim picture that

21

my eyes were looking at. Slowly I began to turn one page after
another. The tale of grief and horror began to unfold.

Jews of Europe
1939—9 1/2 million
dead—6 million
remaining—3 1/2 million

That was all! That was the "Balance Sheet of Extermination."
Seventy-two percent Jews annihilated. My eyes ran down a list of
percentages of Jews lost in Nazi-occupied countries. Poland 85 percent, Germany 81 percent, Yugoslavia 73 percent, Lithuania, 90 percent. I stopped at this figure. Lithuania 90 percent! God in heaven!
So that's why my family had not heard trom even one of its many
relatives who had been living in Lithuania. 90 percent of the
country's Jews had been driven to death, death by the sword, hunger, and fire. I had known previously that the country of my birth
and early childhood had suffered heavily, but never did I imagine
that the extermination had been so brutally thorough. I could read
no further. I placed the pamphlet in my pocket, again leaned back,
and closed my eyes. All this had occurred during the interim of two
stops. The train was rushing away once more, but now the wheels
were screaming in my ears: 90 percent, 90 percent, 90 percent . . .

As if in a dream I began to visualize the little Luthuanian town
which I had left as a child eleven years ago. Pictures of *mein shteteleh*
Utian, for that was its name, and my own childhood years in it sped
with amazing clarity through my mind. In all its simple yet diversi-
fied colors this little town, most of whose population consisted of
about 8,000 Jews—began to unfold itself.

I saw its outskirts: the single asphalt highway, part of which was
still in a stage of construction when I left for America; the several
roads of lesser grandeur, leading into the town, dusty in the summer, muddy in the winter; the almost miniature railroad station
with its rotting water tower; the old flour mill around which men
with powdery white faces went about their business; the newly-built
prison with the foreboding wall which surrounded it on all sides;
the silent World War I military cemetery with its gray moss-covered

monuments; the Russian Orthodox church which stood high upon a hill. These were the familiar sights which greeted the traveler entering the town from any direction.

As one penetrated it further, there appeared the main street with its cobbled stones in the center and its cement sidewalks on both sides. This street was mainly lined with single-story wooden houses, although occasionally a brick building of two or even three stories proudly reared itself. These were the town's skyscrapers and were not too common indeed. This "King's Highway" led one to the center of the town, a rather large square in whose immediate vicinity many shops and stores of all descriptions were located. On Thursdays, known as "market day," this square was almost entirely covered with booths and wagons which displayed the multitude of wares brought to the town by the inhabitants of the surrounding countryside. Once a year it also served as the pitching ground for the circus when that merry cavalcade came to town.

There were perhaps about a dozen other good streets in the town, lined with sturdy houses, and small shops; but the rest were mostly hard, dirt roads or even less dignified narrow alleys which had wooden sidewalks or no sidewalks at all. The town's traffic was predominantly horse and wagon, with an occasional auto or bus racing through. Private cars were, of course, unheard of. In general, self-propelled vehicles were still a rarity.

The religious life and activity of the town stood on firm, solid ground, supreme and almost unchallenged. There were four synagogues, which were always well attended, whether it was during the weekdays or on Sabbath. Two ḥaderim, where one studied from 9:00 A.M. to 5:00 P.M., accommodated most of the town's children acquiring a traditional education. Needless to say, these were in the great majority. A few years after my departure for America, a fairly large yeshiva was established. Saturday was a day of complete rest and absolute cessation of all weekday activity. Few, if any, dared to break the Shabbat openly. All shops and stores were closed. Traffic was at a standstill. The atmosphere was filled with calm and restfulness. The Sabbath Queen reigned in all her majesty. About ten o'clock in the morning crowds of people streamed toward their homes from services. All were visibly benign and cheerful, having divorced themselves from everyday care. The little children especially were gay and full of holiday spirit. In the afternoon some people visited friends, others rambled through the town's streets talking and joking, while still others attended a lecture or meeting of some sort. Nowhere in the world did anyone observe the Sabbath or celebrate the holidays more joyously or more sincerely than in this small Jewish community, typical of so many others of its kind in Eastern Europe.

The town's cultural and social standard was also remarkably high. There existed a secular, government-supported, Jewish public school attended by those boys who did not go to a ḥeder, as well as by girls. In this school, every subject was taught in Hebrew. A similar school existed where Yiddish was the language of instruction. If one wished to continue his secular education there was a Hebrew pro-gymnasium, or what in America would be equivalent to a junior high school. The town also possessed a gymnasium on par with our high school plus two years of college, but since this was under Catholic influence and authority it was frequented by a very limited number of Jewish students. It is interesting to note that even public school pupils had to pay for their books and whatever other supplies they needed. This, no doubt, was instrumental in excluding a number of poor children from study. Generally speaking, however, the opportunities and facilities for learning were open for anyone who so desired. Hebrew, Yiddish, Lithuanian, and Russian books were easily accessible through a well-stocked library. The newspaper which was read most by Utian's Jewish residents was the *Yiddish Shtime,* published in Kaunas. Utian prided itself upon the fact that the editor of this distinguished daily had been born and raised there. A number of people, having relatives in the United States, were fortunate enough to be sent the *Jewish American,* a magazine which was greatly admired.

The young people of the town, ranging in age from eight to the middle twenties, were almost without exception, members of some organization or another, most of them with Zionist aspirations. I remember distinctly that the following groups existed: Halutz, Mizrachi, Betar, and Maccabee. There were several others of less importance which I cannot recall by name any longer. All of these, whether small or large in number, were extremely energetic in many fields of activity. Meetings, always well attended, were held regularly, usually on Friday or Saturday nights. Lecturers from larger cities were often invited to speak on problems of vital importance either to Jewry in particular or the world in general. Plays, usually on Jewish themes, were staged several times during the year. During the spring and summer months soccer games were played almost weekly by the local Maccabee team versus one of the out-of-town teams. Few of the town's younger generation failed to miss these games. Great excitement was especially aroused when the Maccabee team would pit its strength against a non-Jewish soccer team. During this season of the year, too, each organization arranged a hike to some lake or forest of the nearby countryside. All groups placed no small emphasis upon scouting activities, often incorporating them as a vital part of their program.

Although Lithuania, at this time, was comparatively free of the virus of anti-Semitism, few were the Jews who were so blind as not to see the symptoms of this disease. Here and there Jews were being excluded from various industries. Upon several occasions anti-Jewish riots by Lithuanian students were reported in the Yiddish press. A number of super-national, fascist-minded groups began the familiar chorus of "Boycott the Jews." The signs were unmistakable. The anti-Semitic plague was brewing and about to break in all its fury. All of Lithuania's 150,000 Jews, the youth perhaps more than all others, were aware of the impending storm.

This, without doubt, was no small factor in the explanation of Zionist influence upon Lithuanian Jewry. Already for thousands there existed but one ambition, one aspiration. That was to go to Palestine. Some were fortunate enough to have their dreams real-

ized before the Nazi onslaught wrote a finish to the glorious period
of Lithuanian Jewish history. But, unfortunately, compared with the
number who perished, few indeed were these happy ones.

Sitting in the subway train, all these thoughts went racing
through my mind. One scene after another, beginning with those of
earliest childhood, flashed on and off, almost miraculously vivid and
lifelike. I saw my aged grandfather bringing me to ḥeder for the first
time, that wonderful old ḥeder whose simple virtues many of our
modern Hebrew and Yiddish authors have so gloriously described. I
saw its bare walls, the long wooden table with the little children seated about it, the rebbe with the flowing white beard and the sparkle
in his eye. Then there was recess and we played in the sand making
miniature tunnels and dams. A few years passed and we were already
learning Ḥumash with Rashi. How grandfather's face would shine
when on Sabbath, I showed him how well I knew the sedrah of the
week. Another year or two and our little backs were bent over Eilu
Meẓiot and Arba'ah Avot. We were learning Gemora! During the
winter it was dark when we went home from ḥeder. How well do I
remember the pretty little paper lanterns we made, each one of us
claiming the greater craftsmanship. Then came the joy and glory of
the first *siyum*. I was only nine then, but nobody could have felt big-
ger or better. We had finished one complete *perek* in Bava Kamma,
the ninth, I believe. What excitement when each of us contributed
his fifty cents toward the covering of expenses for the little party we
were going to make in the ḥeder. How proud every single one of us
was!

Then the scenes changed and I remembered those long, cold Friday nights when I would leave the house immediately after the Sabbath meal and make my way through the dark streets toward the
house where the Betar group, of which I was a member, met regularly. Clearly, I saw the giant blue menorah painted on a white wall,
the picture of that famous one-armed hero Joseph Trumpeldor, the
blue-and-white flag looking down upon the militant little group of
youngsters in their brown uniforms.

Finally, there came to me the last days in Utian: bidding a sad farewell to all my friends, the last day in ḥeder, the eyes filled with tears, the early morning dew, the old bus that took me from Utian to Kaunas, Lithuania's capital. In quick succession there flew by the pictures of Berlin, Paris, Cherbourg, America.

Now, it was eleven years later, and I was sitting half-slouched in a seat of a subway train that was speeding from one station to another. And what was back there, back in little Utian, back in all those towns and cities of Lithuania where but a few years ago Jewish life and culture had flourished to such a high degree? No more! Finished! Ninety percent of the Jewish population exterminated. Gone are the shuls and batei midrashim, gone are the yeshivot and Talmud Torahs, gone are the schools where secular culture was provided for thousands. Gone are all those bright happy children, all those good pious Jews. A terrible fire had come and all in its way was consumed. Ninety percent! God in heaven! How? Why? Again the train wheels began to scream that song of death in my ears: Ninety percent, 90 percent, 90 percent . . .

This article was originally published in the 1946 edition of *Masmid,* Yeshiva University's student yearbook.

The Blessing of Small Beginnings

Rabbi David B. Hollander

This shall be the punishment of Egypt, and the punishment of all the nations that go not up to keep the feast of Tabernacles.
— *Zechariah 14:19*

The festival of harvest brings to our mind this year [1944] not a harvest of crops and of food to gladden the heart of man but a grim harvest of death. The fields which God intended to produce for man the staff of life, have been turned into huge battlefields and graveyards for the flower of youth. Perhaps never before in the history of man's corruption has his capacity for crime reached such terrifying proportions and taken such a heavy toll of human life. Our consciousness of man's utter depravity and his inhumanity to his own kind has been greatly sharpened by the age of horror that the last decade constitutes. Our text, therefore, which centers its theme around the cardinal sin of the nations of the world, seems to form an anticlimax, when of all the accumulation of evil with which the nations of the world are supersaturated today it should select the failure to observe the festival of Sukkot as the quintessence of the crime of man.

Think of the apparent irony inherent in our text. In the last ten years, twenty-five million people have been murdered in cold blood. The heartlessness and the bestiality of man, his utter lack of mercy toward the defenseless, the aged, the young, and the sick is a record unsurpassed in the history of crime. There was a time not so very long ago when we used to refer to the Dark Ages as a period when the light of humanity was extinguished. But surely, if there are any among us in whom there still dwells a grain of intellectual honesty they will admit freely, though sadly, that the Dark Ages were by no means as dark as our own day. Wherever we cast our eyes we see nothing but the destruction of thousands of cities, towns, and villages with their inhabitants blown off the face of the earth. Cities formerly inhabited by tens of thousands of Jews became overnight cities without Jews. Our hearts ache as we think of the huge centers of Jewish intellectual and religious endeavor, the great centers of commerce and industry built with weary but determined hands, that are today no more than a graveyard of nameless tombs. Vilna, the cradle of Jewish learning in Lithuania, Minsk, the great White Russian center, Warsaw, Kovno, Bialystok, Pressburg, Lemberg, unthinkable but true—cities without Jews!

If ever a text presented a complex moral issue, it is our text. (Zechariah 14:19) For how can we lump all this unspeakable horror into the one relatively minor failure of celebrating the festival of Sukkot. If we examine, however, the psychological factors which precede and induce the corruption of man, we shall find in the words of the prophets a clear exposition of the fundamental cause for the repeated moral crises that plague the structure of civilization.

If we are to arrive at this great diagnosis of the ills of the world as well as to the prescribed cure, we must ask ourselves: what is the spiritual significance of the tiny sukkah which holds within its frail walls the one enduring answer to suffering humanity yearning for a real festival of harvest?

Our sages of old have given us in a few brief words the true spiritual quality of the sukkah when they said, "Get out of your permanent abode and dwell in a place of insecurity" (Sukkah 2a). Nothing so well describes the pilgrimage of man on the face of the earth as the constant shifting from transitoriness to permanence. Examine the early records of individuals and nations and you will discover that their moral depravity varied directly with their ascent toward the summit of power, security and expansion.

The Torah has told us as much when it predicated only too

accurately that "then thy heart He lifted up, and thou forget" (Deuteronomy 8:14). It is in the last word of this verse ve-shakhahta, "and thou forget," that our greatest moral defect is implied. It is this almost criminal forgetfulness that has consistently blighted our lives. Would God that our memories were not so short, that we would remember in the days of prosperity the time of our small and modest beginnings.

A story is told of a poverty-stricken and hapless young man who, contrary to his wildest dreams, became, by marriage, a member of a well-to-do family. His future father-in-law, who admired his intellectual and spiritual qualities, decided to improve his outward appearance. So he replaced the tattered and threadbare garments of the groom with the finest and best-tailord clothes made of the most luxurious fabrics. The groom was, of course, greatly pleased by the attention lavished upon him. He began to look into his future and saw there a new world unfolding, a world of wealth and luxury. He was very anxious to sever his ties with the miserable years that had preceded the stroke of good fortune. But to his great surprise, he noticed that his intended father-in-law picked up his torn clothes, folded them carefully, and placed them in a special chest where only treasured articles were stored. Years later, a poor man in great financial straits turned to this young man for assistance, which however, was not forthcoming. Thereupon the father-in-law, who was disappointed by the heartlessness of his son-in-law, led him to the chest and pointing his finger to the tattered clothes, said, "If you would but recall the yesterday when you were in the predicament of crushing poverty, you would today act with compassion and with sympathy toward the needy."

The ruthless powers of the world, those that plunged mankind into this great war, have chosen that criminal course primarily because they forgot that once they, too, were no greater than the small nations they now chose to devour. In short they did not observe and study the character of the sukkah. They did not heed the counsel of our sages to get out of your fool's paradise, out of your vaunted security, and place yourself in the precarious and insecure positon that you were in and to which you will inevitably be relegated if you allow your heart to be petrified into an insensitive rock.

But it is not only the enemy countries that are now reaping the harvest of their failure to recall that the *dirat arai* (temporary abode) preceded their *dirat keva* (permanent abode), and consequently they lost all sense of justice, but also the enlightened nations of the world, those in whose hands has been entrusted the destiny of freedom and democracy, they, too, are desperately in need of the message of the sukkah. To them also the prophet addresses his fiery warning: "This shall be the punishment of all the nations." There was a time when America was small—a handful of colonies whose inhabitants were refugees from the prejudices and persecutions of the Old World. Their desire for liberty and justice was so great that they undertook the most perilous journey in battered and broken ships. Tossed by the turbulent and threatening waves of the Atlantic, they finally reached the comparatively safety of the New World. But no sooner were the seekers of religious freedom settled in New England, than the erstwhile refugees and immigrants became suspicious of the so-called foreigner and stranger. The victims of religious bigotry of yesterday became the fanatical Inquisitors of today. New settlements had to be established by those banished for religious reasons. But America still was the embodiment of the hope of humanity to the world. Wherever oppression raised its threatening hand, the victims survived by the mere magic charm of a prospective escape to America. Later, in Revolutionary days, America experienced a Valley Forge. It was the critical phase of the Revolutionary War. Washington and his men were hungry, cold, and sick. Only their towering spirit sustained them in battle and brought them to victory. Today, when America is great and strong and rich, at a time when its vast expanse of fertile land and natural resources could sustain half the world, it would be very beneficial indeed, if the immigrant haters, the race mongers, and that whole lunatic fringe of native Fascists would go over to the chest as it were and look down upon that curious array of Dutch, French, and English immigrants, yes, not pioneers, but immigrants, refugees. Then perhaps they would not employ the term "foreigner" as the most disgraceful epithet in the American vocabulary. If ever, the Lord forbid, America should, as some ancient empires have, decline by the sheer weight of its own top-heavy riches and wealth, it will owe the decline to that segment of its population that refuses to observe the sukkah that deliberately turns its eyes away from that period of early American history when the possibilities of its security and future growth were epitomized by the frailty of the sukkah.

Even in this war, when America has had its chance to rediscover its early spirit, when under the urgency of great crises it has masterfully built a tremendous and unconquerable machine of war, paralleled by a rededication to the principles of liberty and justice, we have noticed again and again the manifestation of the evil of forgetting one's initial insecurity, of the failure to reenter the sukkah.

In 1941, when America was militarily weak and when the dictator nations were riding the crest of the waves of military success, America poured out its heart in sincere and genuine sympathy to all those under the crushing heel of the foe. There was a true and real desire to right the wrongs, to bring Americanism into every corner of the earth, to make equality and justice the enduring pillars of our society. There was a determination to defend and to shelter those who were homeless and defenseless. In brief, America moved back into the *dirat arai,* as it were. It dropped, temporarily at least, its *dirat keva* its complacency, its smugness, its feeling of being protected by two oceans against all possible attack. But it seems that we did not even carry out the biblical injunction of dwell in the sukkah for seven days (Leviticus 23:42). It was a fleeting sensation, a vanishing upsurge of idealism, and with the approach of the early stages of victory, there came also a much-too-hasty return to the *dirat keva.* Once again we hear the voices of those who speak derisively of international cooperation. The narrow doctrines of nationalism are again heralded from high and responsible places. To such nations, too, the prophet cries: "This shall be the punishment of Egypt and the punishment of all the nations."

But an even more glaring example of the sin of not celebrating Sukkot is presented by Great Britain. Here is a country which has been the exponent of freedom and human dignity for centuries past, but has carefully marshaled these progressive gains to its own citizenry. It has preferred a *dirat keva* behind the White Cliffs of Dover. England did not count on the possibility that that *dirat keva* would or could be breached, and because of its refusal to voluntarily withdraw into the *dirat arai* because of its unwillingness to think back to the days of its small and precarious origin, the enemy of mankind made out of a *dirat keva* a perilous *dirat arai,* with gaping holes such as London and Coventry. But at this moment of crisis, England found itself. It resolved then and there that for all future time she will observe the spirit of the sukkah. She began to have genuine feeling for those nations and peoples under its mandate, whose world still consisted of frail, shaky sukkot. But as in the case of America, the prescribed period of time of dwelling in the booth was not observed. At the critical battle of Dunkirk, England reached the pinnacle of its spiritual regeneration. But this peak was, unfortunately for mankind, too narrow in its dimension. It had no staying ground. The descent to the other side of the mountain began so that even its great Prime Minister, who symbolized for a time the will of free humanity, freely admitted that the ideology of this war is no more. And perhaps its first manifestation of the abandonment of the sukkah and the return to its haughty feeling of empire has been toward the question of the Jewish National Home. The sympathy of this great power for wretched world Jewry, for the tattered remnants of Israel, has varied inversely with its successes in this war. If only England could place itself into the *dirat arai* in which the Jew has been living all these centuries, if only England would remember that the Jews have suffered a thousand Dunkirks to its one, without the facilities of naval evacuation at their command, it would no doubt fulfill its obligations toward the people who wrote and lived the sacred writ—the Bible—which the English people cherish.

But not the least tragic consequence of the failure to properly observe and understand the festival of Sukkot has been suffered by our own Jewish people. For surely there is no other people in the world who have such painful and compelling reason to remember the sukkah in their lives as we have, for there is no group of Jews who at one time or another has not been exposed to the insecurity and defenselessness and frail existence so characteristic of the sukkah.

Times innumerable it has been hammered into the consciousness of the Jew that no matter what the political philosophy of his land, no matter how salutary his achievements, how heroic his sacrifice, his right to live is definitely and at best a *dirat arai*.

From the genesis of our history down through the unparalleled bloody events of our own sorrowful day this hostile refrain, *dirat arai,* has been dinned into our ears. Beginning with Abraham, the Jew learned that he had no permanent place of abode. The staff of the wanderer became his permanent companion. He already learned the lessons of living in a *dirat arai.* Isaac, too, was told "Go from us; for thou art much mightier than we" (Genesis 26:16). And so his son Jacob was taunted with the false claim "Jacob hath taken away all that was our father's" (Genesis 31:1). And down through the ages in every language we were told over and over again: "Get out of your permanent abode!" And despite all this we have not learned the importance of remembering that our whole life is typified by the sukkah. Had we learned it, we might have been foresighted enough to prepare in advance, before the storm crashed about our heads, "cities of refuge," where to save the remnant of Israel, we should have learned from Rebekah, the mother of Jacob, who understood that the precarious life of her son and his descendants would be sukkah-like and she advised him in the *planning* stage "Behold, thy brother Esau doth comfort himself, purposing to kill thee. . . . rise, flee thou" (Genesis 27:42).

It is thus that our text, although addressed to Egypt and the nations of the world as distinguished from the Jewish people, holds nevertheless a challenge to the children of Israel and particularly to those of them who are known as the American Jews. For the status of the latter against the background of contemporary events is nothing short of the legendary wonderland. This great, prosperous, and influential Jewish community had a very modest and perilous beginning. The early history of the Jewish immigrant coming to America is an inspiring epic of pioneering on the part of an uprooted people swept by the tides of prejudice and persecution to a strange continent on the other side of the world. The Jewish immigrant started out in abject poverty, toiling like a beast in the sweatshops or carrying the heavy load of the peddler's pack, covering the continent on foot; and then almost overnight the bent backs are straightened, the sweatshop worker has undergone a strange metamorphosis. He has become the prosperous, confident, successful manufacturer. The peddler, too, has assumed a new role as the owner of fine department stores. His children, educated, Americanized, healthy, vigorous, active in business, professions, and government. For all this the Jew is grateful to God and the country. But within the recesses of our own intimate privacy we ask, fearfully, whether the Amercan Jew is not forgetting sooner than is good for him the sukkah that preceded his affluence. Perhaps the American Jew has failed, like the young man in our story above, to carefully store his threadbare clothes of immigrant days so that he may be reminded of his precarious beginnings, so that he may transplant himself from the *dirat keva* to the *dirat arai.* Yes, my friends, the American Jew had better enter the sukkah and while there allow himself to be saturated with its teachings lest he suffer the fate of "Egypt and all the nations." The time of our joy, *zeman simḥatenu,* is indivisible from the celebration of Ḥag Ha-Sukkot, the two go together. Our continued preferred status in America where we have, thank God, a year-round *zeman simḥatenu,* depends on our looking to the sukkah, for only under its influence will we cheerfully dedicate ourselves to the herculean task of salvaging the shattered lives of our brothers and sisters, binding up their wounds and rehabilitating them to their former selves. Only by remembering the sukkah will we escape the callousness that unfortunately is all too apparent. Only by walking out of our *dirat keva* will we save ourselves from the disgraceful and inexcusable habit of shouting "refugee" at those who took the boat a little behind schedule. "All that are home-born in Israel shall dwell in booths" (Leviticus 23:42). It is of particular importance, then, that American Jewry, which is the only segment in Israel whose status and circumstances warrant its classification under the category of "home-born in Israel" should dwell in the sukkah and thus remember that our history records more than one instance when the "home-born," those of our people who deemed themselves permanent and secure residents and consequently attempted to erase their religious identity, found nevertheless that they were relegated to a sukkah-like existence.

Whether we like it or not, it seems that man is not big enough to graciously accept the bounties of life. His festival of ingathering must be tempered with a requirement to dwell in a sukkah, his time of joy is sobered by the reading of Kohelet, which stressed the utter futility of life and almost mockingly asks about joy: "What doth it accomplish?" (Ecclesiastes 2:27).

That a good and God-blessed life shall turn man away from God instead of toward Him is a sad commentary on the efficacy of man's progress and civilization, but this observation does not diminish its truth. In the words of our sages: "The Shekhinah is over the head of a sick person" (Shabbat 12b). When man suffers from some kind of malady, physical or moral, that seems to be the time when the Shekhinah is uppermost in his mind.

But shall we wait till we are, God forbid, afflicted? Shall we the world's most ancient people act like incorrigible children who react properly only under the pressure of harsh treatment? Shall mankind in general sink morally when it lives in peace and security and rise to its high duties and ideals only under the crushing horror of bloody war and strife? The sukkah gives us the answer. No, you need not actually experience disaster to find yourself. It is high time for you to have outgrown the stage where the rod must not be spared. But you must dwell in the sukkah. You must relive symbolically and temporarily your sukkah status in order that you may not so deteriorate morally that your *dirat keva* will have to become a *dirat arai* before you reawaken to your sense of duty and righteousness.

Let this sukkah then teach us how to derive permanence from insecurity—the privilege of the *dirat keva* from the lesson of *dirat arai*. In heeding this message of the sukkah we have a great and revealing precedent in the life of the incomparable prophet and unequaled leader Moses. Our sages tell us that Moses was endowed with ten names. Of all the ten, the name Mosheh is the one by which God always addressed him, and that is the name by which the Torah is identified when we say *Torat Mosheh* or *halakhah le-Mosheh mi-sinai*. Yet this name Mosheh was given by the daughter of Pharaoh. Why did she merit that the name of her choice should find divine sanction and enduring life? The preference for the name Mosheh, however, is based on its origin, "because I drew him [*meshitihu*] out of the water" (Exodus 2:10). Here lies the deathlessness of the name. For years later, when Moses became the prophet, the leader of a people before whom nations trembled, the man with whom God spoke, he did not forget his perilous beginnings, when his life was in great danger, hidden as he was in a basket of reeds at a time when all Jewish male children were put to death. Moses did not forget that it was only by the grace of God that he was saved. No, he never wanted to forget that phase of his life. Furthermore, he not only clung to that name which would serve as an everlasting reminder to him in the days of his greatness in the days of his *dirat keva* but he understood that his having been saved was not a gesture to him personally, but that he was saved so that through him others might be saved.

Will American Israel remember that he too was pulled out of the holds of ships coming over the Atlantic, drawn out of the flood of hatred and pogroms? Will he remember now that he considers himself as living in a *dirat keva*? Will he remember that but for the grace of God his fate today might have been indescribably tragic? Will he remember? Our ancient sukkah answers in the affirmative. Let the world as a whole, then, follow the example of Israel in the words of the prophet: "And it shall come to pass, that every one that is left of all the nations that came against Jerusalem shall go up from year to year to worship the King, the Lord of Hosts, and to keep the feast of Tabernacles" (Zechariah 14:16).

Experiences with Holocaust Survivors

Rabbi Manuel Laderman

In 1948 the Agudat ha-Rabbanim invited me to go to Europe for a year as the head of the Central Orthodox Committee which would be in association with the Joint Distribution Committee. Dean Samuel Sar, of blessed memory, was the director of the COC and had asked to be relieved of his duty, and I had been selected to replace him. My family and I went to Europe at the end of 1948, after I took a leave of absence from my congregation in Denver, and Rabbi Benzion Kaganoff came to substitute for me during my absence.

The office of the Central Orthodox Committee was 13 rue de Teheran, Paris, with connections to the JDC in Paris and in every one of its offices in Europe and North Africa.

My children were fourteen and nine, and we had to find a school for them to attend. Fortunately I knew French, so I could conduct my office with very little difficulty.

I made connection with the École Rabbinique in Paris, with the chief rabbi, and with the special office for France of the JDC.

My responsibilities were to be helpful to the Orthodox Jewish refugees in France and Germany and Austria and Belgium and Holland and Italy. I discovered very soon that I could be completely overwhelmed by the people in Paris and throughout France who came to see me, morning, noon, and night, with their problems, and their requests and their petiotions. I had nightmares for a year listening to the horror stories they had to tell.

I was also in telephone communication with parts of Europe that were not available for an American traveler, like Rumania. One of my greatest satisfactions was that I was able to assure the people in

39

Rumania, when the JDC was officially banned from operating there, that the yeshiva which they were conducting would be funded in some manner, and not to lose hope. In the course of the year I was able to make good on that promise, through various sources.

There were three of us who had the privilege of serving in the COC: Dean Samuel Sar, who was the first occupant of the office of director in Paris, for a period of six months; and I, who had that office for one year; then Rabbi Solomon Shapiro, who succeeded me in that responsibility. The arrangement had originally been made through a delegation from the Agudat ha-Rabbanim consisting of Rabbi Eliezer Silver of Cincinnati and Rabbi Ephraim Epstein of Chicago, both of them now in eternal bliss.

Their motivation was, as representatives of the Agudat ha-Rabbanim, that there were special needs of Orthodox refugees. They persuaded the leadership of the Joint Distribution Committee of America to create this special office, the Central Orthodox Committee, which would have a liaison relationship with JDC in Paris, the European headquarters of the American Jewish Joint Distribution Committee, AJJDC.

The idea of creating such an office was commendable. It gave people who had religious needs a special entree to the relief agency. People who were leaving for the Western Hemisphere and discovered that the boats that they were to sail on were leaving Shabbat, for example, who needed all kinds of religious articles, and many other problems.

It was reassuring to me throughout the year, as I traveled all over the continent as well as to North Africa, that I was, in a sense, in a position of showing the interest and the good will of American Jews toward those of our brethren who had remained faithful to the Torah and who wanted to resume a good religious life.

Whenever I read any of the Holocaust studies, or view the tremendously moving portrayal in the cinema *Shoah,* I recall those many searing stories that I heard day by day, night by night, from the people who came to my office in Paris, or when I was visiting in the various countries in Europe, to try to bring them a feeling of being cared for.

Perhaps the very words that I used when I spoke in the synagogue in Munich on the Asarah be-Tevet, on the observance of the Hurban, and quoted those words from Bereshit, when Joseph goes looking for his brothers, "I have come to seek thy brethren," are the keynote of what we were trying to do. From the most trivial to the most demanding kinds of requests, all came to us. It gave practical evidence of the sense of *ahdut* of American Jewry with the unfortunate decimated survivors of the horrors.

There are many instances of how this sense of fellowship manifested itself. It needs to be understood that the JDC, at the end of World War II, was a significant part of what the international rehabilitation effort was like. I had the best example when I was on a train going to Germany on one of my visits. I met with a Lutheran emissary who also was on a relief mission, but who expressed his admiration and envy at how carefully the Jewish community of America was looking after its coreligionists.

In those days right after the war, the JDC had branch offices in every European country. As the representative of Orthodoxy, I had entree to all these offices whenever I came to visit.

For example, on my first visit out of Paris to Belgium, I discovered a problem about an orphanage which had been set up for refugee children and a dispute that the Orthodox communities in Brussels and Antwerp were having. Because I had the privilege, as a spokesman for American Orthodoxy, I could help to resolve what had become a very tangled kind of misunderstanding.

Because of my own partiality to Mizrachi in America, I felt it necessary to establish my credentials with the other Orthodox groupings, such as our Agudat Yisrael. One of the first successes I had was in the establishment of a Beth Jacob School in Paris at the request of the Agudat Yisrael, because I felt that it was extremely important to be impartial in providing the services of our office.

I don't know if there is any way of conveying what this physical

presence of an American Orthodox rabbi in Paris meant to the
people, particularly of France, but the other parts of Europe as well.
The fact that they had a spokesman, a friend, a *ḥaver*. Across my desk
daily there came requests of many kinds from all over Europe,
because the word had spread, as a result of the fine efforts that Dean
Sar had initiated, that there was a listening ear for their needs.

Occasionally the gravity of the situation was eased by some
lighter moments. I remember the time when a couple with fourteen
children were about to leave for America. They had come to say
good-bye, to thank me for whatever had been done by our office,
and then whispered into my ear, in Yiddish, "I fooled the American
government; we have visas for only fourteen children, but there is
another one on the way."

The time that I was in Europe was one of the gradual closing of
refugee camps. The last holdout was at Föhrenwald in Germany. I
remember coming there to speak, coming to say a *devar torah* to the
yeshiva and discovering that different accents of Yiddish were necessary. My public Litvishe Yiddish was a little too harsh for those who
were more accustomed to the Polish and Galician pronunciations
and dialects.

When I visited a yeshiva in Leiden, Holland, I amazed the students by telling them that this was the city from which the great new
immigration to the New World had begun back in the seventeenth
century. They had never heard of it before, or of the new Jewish
colossus which had grown up in the three hundred years since.

In France I had the privilege of helping to maintain a yeshiva
that had been transplanted from a German refugee camp to Aix-les-
Bains, up in the mountains of the French Alps. It was fascinating to
visit there and to hear the *Yoreh De'ah* being taught in French to
those who had been born in France, as well as those transplanted
from Germany.

In Grenoble, a fine Jewish community under the French Consistoire, I had the opportunity of meeting with the rabbi, who was of
Eastern European origin, and had a hard time breaking into the

monopoly of French-born Jews who were the only rabbis until that day accepted by the Consistoire.

At Aix-les-Bains I was instrumental in carrying out the beginning made by Dean Sar of the creation of a beautiful mikveh, which took a lot of doing both in getting the money from the JDC and also in having it built, and became a resource for the observant Jewish women in the southern part of France.

Closer to our office in Paris itself, in the French suburb of Bailly, which is near Versailles, we established a very important yeshiva, which brought together students from all of the schools of higher Jewish learning from Germany and Eastern Europe who had survived the Holocaust. The roshei yeshiva were renowned for their learning and their piety. It was a great personal pleasure to me, when the chief rabbi of Israel, Rabbi Isaac Herzog, stopped off in France on his return trip from America, to accompany him to give a *shiur* at the yeshiva there, so that these refugee students, who were destined, most of them, to be going on to Israel, would have feeling that the highest rabbinic authority in the Holy Land was ready to welcome them.

One of the most exciting successes that our office was able to record was to bring about the release of a person who had been one of the leaders of the rescue movement in Eastern Europe, who had been in prison in Prague, Czechoslovakia, for a considerable period of time. It took a great deal of effort from our side in Paris to bring about his release. It was another instance of cooperation between the JDC, the organization of Hasidic rabbis in America, and our office in Paris.

At that time the Communist takeover in Hungary had brought about the closing of the Joint Distribution Committee offices in Budapest. There were a number of very unhappy circumstances related to that event which are part of JDC history. It happened, however, that the Hungarian authorities were anxious to make it appear that they were not against religion. It was the time when the Catholic Cardinal Mindszenty had been forced to take refuge in the

American embassy. For that reason the authorities, who would not allow any other JDC official to come from outside Hungary, welcomed my application for a visa and made it possible for me to spend ten days in their country. I met with the minister of religion and culture, who tried to persuade me that religion had nothing to fear from the Communist takeover. One of the ironic experiences I had was to visit a Talmud Torah in Budapest and see two pictures on the wall facing the students, one of the Ḥafeẓ Ḥayyim, and the other of Karl Marx.

Hungary had a flourishing Jewish Community Organization, which looked after the sheḥitah, the mikveh, the moshav zekenim, and helped to maintain the magnificent rabbinic library and the rabbinic seminary. The Hungarian part of the Holocaust has many very inspiring stories. It is a reflection of the ingenuity of the Jewish religious tradition that was so very recently when the Jewish Cultural Organization, which is trying to rebuild Jewish life in Europe today, had their international meeting in Budapest and gave a new impetus to the revival of a Jewish identity in that beautiful city.

Italy has, of course, a special place in the entire postwar history. Italy had made it possible for the Beriḥah organization to operate in bringing people out of the camps, running the blockade which England had made on the shores of Palestine and providing for the influx of Aliyah Bet, which is the historic tale of so many novels, plays and movies.

In the Scandinavian countries I had the opportunity of seeing the visible signs of the heroism of both the native populations and of Jews who had outwitted the Nazis. Denmark has its own famous story, which is well-known, when King Christian made it possible for the Jews of his country to escape to Sweden.

Oslo, Norway, was a special chapter, where the Jewish women took over the preparation of the bodies of those who died after the Jewish men escaped. They continue, down to this day, to hold it as a mark of their special place, to act as the Ḥevra Kaddisha.

Sweden, which stood on the sidelines in the war, as did Switzerland, was also the haven of refuge of the Jews of Denmark and of others who had escaped from Nazi camps.

In the year in which I was serving, the opportunity of visiting in Eastern Europe was not available. The Rumanian and Polish governments both refused my applications for visas, so that communication with those countries had to be done by correspondence and by telephone. When we telephoned we had to be particularly discreet because we knew that we were being monitored and under surveillance.

I also made visits to the German refugee camps. It required military approval to enter into the United States–occupied zone of Western Germany. I had the unofficial rank of a brigadier general, which allowed for lodging in hotels and at military bases.

To see the people who had managed to survive as they began to pick up the pieces and try to create a new life was, on the one hand, very sad, and on the other, inspiring. When the first wedding of survivors, each of whom had lost his and her original mate, took place in a German camp, there were more tears than joy. It took a great deal of courage on the part of the widow and the widower to agree to start a new life for themselves. It was encouraged by the German rabbis as well as by those of us who came from afar.

All of us ought to be aware of the magnificent gesture made by the American Army—acceding to the suggestion made by the rabbis in Germany, strongly supported by Dean Sar, showing what the American attitude was—by publishing a special edition of the Talmud. Requisitioning the paper, arranging for the presses, was a remarkable sign of American friendliness and understanding. When the Talmud was finally published, only five hundred sets were printed. It was most appropriate that it should be dedicated to General Eisenhower and the United States Army, which had shown the American encouragement of rebuilding the spiritual as well as the physical life of the survivors. Those of us who were privileged to receive a set of this *Shas* were singularly honored. As Rabbi Herzog liked to say, "I received the Talmud, President Truman received a copy, and so did President Chaim Weizmann of Israel."

Austria was a special case. Vienna was under four-government rule, and one had to step carefully as an American, knowing that the Russians, the French and the British were extremely jealous of

American prerogatives. Austria had many D.P. camps, and visiting them was another of the privileges that our office was able to exercise. One of the outstanding experiences was visiting with the commanding general of the American zone in Austria and being confronted by the question, "When do you suppose the last refugees will have left the occupied zone?" I confessed that I did not know, but he kept pressing me for some kind of an answer. I did not fall for the bait and discovered that he took special delight having predictions made about when all of the refugees would be out of the occupied zones and discovering that they were all premature.

To visit in North Africa was an eye-opener. These were our Sephardic brethren. On the one hand, one got the impression that they had been rather remote from the entire Holocaust scene. Hitler had not affected their lives as he had all Jews of the European continent. That was a strange feeling, to think that though geographically close they could be, so distant in this particular situation. One of the striking incidents of my visit to the chief rabbi of Casablanca in Morocco was his question, "How many wives do you have? I have four." He had difficulty understanding that we American Jews followed the European tradition, inaugurated by Rabbenu Gershom, and was not very happy with my explanation.

We saw the poverty of Morocco and Algeria and Tunisia, which was staggering. On the other hand, there was the fabulous experience of visiting a Talmud Torah where the children studied by heart, because books were not easily available to them, and on their eager faces when hearing a word of Torah. There was the joy that I saw when a youngster in one of their higher classes proved to me how much he had learned in his Gemara studies by rattling off several pages of Ketubbot and then saying very modestly, "I only know a few pages; you as a rabbi must know the whole volume by heart." I assured him that I couldn't even match him in memory, and the boy was flattered and delighted.

Tunisia is, of course, the seat of an ancient Jewry. There is an island in the country called Jerba where they still follow the opinion of Bet Shammai, as recorded in the Talmud, that a divorce is possible only on the basis of adultery and not for any other reason.

One had the feeling when visiting there that one was walking in the footsteps of the great medieval rabbis, Alfasi, Ibn Migash, and of course Maimonides.

Visiting in Carthage brought back all the memories of our studies in school about Hannibal and the denunciations of the city of Carthage by Roman senators.

In the line of present-day world politics, it is interesting to recall that Libya was then difficult to get into. To get a visa for Libya one had to go back from Tunis to Rome or to London because they insisted on special entry requirements.

Anyone who visits Israel today is aware of the immense strides made by the ORT organization in Israel. Historically, of course, ORT goes back to Poland at the end of the nineteenth century and then to the great development of ORT International, which centered around Geneva, Switzerland, under the direction of one of our own RCA *Haverim,* Rabbi Max Braude, one of the first chaplains with the American forces.

Visiting in Greece brought the horror of that country's suffering very much to the fore, and the knowledge that so old a community as Saloniki had been victimized by the Nazis in some of the cruelest and most barbarian of their activities. Its rebirth is another example of the innate heroism of Jews of every age and geography.

The Holocaust has left searing marks on all of us. Whether we lived through it or have read about it since, we know that it will occupy a somber place in our minds and thoughts. We shall be disturbed theologically in understanding it for generations. There are no easy answers, and there are no explanations. Theodicy has a particular importance for us who lived in the shadow of these decimating years. We shall always have to defer to our brethren who were able to come out of it with some wholeness. It is very fitting that the observances for the Holocaust should be made more significant each year. It is appropriate that memorials shall be established in all of our communities. It is commendable that an organization calling itself Children of the Holocaust should be making significant efforts to keep our memories alive.

Long ago the Torah warned us that about those who were the enemies of the Jewish people, we have twin obligations, *zakhor,* "remember," and *lo tishkah,* "do not forget." That twin obligation will be ours forever. May the Almighty spare future generations.

Theological and Halakhic Reflections

Kol Dodi Dofek:
It Is the Voice of My Beloved That Knocketh

Rabbi Joseph B. Soloveitchik

THE RIGHTEOUS WHO SUFFERS

One of the darkest enigmas with which Judaism has struggled from the very dawn of its existence is the problem of suffering in the world. Already Moses, the master of the prophets, in a moment of mercy and grace, of divine acceptance, pleaded with the Lord that He enlighten him concerning this obscure matter.[1] Moses knocked at the gates of heaven and cried out: "Show me now Thy ways, that I may know Thee, to the end that I may find grace in Thy sight. . . . Show me, I pray Thee, Thy glory" (Exodus 33:13, 18). Why and wherefore do afflictions and pain befall man? Why and wherefore do the righteous suffer and the wicked prosper? From that wondrous morn when Moses, the faithful shepherd, communed with the Creator of the world and sought a comprehensive solution to this question of questions, prophets and sages, through all the generations, have continued to grapple with it. Habakkuk demanded satisfaction for the affront to justice; Jeremiah, King David in his Psalms, and Koheleth pondered this quandary. The entire Book of Job is devoted to this ancient and mysterious query which still agitates and disturbs our world and demands an answer: why has God allowed evil to reign over His creation?

Judaism, in its strenuous endeavor to reach a safe shore in a world torn asunder by pain and affliction, in its search for an answer to the profound dilemma posed by the evil which—apparently—reigns unboundedly, arrived at a new formulation and definition of the problem, possessed of both depth and breadth. The problem of suffering, Judaism claims, may be raised in two distinct dimensions: fate and destiny. Judaism has always distinguished between an existence of fate and an existence of destiny, between the "I" subject to fate and the "I" endowed with destiny. It is in this distinction that our teaching regarding suffering is to be found.

What is the nature of an existence of fate? It is an existence of compulsion, an existence of the type described by the Mishnah, "Against your will[2] do you live out your life" (Avot 4:29), a purely factual existence, one link in a mechanical chain, devoid of meaning, direction, purpose, but subject to the forces of the environment into which the individual has been cast by providence, without any prior consultation. The "I" of fate has the image of an object. As an object he appears, as made and not as maker. He is fashioned by his passive encounter with an objective, external environment, as one object vis-à-vis another object. The "I" of fate is caught up in a blind, wholly external dynamic. His being is empty, lacking any inwardness, any independence, any selfhood. Indeed, an "I" of fate is a contradiction in terms. For how can "I"-awareness and selfhood coexist with pure externality and objectlike being?

It is against this background that the experience of evil arises in all its terror. There are two stages to this fate-laden experience of evil. To begin with, man the object, bound in the chains of an existence of compulsion, stands perplexed and confused before that great mystery—suffering. Fate mocks him; his being, shattered and torn, contradicts itself and negates its own value and worth. The dread of annihilation seizes hold of him and crushes him, both body and soul. The sufferer, quaking and panic-stricken, wanders in the empty spaces of a world upon which the wrath and terror of God weigh heavily. His afflictions appear shadowy and murky, like satanic forces, the offspring of the chaos and the void which pollute the cosmos that had been destined to clearly reflect the image of its Creator. In this stage of perplexity and speechlessness, of confusion of both mind and heart, the sufferer does not pose any questions about the cause and nature of evil. He suffers in silence, groaning under the weight of an agony that has stifled all complaint and suppressed all queries and inquiries.

After this psychic upheaval of the sufferer as the immediate reaction to evil has passed, there follows the intellectual curiosity which endeavors to understand the cosmos and thereby undergird man's confidence and security. In this stage, a person begins to contemplate suffering and to pose grave and difficult questions. He tracks the intellectual foundations of suffering and evil, and seeks to find the harmony and balance between the affirmation and the negation and to blunt the sharp edge of the tension between the thesis—the good—and the antithesis—the bad—in existence. As a result of the question and answer, problem and resolution, he formulates a metaphysics of evil wherewith he is able to reach an accommodation with evil, indeed to cover it up. The sufferer utilizes his capacity for intellectual abstraction, with which he was endowed by his Creator, to the point of self-deception—the denial of the existence of evil in the world.

Judaism, with its realistic approach to man and his place in the world, understood that evil cannot be blurred or camouflaged and that any attempt to downplay the extent of the contradiction and fragmentation to be found in reality will neither endow man with tranquility nor enable him to grasp the existential mystery. Evil is an undeniable fact. There is evil, there is suffering, there are hellish torments in this world. Whoever wishes to delude himself by diverting his attention from the deep fissure in reality, by romanticizing human existence, is nought but a fool and a fantast. It is impossible to overcome the hideousness of evil through philosophico-speculative thought. Therefore, Judaism determined that man, entrapped in the depths of a frozen, fate-laden existence, will seek in vain for the solution to the problem of evil within the framework of speculative thought, for he will never find it. Certainly, the testimony of the Torah that the cosmos is very good is true. However, this affirmation may only be made from the infinite perspective of the Creator. Finite man, with his partial vision, cannot uncover the absolute good in the cosmos. The contradiction in existence stands out clearly and cannot be negated. Evil, which can neither be explained nor comprehended, does exist. Only if man could grasp the world as a whole would he be able to gain a perspective on the essential nature of evil. However, as long as man's apprehension is limited and distorted, as long as he perceives only isolated fragments of the cosmic drama and the mighty epic of history, he remains unable to penetrate into the secret lair of suffering and evil. To what may the matter be compared? To a person gazing at a beautiful rug, a true work of art, one into which an exquisite design has been woven—but looking at it from its reverse side. Can such a viewing give rise to a sublime aesthetic experience? We, alas, view the world from its reverse side. We are, therefore, unable to grasp the all-encompassing framework of being. And it is only within that framework that it is possible to discern the divine plan, the essential nature of the divine actions.

In a word, the "I" of fate asks a theoretical-metaphysical question regarding evil, and this question has no answer. It is insoluble.

In the second dimension of human existence, destiny, the problem of suffering assumes a new form. What is the nature of the existence of destiny? It is an active mode of existence, one wherein man confronts the environment into which he was thrown, possessed of an understanding of his uniqueness, of his special worth, of his freedom, and of his ability to struggle with his external circumstances without forfeiting either his independence or his selfhood. The motto of the "I" of destiny is, "Against your will you are born and against your will you die, but you live of your own free will." Man is born like an object, dies like an object, but possesses the ability to live like a subject, like a creator, an innovator, who can impress his own individual seal upon his life and can extricate himself from a mechanical type of existence and enter into a creative, active mode of being. Man's task in the world, according to Judaism, is to transform fate into destiny; a passive existence into an active existence; an existence of compulsion, perplexity, and muteness into an existence replete with a powerful will, with resourcefulness, daring, and imagination. God's blessing to the work of His hands sums up their entire purpose in life: "Be fruitful, and multiply, and fill the earth and subdue it" (Genesis 1:28). Subdue the environment and subject it to your control. If you do not rule over it, it will subjugate you. Destiny bestows upon man a new rank in God's world, it presents him with a royal crown, and man becomes transformed into a partner with the Almighty in the act of creation.

As was stated above, man's existence of destiny gives rise to an original approach to the problem of evil. For so long as a person grapples with the problem of evil, while still living an existence of fate, his relationship to this problem expresses itself only in a theoretical-philosophical approach. As a passive creature, the man of fate lacks the strength to struggle with evil in order to contain it or in order to utilize it to achieve an exalted goal. For the "I" subject to fate is unable to effect any matter of consequence in the sphere of his own existence. He is nourished by his external environment, and his life bears the imprint of that environment. Therefore, he relates to evil from a nonpractical standpoint and philosophizes about it from a purely speculative perspective. He wishes to deny the existence of evil and to create a harmonistic worldview. The end of such an effort can only be complete and total disillusionment. Evil derides the captive of fate and his fantasy about a world which is wholly good and wholly beautiful.

However, in the realm of destiny man recognizes the world as it is and does not wish to use harmonistic formulas in order to gloss over and conceal evil. The man of destiny is highly realistic and does not flinch from confronting evil face to face. His approach is an ethico-halakhic one, devoid of the slightest speculative-metaphysical coloration. When the man of destiny suffers he says to himself: "Evil exists, and I will neither deny it nor camouflage it with vain intellectual gymnastics. I am concerned about evil from a halakhic standpoint, like a person who wishes to know the deed which he shall do; I ask one simple question: What must the sufferer do so that he may live through his suffering?" In this dimension the center of gravity shifts from the causal and teleological aspect of evil (the only difference between causality and teleology being a directional one) to its practical aspect. The problem is now formulated in straightforward halakhic language and revolves about one's daily, quotidian tasks. The fundamental question is: What obligation does suffering impose upon man? This question is greatly beloved by Judaism, and she has placed it at the very center of her world of thought. The halakhah is concerned with this problem as it is concerned with other problems of permitted and forbidden, liability and exemption. We do not inquire about the hidden ways of the Almighty but, rather, about the path wherein man shall walk when suffering strikes. We ask neither about the cause of evil nor about its purpose but rather about how it might be mended and elevated. How shall a person act in a time of trouble? What ought a man to do so that he not perish in his afflictions?

The halakhic answer to this question is very simple. Afflictions come to elevate a person, to purify and sanctify his spirit, to cleanse and purge it of the dross of superficiality and vulgarity, to refine his soul and to broaden his horizons. In a word, the function of suffering is to mend that which is flawed in an individual's personality. The halakhah teaches us that the sufferer commits a grave sin if he allows his troubles to go to waste and remain without meaning or purpose. Suffering occurs in the world in order to contribute something to man, in order that atonement be made for him, in order to redeem him from corruption, vulgarity, and depravity. From out of its midst the sufferer must arise ennobled and refined, clean and pure. "It is a time of agony unto Jacob, but out of it he shall be saved" (Jeremiah 30:7); i.e., from out of the very midst of the agony itself he will attain eternal salvation. The agony itself will serve to form and shape his character so that he will, thereby, reach a level of exaltedness not possible in a world bereft of suffering. Out of the negation grows the affirmation, out of the antithesis the thesis blossoms forth, and out of the abrogation of reality there emerges a new reality. The Torah itself bears witness to man's powerful spiritual reaction to any trouble that may befall him when it states: "In your distress, when all these things come upon you . . . and you return unto the Lord your God" (Deuteronomy 4:30). Suffering imposes upon man the obligation to return to God in complete and whole-hearted repentance.[3] Afflictions are designed to bestir us to repent, and what is repentance if not man's self-renewal and his supernal redemption?

Woe unto the man whose suffering has not precipitated a spiritual crisis in the depths of his being, whose soul remains frozen and lacking forgiveness! Woe unto the sufferer if his heart is not inflamed by the fires of affliction, if his pangs do not kindle the lamp of the Lord that is within him! If a person allows his pains to wander about the vast empty spaces of the cosmos like blind, purposeless forces, then a grave indictment is drawn up against him for having frittered away his suffering.

Judaism has deepened this concept by combining the notion of the mending and elevation of suffering with that of the mending and elevation of divine lovingkindness, divine *hesed*. God's acts of *hesed*, Judaism declares, are not granted to man as a free gift. Rather, they impose obligations, they make ethico-halakhic demands upon their beneficiary. To be sure, the overflow of divine *hesed* derives from God's open, superabundant, and generous hand, but it is not an absolute gift, without conditions or restrictions. The bestowal of good is always to be viewed as a conditional gift—a gift that must be returned—or as a temporary gift. When God endows a person with wealth, influence, and honor, the recipient must know how to use these boons, how to transform these precious gifts into fruitful, creative forces, how to share his joy and prominence with his fellows, how to take the divine *hesed* that flows toward him from its infinite, divine source and utilize it to perform, in turn, deeds of *hesed* for others. A person who is not brought by divinely bestowed bountiful good to commit himself, absolutely and unreservedly, to God perpetrates a dire sin, and in its wake he finds himself in very difficult straits which serve to remind him of the obligation he owes to God for His gift of *hesed*. Our great tannaitic masters have taught us: "A man must pronounce a blessing over evil just as he pronounces a blessing over good" (Berakhot 9:5). In the same way that

God's goodness imposes upon man the obligation to perform exalted, sublime deeds, and demands of either the individual or the community original, creative actions, so too do afflictions require of a
person that he improve himself, that he purify his life—if he was
previously not bestirred to action when God's countenance shined
upon him, when God's *hesed* overflowed toward him. For there are
times when a person is called upon to mend through his afflictions
the flaws that he was inflicting upon creation when God "extended
peace to him like a river" (cf. Isaiah 66:12). The awareness of the
requirement to commit oneself entirely to God and the understanding of one's obligation to purify and sanctify oneself from precisely
out of the midst of one's suffering must shine brightly in the soul of
a person when he finds himself in the straits and inquires into the
meaning of his very existence. At that very moment, he is obliged to
mend his unfeeling heart, the moral callousness that caused him to
sin while he was yet standing in the great expanses. In a word, man
is obliged to resolve not the question of the causal, or teleological,
explanation of suffering in all of its speculative complexity but
rather the question of the rectification of suffering in all of its halakhic simplicity. He does this by transforming fate into destiny,
elevating himself from object to subject, from thing to person.

JOB

Consider: This was precisely the answer that the Creator gave to
Job. As long as Job philosophized, like a slave of fate, regarding the
cause of and reason for suffering, as long as he demanded of God
that He reveal to him the nature of evil, as long as he continued to
question and complain, asking why and wherefore afflictions befall
man, God answered him forcefully and caustically, posing to him
the very powerful and pointed question, "Dost thou know?" "Who
is this that darkeneth counsel by words without knowledge? Gird up
now thy loins like a man; for I will demand of thee, and declare
thou unto Me. Where wast thou when I laid the foundations of the

earth? Declare if thou hast the understanding. . . . Dost thou know the time when the wild goats of the rock bring forth? Or canst thou mark when the hinds do calve?" (Job 38:2-4, 39:1). If you do not even know the ABC of creation, how can you so arrogantly presume to ask so many questions regarding the governance of the cosmos? However, once Job understood how strange and inappropriate his question was, how great was his ignorance, once he confessed unashamedly, "Therefore have I uttered that which I understood not, things too wonderful for me, which I knew not" (Job 42:4), the Almighty revealed to him the true principle contained in suffering, as formulated by the halakhah. God addressed him as a man of destiny and said: Job, it is true you will never understand the secret of "why," you will never comprehend the cause, or telos, of suffering. But there is one thing that you *are* obliged to know: the principle of mending one's afflictions. If you can elevate yourself via your afflictions to a rank that you had hitherto not attained, then know full well that these afflictions were intended as a means for mending both your soul and your spirit. Job! when My lovingkindness overflowed toward you in the manner described by the verse, "Behold, I will extend peace to her like a river" (Isaiah 66:12), when you were a prominent and influential person—"And this man [Job] was the greatest of all the people of the East" (Job 1:3)—you did not fulfill the task that My abundant lovingkindness imposed upon you. True, you were a wholehearted and upright man, you feared God and shunned evil; you did not use your power or wealth for bad; you dispensed a great deal of charity—"I put on righteousness, and it clothed itself with me: my justice was as a robe and a diadem" (Job 29:14)—nor were you ever loath to extend your help and support to the needy, but you came to their aid in times of distress—"For I delivered the poor that cried, the fatherless also, that had none to help him" (Job 29:12). However, in two respects you were lacking in that great attribute of *ḥesed,* of lovingkindness: (1) you never assumed your proper share of the burdens of communal responsibility and never joined in the community's pain and anguish; (2) nor did you ever properly empathize with the agonies of the individual

sufferer. As a kind, good-hearted person, you took momentary pity
on the orphan, you were very wealthy and could afford to give substantial charitable contributions without straining your financial
resources. However, *hesed* means more than a passing sentiment, a
superficial feeling; *hesed* demands more than a momentary tear or a
cold coin. *Hesed* means to merge with the other person, to identify
with his pain, to feel responsible for his fate. And this attribute of *hesed* you lacked in your relationships with the community and with
the individual.

You were a contemporary of Jacob, who struggled with Laban,
with Esau, and with the man at the ford of the Jabbok.[4] Did you seek
to help him and offer him of your counsel and wisdom? Who was
Jacob? A poor shepherd. And you? A wealthy and influential man.
Had you accorded Jacob a proper measure of sympathy, of caring,
had you treated him with the attribute of steadfast lovingkindness,
then he would not have had to endure so much suffering. You lived
during the time of Moses and were numbered among Pharaoh's
advisers. Did you lift a finger when Pharaoh decreed, "Every son
that is born shall ye cast into the river;; (Exodus 1:22), when the
taskmasters worked your brethren with rigor? You were silent and
did not protest, for you were afraid to be identified with the
wretched slaves. To slip them a coin—fine, but to intervene publicly
on their behalf—out of the question. You were fearful lest you be
accused of dual loyalty. You were active during the generation of
Ezra and Nehemiah and those who went up with them from Babylon. You, Job, with your wealth and influence, could have signifi-
cantly accelerated the process of *yishuv ha-arez,* of settling the land of
Israel and building the Temple. However, you were deaf to the
historical cry of the people. You did not storm and protest against
the Sanballats, the Samaritans, and the other Jew-haters who sought
to destroy the small Jewish community in Judea and thereby extinguish the last glimmer of hope of God's people. What did you do
when those who went up from Babylon cried out, from the depths of
pain and despair, "The strength of the bearers of burdens is
decayed, and there is much rubbish; so that we are not able to build

the wall" (Nehemiah 4:4)? You stood by idly! You did not participate in the struggle and suffering of those who fought for Judaism,
for the land of Israel, and for the redemption; you never offered a
single sacrifice on their behalf. You were concerned only about your
own welfare, you would pray and offer a burnt-offering only on
your own behalf. "And it was so, when the days of their [Job's sons']
feasting were gone about, that Job sent and sanctified them, and
rose up early in the morning, and offered burnt-offerings according
to the number of them all; for Job said: It may be that my sons have
sinned, and blasphemed God in their hearts" (Job 1:5). Did you
ever once offer a prayer on behalf of a stranger in a spirit of sharing
in his grief? No! Don't you know, Job, that prayer is the possession
of the community as a whole, and that an individual cannot
approach the King and appeal to Him and present his requests
before Him unless he redeems himself from his isolation and seclu-
sion and attaches himself to the community? Have you forgotten
that Jewish prayer is recited in the plural—"a man should always
associate himself with the congregation" (Berakhot 30a), that Jewish
prayer means that one soul is bound up with another soul, that
stormy and tempestuous hearts merge and blend? You did not know
how to utilize the formulation of prayer in the plural as fixed by the
nation in order to include yourself among the many and in order to
bear the yoke of your fellow man. Job, if you but wish to learn the
teaching of the mending of one's afflictions, you must first apprehend the secret of prayer that brings the "I" closer to his fellow, you
must first be able to recite clearly the authentic text of prayer whereby the individual partakes of the experience of the many, and you
must first understand the idea of *hesed* as it is embodied by the
prayerful person who rises above his individual uniqueness to
achieve a sense of communal unity. You cannot discharge your obligation by merely dispensing a few clattering coins from amidst the
abundant wealth with which you have been blessed. Only through a
prayer fraught with the experience of a shared communal suffering
will you be redeemed. You did not understand the teaching contained in lovingkindness and you frittered away the blessing which I

bestowed upon you. Now seek to apprehend the teaching contained in suffering. Perhaps now you will be able to mend, in pain and grief, the sinful behavior you indulged in while in your previous state of self-satisfaction and pseudo-happiness.

God addressed the friends of Job: "Now therefore, take unto you seven bullocks and seven rams, and go unto My servant Job, and offer up for yourselves a burnt-offering; and My servant Job shall pray for You" (Job 42:8). Behold, I will test Job yet again. Let him be scrutinized publicly; will he now know how to pray for his fellow man, how to share in his suffering? Has he learned anything in this hour of calamity and wrath? Has he properly appropriated a new formulation of prayer which includes and encompasses the community? If he pleads on your behalf, then both he and you will be redeemed, "for him I will accept" (Job 42:8). Then you will know that Job has been delivered from the straits of egoism and has entered into the wide expanses of sympathy with the community and solidarity with one's fellowman, that his sense of detachment has disappeared and in its place a true spirit of communion has emerged. The great miracle occurred. Job suddenly grasped the true nature of Jewish prayer. In a moment he discovered its plural form, he descried the attribute of *ḥesed* which sweeps the individual from the private to the public domain. He began to live the life of the community, to feel its griefs, to mourn over its calamities, and to rejoice in its happiness. The afflictions of Job found their true rectification when he extricated himself from his fenced-in confines, and the divine wrath abated. "And the Lord turned the captivity of Job, *when he prayed for his friends*" (Job 42:10).

MISSING THE MOMENT

Now, as well, we are living in troubled times, in days of wrath and distress. We have been the victims of vicious attacks; we have been stricken with suffering. During the last fifteen years we have been afflicted with torments which are unparalleled in the thousands of years of exile, oppression, and religious persecution. This era of suffering, this dark chapter in our history, did not come to an end with the establishment of the State of Israel. Even now, today, the State of Israel still finds itself in a crisis situation, fraught with danger, and we are all filled with fear and trembling regarding the fate of the *Yishuv,* of the struggling Jewish community in the land of Israel. We are witnesses to the rising star of the wicked and the international perversion of justice, deriving from the indifference to the principles of righteousness and equity exhibited by the states of the West. Everyone flatters our enemies and adversaries, they all grovel before them in a display of hypocrisy and sycophancy of the worst order. Everyone seeks their well-being, while they treat our beleaguered and fragile *Yishuv* in the same manner as that wealthy man who stole the little ewe lamb from his poor, weak, and helpless neighbor.

The well-known metaphysical problem arises yet again and the sufferer asks: "Why dost Thou show me iniquity and beholdest mischief? . . . For the wicked doth beset the righteous; therefore, right goes forth perverted" (Habakkuk 1:3–4). However, as we emphasized earlier, God does not address Himself to this question and man receives no reply concerning it. The question remains obscure and sealed, outside the domain of logical thought. For "Thou canst not see My face, for man shall not see Me and live" (Exodus 33:20). When the impulse of intellectual curiosity seizes hold of a person, he ought to do naught but find strength and encouragement in his faith in the Creator, vindicate God's judgment, and acknowledge the perfection of His work. "The Rock, His work is perfect; for all His ways are justice" (Deuteronomy 32:4). If we wish to probe deeply, to question profoundly during a period of nightmarish terrors, then we have to pose the question in a halakhic form and ask: What is the obligation incumbent upon the sufferer, deriving from the suffering itself? What commanding voice, what normative principle arises out of the afflictions themselves? Such a question, as we stated above, has an answer which finds its expression in a clear halakhic ruling. We need not engage in metaphysical speculation in order to clarify the law of the rectification of evil. "It is not in heaven" (Deuteronomy 30:12). If we should succeed in formulating this teaching without getting involved in the question of cause and telos, then we will attain complete redemption, and the Biblical promise, "Take counsel together and it shall be brought to naught; speak the word and it shall not stand; for God is with us" (Isaiah 8:10), shall be fulfilled with regard to us. Then, and only then, will we rise from the depths of the Holocaust, possessed of a heightened spiritual stature and adorned with an even more resplendent historical grandeur, as it is written: "Also the Lord gave Job twice as much as he had before" (Job 42:10)—double, both in quantity and in quality.

The teaching of the rectification of suffering—when it is put into practice—demands of the sufferer both courage and discipline. He must find within himself and draw upon prodigious resources, and subject himself to a rigorous self-examination and self-evaluation, untainted by the slightest hint of partiality or self-indulgence; he must contemplate his past and envisage his future with complete and unwavering honesty. It was not easy for Job to mend his suffering. And we as well, faint-hearted and weak-willed as we are, bound in the chains of fate and lacking personal fortitude, are now called upon by divine providence to clothe ourselves in a new spirit, to elevate ourselves to the rank of the rectification of our afflictions, afflictions which are demanding of us that we provide them with their deliverance and redemption. For this purpose, we need to examine our own reflection with spiritual heroism and total objectivity. This reflection breaks through both past and present together in order to confront us directly.

If the gracious divine bounties which have been showered upon both the individual and the community obligate their beneficiary to perform special, concrete deeds, even if these bounties (like wealth, honor, influence, power, and the like, which are acquired through exhausting labor) have been bestowed upon man in a natural manner, how much more so do the divine bounties which are bequeathed in a supernatural manner, in the form of a miracle which takes place outside the context of the basic lawfulness governing the concatenation of historical events, bind the miracle's beneficiary to God. God's miraculous boon of *ḥesed* imposes upon man the absolute obligation to fulfill the great commandment which cries out from the very midst of the miracle itself. A transcendental commandment always accompanies a miraculous act—"Command the Israelites!" Woe unto the beneficiary of a miracle if he does not recognize the miracle performed on his behalf, if he is deaf to the imperative which echoes forth from the metahistorical event. How unfortunate is he who has enjoyed God's wonders if the spark of faith has not been kindled within him, if his conscience does not tremble and take heed at the sight of the extraordinary occurrence.

When a miracle does not find its proper answering echo in the form of concrete deeds, an exalted vision degenerates and dissipates, and the divine attribute of justice begins to denounce the ungrateful beneficiary of the miracle. "The Almighty sought to make Hezekiah the Messiah, and Sennacherib, Gog and Magog. The attribute of justice objected, 'You performed all these miracles on behalf of Hezekiah, yet he did not utter song before You. Shall You, then, make him the Messiah?'"[5] Then come times of distress; the hour of suffering makes its appearance. Suffering is the last warning wherewith divine providence alerts the man lacking any sense of appreciation for the good he has received. One must respond to this last pronouncement, arising out of suffering, with alacrity, and must answer the voice of God calling out to man, "Where art thou!" Judaism has always been very strict regarding the prohibition against missing the moment. It possesses a highly developed and sensitive time-consciousness and views the slightest delay as a sin. There are occasions when a person can lose his entire world on account of one sin—"and he lingered." What is the prohibition against overdue sacrifices (*notar*) if not a matter of being late? In what does the grave sin of the profanation of the Sabbath consist if not in the performance of work one moment after sunset, the very same work that had been permitted one moment before sunset? Does not the culpable nonfulfillment of commandments often take the form of lingering for but a few minutes: for example, reciting the *Shema* after its set time has elapsed, taking the *lulav* after sundown, and the like. Two kings of Israel, anointed of God and national heroes, sinned, repented fully, and confessed. The sin of one was not pardoned right away, while God reconciled Himself to the other and forgave him the very moment he confessed. God treated Saul in accordance with the attribute of strict justice and tore his kingdom away from him. However, with regard to David, God tempered justice with mercy, and He did not deprive David's descendants of the Davidic kingship. Why did God treat Saul with such severity and act so graciously toward David? But the question is not a particularly difficult question! The answer is very simple. David did not miss the opportune moment and confessed his sin immediately. Saul lingered just a bit, and because of this delay his kingdom was taken away from him. When Nathan the prophet came to David and exclaimed, "Thou art the man!" (2 Samuel 12:7), David started to confess immediately and did not put off his plea to God for even the slightest moment. "And David said unto Nathan: I have sinned against the Lord" (2 Samuel 12:13). Saul squandered that precious, inestimable moment. After he heard Samuel's rebuke— "Wherefore then didst thou not hearken to the voice of the Lord, but didst fly upon the spoil?" (1 Samuel 15:19)—he began to argue with Samuel prior to confessing. "And Saul said unto Samuel: Yea, I have hearkened to the voice of the Lord, and have gone the way which the Lord sent me" (1 Samuel 15:20). It is true that in the very same encounter with Samuel, Saul confessed his sin, broken–hearted and contrite. "And Saul said unto Samuel: I have sinned; for I have transgressed the commandment of the Lord and thy words" (1 Samuel 15:24). But his confession was not forthcoming at the desired moment, and this slight delay brought about the loss of his kingdom. By the time he confessed, the decree had already been sealed and his situation was irremediable. "The Lord hath torn the kingdom of Israel from thee this day" (1 Samuel 15:28). Had Saul not missed the right moment, had he not tarried, then his kingdom would have endured.[6]

What is the gist of the Song of Songs if not the description of the tragic and paradoxical delay of the Shulammite maiden, drunk with love and overwhelmed with yearning, when a favorable moment, replete with awe and majesty, beckoned to her—if not her missing that great, exalted, and momentous opportunity that she had dreamed about, fought for, and sought so passionately? The tender and delicate Shulammite maiden, impelled by longing for her bright-eyed beloved, roamed during sun-drenched days through the bypaths of vineyards and over the crests of mountains, through fields and gardens, and during pale, magical moonlit nights, during pitch-black nights, between the walls, searching for her beloved. One cold and rainy night she returned to her tent, tired and worn out, and fell fast asleep. The sound of quick and light footsteps could be heard in the silence of the tent. On that strange and mysterious night, suddenly the beloved emerged from out of the dark and knocked on the door of his darling, who had intensely yearned for and awaited him. He knocked and pleaded with her to open the door of her tent. "It is the voice of my beloved that knocketh. 'Open to me, my sister, my darling, my dove, my undefiled; for my head is filled with dew, my locks with the drops of the night'" (Song of Songs 5:2). The great moment that she had looked forward to with such impatience and longing materialized unexpectedly. Her elusive, self-concealing beloved, tired of wandering and hardships, appeared with his curly hair, black eyes, powerful build, and radiant countenance. He stood by her door, stretched his hand in through the hole in the latch, sought refuge from the damp of night, and wished to tell her about his powerful love, about his desires and yearnings, about a life of companionship, filled with delight and joy, about the realization and attainment of their aspirations and hopes. Only the slight movement of stretching out her hand and turning the latch intervened between her and her beloved, between the great dream and its complete fulfillment. With a single leap the Shulammite maiden could have obtained her heart's longings—"Draw me, we will run after thee . . . we will be glad and rejoice in thee" (Song of Songs 1:4). But the heart is deceitful, and who can discern it? Precisely on that very night, a strange, stubborn indolence overcame her. For a brief moment the fire of longing that had burned so brightly was dimmed, the fierce passion ebbed, her emotions were

stilled, her dreams, extinguished. The maiden refused to descend
from her bed. She did not open the door of the tent to her hand-
some beloved. A cruel madness swept her into an abyss of oblivion
and indifference. The maiden proved stubborn and lazy and rained
down a multitude of excuses and rationalizations to account for her
peculiar behavior: "I have put off my coat; how shall I put it on? I
have washed my feet; how shall I soil them?" (Song of Songs 5:3).
The beloved knocked again and again, and the more insistent his
knocks, the louder they grew, the more her icy, defiling madness
increased in intensity. As the whispered entreaties of the beloved
pierced the silence of the night, the heart of his darling became
harder and harder—like stone. The beloved continued to knock,
pleading patiently, and together with his knocks the clock sounded
the minutes and hours. The maiden paid no heed to the voice of her
beloved; the door to her tent remained shut up tight. The moment
was lost; and the vision of an exalted life faded away. It is true that
after a brief delay the maiden awoke from her slumber and, confused and startled, leapt from her bed to welcome her beloved: "I
rose up to open to my beloved" (Song of Songs 5:5); but she arose
too late. Her beloved had stopped knocking and vanished into the
darkness of the night—"My beloved had turned away and gone"
(Song of Songs 5:6). Her life's joy was fled; her existence—a desolate
wilderness, an empty waste. The saga of her passionate quest began
anew. She is still wandering amidst the shepherds' tents—searching
for her beloved.

SIX KNOCKS

Eight years ago, in the midst of a night of terror filled with the
horrors of Maidanek, Treblinka, and Buchenwald, in a night of gas
chambers and crematoria, in a night of absolute divine self-concealment (*hester panim muḥlat*), in a night ruled by the satan of doubt
and apostasy which sought to sweep the maiden from her house into
the Christian church, in a night of continuous searching, of questing

for the Beloved—in that very night the Beloved appeared. "God who conceals Himself in His dazzling hiddenness" suddenly manifested Himself and began to knock at the tent of His despondent and disconsolate love, twisting convulsively on her bed, suffering the pains of hell. *As a result of the knocks on the door of the maiden, wrapped in mourning, the State of Israel was born!*

How many times did the Beloved knock on the door of the tent of His love? It appears to me that we can count at least six knocks.

First, the knock of the Beloved was heard in the political arena. No one can deny that from the standpoint of international relations, *the establishment of the State of Israel, in a political sense, was an almost supernatural occurrence.* Both Russia and the Western countries jointly supported the idea of the establishment of the State. This was perhaps the only proposal where East and West were united. I am inclined to believe that the United Nations organization was created specifically for this purpose—in order to carry out the mission which divine providence had set for it. It seems to me that one cannot point to any other concrete achievement on the part of the U.N. Our sages, of blessed memory, already expressed the view that at times "rain" descends "for a single person," or for a single blade of grass. I do not know whom the journalists, with their eyes of flesh and blood, saw sitting in the chairman's seat during that fateful session when the General Assembly decided in favor of the establishment of the State. However, someone who at that time observed matters well with his spiritual eye could have sensed the presence of the true chairman who presided over the discussion—i.e., the Beloved! It was He who knocked with His gavel on the podium. Do we not interpret the verse "That night the sleep of the king fled" (Esther 6:1) as referring to "the sleep of the King of the universe" (Megillah 15b). Were it Ahasuerus alone who could not sleep, it would have been of no consequence, and the salvation of Israel would not have blossomed forth on that night. However, if it is the King of the universe who, as it were, does not slumber, then the redemption will be born. If it had been John Doe who called the session of the United Nations to order, the State of Israel would never have come into being—but if the Beloved knocked on the chairman's podium, then the miracle occurred. It is the voice of my Beloved that knocketh!

Second, the knocking of the Beloved could be heard on the battlefield. *The small Israeli Defense Forces defeated the mighty armies of the Arab countries.* The miracle of "the many in the hands of the few" took place before our very eyes. And an even greater miracle occurred at that time. God hardened the heart of Ishmael and enjoined him to do battle against the State of Israel. Had the Arabs not declared war against the State, and, instead, agreed to the Partition Plan, the State of Israel would have lacked Jerusalem, a large part of the Galilee, and several areas of the Negev. Had Pharaoh, thousands of years ago, allowed the Israelites to depart from Egypt immediately, in accordance with Moses' original request, Moses would have been bound to keep his promise and would have had to return after three days. However, Pharaoh hardened his heart and did not hearken to Moses. The Almighty took the Israelites out of Egypt with a strong hand and an outstretched arm. Consequently, Moses' pledge that they would return to Egypt was no longer binding. A bilateral contract cannot bind one party if the other party refuses to fulfill his obligations. It is the voice of my Beloved that knocketh!

Third, the Beloved began to knock as well on the door of the theological tent, and it may very well be that this is the strongest knock of all. I have often emphasized, when speaking of the land of Israel, that all the claims of Christian theologians that God deprived the Jewish people of its rights in the land of Israel, and that all the biblical promises regarding Zion and Jerusalem refer, in an allegorical sense, to Christianity and the Christian church, *have been publicly refuted by the establishment of the State of Israel and have been exposed as falsehoods,* lacking all validity. It requires a comprehensive knowledge of Christian theological literature, from Justin Martyr down to contemporary theologians, to properly appreciate the great miracle which so clearly invalidated this central premise of Christian theology. We ought to take note of the "learned" explanation of our

Secretary of State, Mr. [John Foster] Dulles, who also serves as an elder in the Episcopal Church, at a meeting of a Senate committee, that the Arabs hate the Jews because the Jews killed the founder of their religion. This "explanation" possesses profound, hidden symbolic significance. I am not a psychologist and certainly not a psychoanalyst; however, I do have some acquaintance with the Talmud, and I remember well what our sages said about Balaam: "From his blessing . . . you may learn what was in his heart" (Sanhedrin 105b; cf. Rashi on Numbers 24:6). When a person speaks at length, the truth may, at times, slip out. When one of the senators asked the Secretary of State: "Why do the Arabs hate the Jews?" he really wanted to reply: "I myself, as a Christian, don't bear any great love for them, for they killed our Messiah and, as a result, lost their share in the inheritance of Abraham." However, an angel intervened or a bit was placed in the Secretary's mouth (as happened to Balaam, according to the sages' interpretation of the verse "and He put a word into his mouth" [Numbers 23:16; cf. Rashi ad loc. and Sanhedrin 105b]), and instead of uttering the words "our Messiah" and "I myself," alternative terms slipped out of his mouth, and he said "the Arabs" and "Muhammed." In his subconscious he is afraid of the "terrible" fact that the Jewish people rule over Zion and Jerusalem. I find special pleasure in reading articles about the State of Israel in Catholic and Protestant newspapers. Against their will they have to use the name "Israel" when they report the news about Zion and Jerusalem which are now in our hands. I always derive a particular sense of satisfaction from reading in a newspaper that the response of the State of Israel is not as yet known, since today is the Sabbath and the offices of the ministries are closed, or from reading a news release from the United Press on Passover eve that "the Jews will sit down tonight at the Seder table confident that the miracles of Egypt will recur today." It is the voice of my Beloved that knocketh!

Fourth, the Beloved is knocking in the hearts of the perplexed and assimilated youths. The era of self-concealment (*hastarat panim*) at the beginning of the 1940s resulted in great confusion among the

Jewish masses and, in particular, among the Jewish youth. Assimilation grew and became more rampant, and the impulse to flee from Judaism and from the Jewish people reached a new height. Fear, despair, and sheer ignorance caused many to spurn the Jewish community and board the ship "to flee unto Tarshish from the presence of the Lord" (Jonah 1:3). A raging, seemingly uncontrollable, torrent threatened to destroy us. Suddenly, the Beloved began to knock on the doors of the hearts of the perplexed, and *His knock, the rise of the State of Israel,* at the very least slowed the process of flight. Many of those who, in the past, were alienated from the Jewish people are now tied to the Jewish state by a sense of pride in its outstanding achievements. Many American Jews who had been semi-, demi-, or hemi-assimilated are now filled with fear and concern about the crisis overtaking the State of Israel, and they pray for its security and welfare, even though they are still far from being completely committed to it. Even those who are opposed to the State of Israel—and there are such Jews—are compelled to defend themselves, without letup, against the strange charge of dual loyalty, and they loudly proclaim, day in day out, that they have no share in the Holy Land. It is good for a Jew not to be able to hide from his Jewishness, but to be compelled to keep on answering the question "Who art thou? and what is thine occupation?" (cf. Jonah 1:8), even if, overcome by cowardice, he lacks the strength and courage to answer proudly: "I am a Hebrew; and I fear the Lord, the God of heaven" (Jonah 1:9). This persistent question, "Who art thou?" binds him to the Jewish people. The very fact that people are always talking about Israel serves to remind the Jew in flight that he cannot run away from the Jewish community with which he has been intertwined from birth. Wherever we turn we encounter the word "Israel"; whether we listen to the radio, read the newspaper, participate in symposia about current affairs, we find the question of Israel always being publicly discussed.

This fact is of particular importance for Jews who are afflicted with self-hatred and wish to escape from Judaism and flee for their lives. They, like Jonah, seek to hide in the innermost part of the ship and wish to slumber, but the shipmaster does not allow them to ignore their fate. The shadow of Israel pursues them unceasingly. Buried, hidden thoughts and paradoxical reflections emerge from the depths of the souls of even the most avowed assimilationists. And once a Jew begins to think and contemplate, once his sleep is disturbed—who knows where his thoughts will take him, what form of expression his doubts and queries will assume? It is the voice of my Beloved that knocketh!

The fifth knock of the Beloved is perhaps the most important of all. For the first time in the history of our exile, divine providence has surprised our enemies with the sensational discovery that *Jewish blood is not free for the taking, is not hefker!* If anti-Semites wish to describe this phenomenon as "an eye for an eye," so be it; we will agree with them. If we wish to heroically defend our national-historical existence, we must, at times, interpret the verse "an eye for an eye" (Exodus 21:24) literally. How many eyes did we lose during the course of our bitter exile because we did *not* return blow for blow. The time has come for us to fulfill the law of "an eye for an eye" in its plain, simple sense. I am certain that everyone who knows me knows that I am a believer in the Oral Law and, consequently, that I do not doubt that the verse refers to monetary compensation, in accordance with the halakhic interpretation. However, with regard to Nasser or the Mufti I would demand that we interpret the phrase "an eye for an eye" in a strictly literal sense—as referring to the removal of the concrete, actual eye. Pay no attention to the fine phrases of well-known Jewish assimilationists or socialists, who continue to adhere to their outworn ideologies and think that they are living in the Bialystok, Minsk, or Brisk of 1905, and who publicly declaim that it is forbidden for Jews to take revenge at any time, any place, and under all circumstances. Vanity of vanities! Revenge is forbidden when it serves no purpose. However, if by taking revenge we raise ourselves up to the plane of self-defense, then it becomes the elementary right of man qua man to avenge the wrongs inflicted upon him.

The Torah has always taught us that a person is permitted,

indeed, that it is his sacred obligation, to defend himself. The Biblical law about the thief breaking into a house (Exodus 22:1-2) indicates that it is a firmly fixed halakhic principle that a person is permitted to defend not only his life but also his property.[7] If the thief who comes to steal the money of the householder is capable of murdering the householder if he does not accede to his demands, then the householder is permitted to rise up against the lawbreaker and kill him. It is not for naught that the Torah informs us that its two great heroes, Abraham and Moses, both took up arms in order to defend their brethren—"and he [Abraham] armed his trained men" (Genesis 14:14 and cf. Rashi ad loc.); "and he [Moses] smote the Egyptian" (Exodus 2:12). Such behavior does not contradict the principles of mercy and lovingkindness. On the contrary, a passive attitude, renouncing self-defense, is likely, at times, to give rise to the worst types of cruelty. "And I will get Me honor through Pharaoh and through all his hosts; and the Egyptians shall know that I am the Lord" (Exodus 14:4). God did not seek honor and fame; He wanted Pharaoh, Moses' contemporary, to know that he would have to pay a high price for the decree, "Every son that is born ye shall cast into the river" (Exodus 1:22). And now, as well, it is God's wish that the blood of the Jewish children who were murdered while reciting the *Shemoneh Esreh* be avenged. When God smote Egypt, He wished thereby to demonstrate that Jewish blood always has claimants. Today, also, it is necessary to convince not only the current Egyptian tyrant but also the self-declared saint, Nehru, the British Foreign Office, and the "moralists" in the United Nations that Jewish blood is not ownerless. Therefore, how grotesque is the attempt to convince us that we ought to rely on the declaration of the three great powers guaranteeing the status quo. We all know from experience how much value there is to the promises of the British Foreign Office and to the "friendship" of certain well-known officials in our own State Department. And, in general, how absurd it is to demand of a people that it be completely dependent upon the good graces of others and that it relinquish the ability to defend itself. The honor of every community, like the honor of every individual, resides in the ability to defend its existence and honor. A people that cannot ensure its own freedom and security is not truly independent. The third phrase in God's promise of redemption is: "And I will redeem you with an outstretched arm *and with great judgments*" (Exodus 6:7). *Blessed be He Who has granted us life and brought us to this era when Jews have the power, with the help of God, to defend themselves!*

Let us not forget that the venom of Hitlerian anti-Semitism, which made the Jews like the fish of the sea to be preyed upon by all, still infects many in our generation who viewed the horrific spectacle of the gassing of millions with indifference, as a ordinary event not requiring a moment's thought. The antidote to this deadly poison that envenomed minds and benumbed hearts is the readiness of the State of Israel to defend the lives of its sons, its builders. It is the voice of my Beloved that knocketh!

The sixth knock, which we must not ignore, was heard when the gates of the land were opened. A Jew who flees from a hostile country now knows that he can find a secure refuge in the land of his ancestors. This is a new phenomenon in our history. Until now, whenever Jewish communities were expelled from their lands, they had to wander in the wilderness of the nations and were not able to find shelter in another land. Because the gates were barred before exiles and wanderers, many Jewish communities were decimated. Now the situation has changed. If a particular people expels the Jewish minority from its midst, the exiles can direct their steps unto Zion, and she, like a compassionate mother, will gather in her children. We have all been witness to Oriental Jewry's settling in the land of Israel in the past few years. Who knows what might have befallen our brethren in the lands in which they had settled had not the land of Israel brought them by boats and planes to her? Had the State of Israel arisen before Hitler's Holocaust, hundreds of thousands of Jews might have been saved from the gas chambers and crematoria. The miracle of the State came just a bit late, and as a result of this delay thousands and tens of thousands of Jews were murdered. However, now that the era of divine self-concealment (*hester pan-*

im) is over, Jews who have been uprooted from their homes can find
lodging in the Holy Land. Let us not view this matter lightly! It is
the voice of my Beloved that knocketh!

THE OBLIGATION OF TORAH JEWRY
TO THE LAND OF ISRAEL

What was our reaction to the voice of the Beloved that knocketh, to
God's bounteous kindnesses and wonders? Did we descend from
our couches and immediately open the door? Or did we, like the
Shulammite maiden, continue to rest and tarry rather than descend
from our beds? "I have put off my coat; how shall I put it on? I
have washed my feet; how shall I soil them?" (Song of Songs 5:3).

All of the trepidation and concern for the geographical integrity
of the State of Israel, on the one hand, and all of our enemies' pro-
posals that are designed to exact territorial concessions from the
State of Israel, all of the brazen demands of the Arabs for boundary
changes, on the other hand, are all based on one and only one fact:
the Jews have not colonized the Negev and have not set up hundreds
of settlements there. Were the Negev settled by tens of thousands of
Jews, then not even Nasser would dream of the possibility of wrest-
ing it from the State of Israel. Desolation, from time immemorial,
endangers political tranquility. The Torah has already emphasized
this truth. "Thou mayest not consume them [the nations of Canaan]
quickly, lest the beasts of the field increase upon thee" (Deuteronomy 7:22). The fact that Jews conquered the Negev does not suffice;
the main thing is to settle it. Maimonides, the great eagle, ruled that
the first sanctification of the land, wrought by Joshua, was not permanent because it derived from military conquest, which was nullified by the invasion of the enemy, whose army was mighty and
weapons many, who conquered the land and seized it from us. The
second sanctification, wrought by Ezra, which derived from taking
possession of the land and settling it—in accordance with the divine
command—with the toil of one's hands and the sweat of one's

brow, was not nullified.[8] The holiness grounded in settling the land—settling, plain and simple—remains in effect for its time and for eternity! We have been remiss and our guilt is great. American Jewry could certainly have accelerated the process of colonization. But why should we search out the faults of others and seek to place the blame on the shoulders of secular Jews? Let us examine our own flaws and confess our own sins. It is precisely Orthodox Jews, more than all other American Jews, who bear the burden of guilt for the slow place of conquest through taking possession. The obligation to pay close attention to the "voice of my Beloved" that knocketh and to respond to Him immediately with mighty deeds and undertakings devolves precisely upon us who are faithful to traditional Judaism. Rashi, basing himself upon the *Sifra,* in his commentary on the verse "And I will bring the land into desolation" (Leviticus 26:32) states: "This is a good dispensation for the Israelites, for the enemies will not find any gratification in their land, since it will be desolate of its inhabitants." The land of Israel cannot be built by just any people or group. Only the Jewish people possesses the capacity to transform it into a settled land and to make the desolate waste bloom. This divine promise became a miraculous fact in the history of the land of Israel during various periods. We must not forget, even for a moment, that the land of Israel drew the nations of the world—Christian and Muslim alike—to it like a magnet. The medieval Crusades were undertaken for the purpose of conquering the land of Israel and colonizing it with a Christian population. All of the efforts of the crusaders were in vain, and they did not take root in the land. Even the Muslims, who were already in the land, did not succeed in colonizing it properly. It remained a desolate waste. "And your land shall be a desolation" (Leviticus 26:33). Even later, in the modern era, when the European nations in the seventeenth and eighteenth centuries settled and colonized entire continents, the land of Israel remained desolate and in a more primitive state than its neighboring Arab countries—Egypt, Syria, and Lebanon. Had the land of Israel been settled by a capable, enterprising, powerful, and cultured nation, had it been properly colonized and

developed, then our tie to it would, in the course of events, have
been obliterated, and no Jewish presence would have established
itself there. Strangers would have consumed its goodness and its
fruit, and our rights and claims would have been completely nullified. However, the land of Israel did not betray the people of Israel;
she remained faithful to them and during all those years awaited her
redeemer. It stands to reason, then, that when the possibility arose
for the Jewish poeple to return to its land, the land which had with-
held its treasures from strangers and guarded them for us, Orthodox Jews would eagerly bestir themselves to perform this great and
important commandment and would plunge, with joy and enthusiasm, into the midst of this holy task—the building and settling of
the land. Alas, we did not act thus. When the "desolate wife," who
had awaited us with such yearning and for so long, invited us, her
sons, to come and redeem her from her desolate condition, and
when the Beloved, who had watched over the desolation for almost
nineteen hundred years, and who had decreed that not a tree would
flourish there, that no springs would fructify its ground, knocked on
the doors of His love, the maiden—we religious Jews—did not rush
to descend from her couch and let in the Beloved. Had we built a
dense network of settlements throughout the entire length of the
land, from Eilat to Dan, then our situation would be entirely
different.

Let us be honest and speak openly and candidly. We are critical
of certain well-known Israeli leaders because of their attitudes to
traditional values and religious observances. Our complaints are
valid; we have serious accusations to level against the secular leaders
of the land of Israel. However, are they alone guilty, while we are as
clean and pure as the ministering angels? Such an assumption is
completely groundless! We could have extended our influence in
shaping the spiritual image of the *Yishuv* if we had hastened to
arouse ourselves from our sleep and descend to open the door for
the Beloved who was knocking. I am afraid that we Orthodox Jews
are, even today, still sunk in a very pleasant slumber. Had we established more religious kibbutzim, had we built more houses for reli-

gious immigrants, had we created an elaborate and extended system of schools, our situation would be entirely other than it is. Then we would not have to criticize the leaders of other movements so severely. We Orthodox Jews suffer from a unique illness which is not to be found among nonreligious Jews (with a few exceptions); we are all misers! In comparison with other American Jews, we do not excel in the attribute of *hesed*. We are content to give a few pennies, and in return for our paltry contributions we demand a hefty this-worldly reward and a place at the head of the line. Therefore, our honor has declined to a new low, and we are not able to exercise the proper influence on Jewish life here and on events in the land of Israel. America, the great and the free, is a land of tzedekah, of charity. The American government itself, during the years 1945 to 1956, disbursed over $55 billion in foreign aid. (The numbers are simply unimaginable.) And it is only philanthropists, who know how to give, who are accorded honor in a land which knows how to give and help on such a scale. Consequently, we Orthodox Jews in America are not entitled to any position of eminence, and such positions are occupied by others. Recently, we have become specialists in criticism and in the detection of plagues—"and the priest shall look on the plague . . . and pronounce him unclean" (Leviticus 13:3). This task—to search out blemishes and offer our expert opinions—we know how to do very well. However, we have overlooked one point, namely, that the priest who declares a person unclean must go outside the camp to the leper, the afflicted individual, the sufferer, in order to purify him. "And the priest shall go outside the camp . . . and the priest shall command . . ." (Leviticus 14:3-4). We have to build not just small, isolated corners whose influence is not discernible, but major institutions throughout the length and breadth of America and Israel. It is incumbent upon us to purify those who are "outside the camp," those who dwell in the great camp of ignorance. For this end we require great sums; and we Orthodox Jews are very far from being generous and liberal, open-hearted and open-handed, in matters of charity. This is why our institutions, both here and in the land of Israel, are so poverty-stricken. In particular, the religious *shivat ẓiyyon* (return to Zion) movement must, perforce, be content with meager sums. Because it is deprived of adequate financial means, it lacks the capacity to operate on a proper scale. Indeed, it is true: the faithful maiden is very lovely, her eyes are like doves, her face shines with grace and charm. She is much more beautiful than the nonreligious maiden. But "grace is deceitful and beauty is vain" (Proverbs 31:30) if the faithful maiden is miserly and slothful. "I have put off my coat; how shall I put it on? I have washed my feet; how shall I soil them?" (Song of Songs 5:3). If one telephones a rich Jew and asks that he contribute to a worthy cause, he replies: "I am going to Florida, and this year have decided to stay in a luxury hotel. I am, therefore, unable to give the amount requested of me." What did the rabbi say to the King of the Khazars? "This is a justified reproach, O King of the Khazars! . . . and that which we say, 'Bow to His holy hill' (Psalms 99:9), . . . is but as the chattering of the starling and the nightingale."[9]

Can we not hear, in our own concern for the peace and security of the land of Israel today, the knocking of the Beloved pleading with His love that she let Him enter? He has already been knocking for more than eight years and still has not received a proper response; nevertheless, he continues to knock. We have been fortunate. The Beloved did not show any special regard to His own cherished darling, but He continues to favor us. On that fateful night, the maiden's Beloved knocked on the door of her tent for only a brief moment and then disappeared, while He treats us with extreme patience. It is eight years now that He has been knocking. Would that we not miss the moment!

THE COVENANT AT SINAI
AND THE COVENANT IN EGYPT

When we probe the nature of our historical existence we arrive at a very important insight, one that constitutes a fundamental element of our world-view. The Torah relates that God made two covenants with the Israelites. The first covenant He made in Egypt: "And I will take you to Me for a people, and I will be to you a God" (Exodus 6:7); the second covenant, at Mount Sinai: "And he took the book of the covenant . . . and said: 'Behold the blood of the covenant, which the Lord hath made with you in agreement with all these words'" (Exodus 24:7-8). (The third covenant, "These are the words of the covenant . . . beside the covenant which He made with them in Horeb" [Deuteronomy 28:69], is identical in content and goals with the covenant at Sinai.)[10] What is the nature of these two covenants? It seems to me that this question is implicitly answered at the beginning of our essay. For just as Judaism distinguishes between fate and destiny in the personal-individual realm, so it differentiates between these two ideas in the sphere of our national-historical existence. The individual is tied to his people both with the chains of fate and with the bonds of destiny. In the light of this premise, it may be stated that the covenant in Egypt was a covenant of fate, while the covenant at Sinai was a covenant of destiny.

THE COVENANT OF FATE

What is the nature of a covenant of fate? Fate in the life of a people, as in the life of an individual, signifies an existence of compulsion. A strange necessity binds the particulars into one whole. The individual, against his will, is subjected and subjugated to the national, fate-laden, reality. He cannot evade this reality and become assimilated into some other, different reality. The environment spits out the Jew who flees from the presence of the Lord, and he is bestirred from his slumber in the same manner as the prophet Jonah, who awoke upon hearing the voice of the ship's captain demanding that he identify himself in both personal and national-religious terms.

This sense of a fate-laden existence of necessity gives rise to the historical loneliness of the Jew. He is alone both in life and in death. The concept of a Jewish burial-plot emphasizes the Jew's strange isolation from the world. Let the sociologists and psychologists say what they may about the incomprehensible alienation of the Jew. All their explanations are naught but vain and empty speculations which do not shed any intelligible light on this phenomenon. Jewish loneliness belongs to, is part of, the framework of the covenant of fate that was made in Egypt. In truth, Judaism and separation from the world are identical ideas. Even before the exile in Egypt, with the appearance of the first Jew—our father, Abraham—loneliness entered our world. Abraham was lonely. He was called Abraham the Hebrew, *Avraham ha-Ivri,* for "all the world was to one side (*ever eḥad*) while he was to the other side (*ever eḥad*)."[11] When Balaam saw the Jewish people dwelling tribe by tribe, he apprehended the mystery of the solitary mode of Jewish existence and proclaimed in a state of amazement: "Lo, it is a people that shall dwell alone, and shall not be reckoned among the nations" (Numbers 23:9). Even if a person achieves the pinnacle of social or political success, he will still not be able to free himself from the chains of isolation. This paradoxical fate has preserved both the separateness and the uniqueness of the Jew despite his supposed integration into his foreign, non-Jewish environment. Even as politically powerful a person as Joseph, who ranked next to the king of Egypt, lived separately from Egyptian society and dwelled alone in his tent—"And they set on for him by himself . . . and for the Egyptians that did eat with him, by themselves" (Genesis 43:32). Before his death, he pleaded with his brothers: "God will surely remember you, and ye shall carry up my bones from hence" (Genesis 50:25). Despite my greatness and glory, I am bound up with you and with your survival, both in my life and in my death. This special, incomprehensible reality of the individual clinging to the community and feeling alienated from the foreign, outside world became crystallized in Egypt. It was there that the Israelites raised themselves up to the rank of a people, peoplehood signifying both togetherness (the Hebrew word for "people," *am,* is related to the Hebrew word *im,* meaning "with," "togetherness")[12] and the uniqueness that derives from togetherness. This consciousness of a covenant of fate in all of its manifestations is an integral part of our historical-meta-physical being.

When the Jew, with this sense of his special, unique fate, con-fronts God face to face, he encounters the God of the Hebrews, who reveals himself to man from out of the very midst of the experience of loneliness and necessity, from out of the very midst of the con-sciousness of the fate which seizes hold of an individual and over-comes him. The God of the Hebrews does not wait for man to search for Him, to freely invite Him into his presence. He imposes His rule over man, against his will. A Jew cannot expel the God of the Hebrews from his private domain. Even if he violates the Sab-bath, defiles his table and bed, and strives to deny his own Jewish-ness, his membership in the Jewish people, he will still not be able to escape the dominion of the God of the Hebrews, who pursues him like a shadow. So long as a person's nose testifies to his origins, so long as a drop of Jewish blood courses through his veins, so long as physically he is still a Jew, he serves the God of the Hebrews against his will. Neither counsel nor understanding can prevail against Him. Yea, if the Jew who rejects his people ascends heavenward, yea, if he takes the wings of the morning, there would the hand of the God of the Hebrews take hold of him. Whither shall the Jew go from the spirit of the God of the Hebrews, and whither shall he flee from His presence? "And they said: 'The God of the Hebrews hath met with us. Let us go, we pray thee, three days' journey into the wilder-ness, and sacrifice unto the Lord our God; lest He fall upon us with pestilence, or with the sword'" (Exodus 5:3). To disregard the com-mands of the God of the Hebrews will, in the end, result in calamity and destruction.

The covenant of fate expresses itself as well in positive categories which derive from the consciousness of a shared fate. There are four aspects to this rare mode of consciousness.

First, the consciousness of a shared fate manifests itself as a con-sciousness of shared circumstances. We all find ourselves in the realm of a common fate which binds together all of the people's dif-

ferent strata, its various units and groups, a fate which does not dis-
criminate between one group and another group or between one
person and his fellow. Our fate does not distinguish between aristo-
crats and common folk, between rich and poor, between a prince
garbed in the royal purple and a pauper begging from door to door,
between a pietist and an assimilationist. Even though we speak a
plethora of languages, even though we are inhabitants of different
lands, even though we look different—one may be short and dark,
the other tall and blond—even though we live in varying and une-
qual social and economic conditions—one may dwell in a magnificent palace, the other in a miserable hovel—we still share the same
fate. If the Jew in the hovel is beaten, then the security of the Jew in
the palace is endangered. "Think not with thyself that thou shalt
escape in the king's house, more than all the Jews" (Esther 4:13).
Both Queen Esther, garbed in royal apparel, and Mordecai the Jew,
clad in sackcloth, were caught in the same web of historical circumstances. *Haverim kol yisrael,* "All Israel are knit together"—We will all
be pursued unto death or we will all be redeemed with an eternal
salvation.

Second, the consciousness of shared historical circumstances
results in the experience of shared suffering. The feeling of sympathy
is a fundamental feature of the consciousness of the unifying fate of
the Jewish people. The suffering of one part of the people affects the
people as a whole. The scattered and dispersed people mourn
together and are comforted together. *Tefillah,* prayer, *ze'akah,* the
human outcry, and *nehamah,* comfort, are all formulated, as I
emphasized above, in the plural. The pleas that ascend from the
abyss of affliction are not restricted to the suffering and pain of the
individual supplicant. They include the needs of the entire community. When a person has a sick relative, he cannot pray for him
alone but has to pray for all the sick of Israel. If one enters into a
mourner's home to comfort him and wipe away a tear from his
grieving face, one directs one's words of comfort to all who mourn
for Zion and Jerusalem. The slightest disturbance in the condition of
a single individual or group ought to grieve all of the various seg-

ments of the people in all of their dispersions. It is both forbidden and impossible for the "I" to isolate himself from his fellow and not share in his suffering. If the premise of shared historical circumstances is correct, then the experience of shared suffering is the direct conclusion of that premise.

A preacher of the last generation put it well. He said that the Jewish people may be compared to the man with two heads, concerning whom the question was posed in the house of study: How is he to be viewed for purposes of inheritance? Does he take two portions like a dual person? Or does he take one portion like a single unified individual?[13] One may similarly ask: Has the dispersion of the Jewish people throughout the lands of its exile and its taking root in its various surroundings resulted in its spiritual and psychic dissolution? Or has the unity of the people not been abrogated, despite the fact that it has grown many heads, that it expresses itself in a multitude of languages and cultures, in differing customs and varying practices? In a word: Is the Jewish diaspora a unity or not?

The answer—the preacher continued—to the question of the unity of the Jewish people is identical with the ruling issued in the house of study regarding the question of the unity of the two-headed heir. Let boiling water be poured on one of his heads, stated the judge, and let us see the reaction of the other head. If the other head cries out in pain, then both heads blend into one complete and unified personality and the heir will take one portion. However, if the second head does not feel the pangs of the first head, then we have two personalities coupled together in one body and they take two portions.

The same holds true with regard to the question of the unity of the Jewish people. The authoritative ruling is that as long as there is shared suffering, in the manner of "I will be with him in trouble" (Psalms 91:15), there is unity. If the Jew upon whom divine providence has shed a beneficent light, and who consequently believes that, at least with respect to him, the venom of hate and rejection has been expunged from his surroundings, still feels the troubles of the people and the burden of a fate-laden existence, then his link with the people has not been broken. If boiling water is poured upon the head of the Jew in Morocco, the fashionably attired Jew in Paris or London has to scream at the top of his voice, and through feeling the pain he will remain faithful to his people. The fragmentation of the people and the blearing of its image are concomitants of the absence of the feeling of sympathy.

Third, shared suffering finds its expression in the awareness of shared responsibility and liability. When Israel went forth from Egypt, Moses and Aaron fell down upon their faces, pleaded with God, and said: "O God, the God of the spirits of all flesh, shall one man sin, and will Thou be wroth with all the congregation?" (Numbers 16:22). This prayer accomplished the aim intended for it by Moses and Aaron, the shepherds of their people, Israel; God agreed that they had acted properly in setting forth their plea and punished only the congregation of Korah. However, God's display of this particular mode of *hesed* was only temporary. On a permanent basis, the "I" is held responsible for the sin of his fellow, if it was in his power to rebuke him, to protest against his behavior and induce him to repent. A collective ethico-halakhic responsibility devolves upon the entire Jewish people. The individuals coalesce into one ethico-halakhic unit, possessed of one conscience and an all-encompassing normative consciousness. The halakhah has already declared that all Jews are guarantors for one another. Consequently, the halakhic ruling is that a person who has already discharged his obligation to fulfill a commandment can still perform the commandment for his fellow Jew who has not as yet performed it and thereby enable him to discharge his obligation. The fact that the first person has already performed the commandment does not result in his being included in the category of those who are exempt from a particular obligation, who cannot enable the many to discharge their obligation. The "I" is not himself exempt as long as his fellow has not performed the commandment required of him. A special covenant was made in order to effect the mutual *arevut* (suretyship) of all Jews for one another. This covenant received its expression in the blessings and curses on Mounts Gerizim and Ebal. It is based on the idea of peoplehood that God revealed to Moses in Egypt. From the idea of peoplehood the covenant of mutual *arevut* directly followed. Moses, the master of the prophets, in referring to this covenant of *arevut,* emphatically proclaimed: "that He may establish thee this day unto Himself for a people and that He may be unto thee a God" (Deuteronomy 29:12). In speaking thus, he used the same phrases employed to describe the covenant in Egypt, "And I will take you to Me for a people, and I will be to you a God" (Exodus 6:7). Here the concept of shared fate has risen from the plane of socio-political suffering to the plane of ethico-halakhic *arevrut.* We are all mutually responsible for one another, we are all each other's guarantors, as the verse states: "but the things that are revealed belong unto us and our children for ever, that we may do all the words of this Law" (Deuteronomy 29:28).[14]

Shared responsibility is not only a theoretical halakhic idea; it is also a central fact in the history of the Jewish people in respect to its relationship to the nations of the world. Our neighbors have always condemned all of us for the sins of one of us; they have, thereby, transformed the rhetorical talmudic query, "Shall Tuviah sin and Zigud be punished?" (Pesaḥim 113b), into a daily reality that does not even surprise anyone. The identification of the actions of the individual with the deeds of the people is a fundamental feature of our history. Our enemies will not allow the individual Jew to remain isolated in his own private, separate sphere. They take him out of his four cubits into the public domain, and there they make use of him in order to level a harsh indictment against the entire community. This criterion they apply only to Jews and not to other nations. No one has ever accused a particular Russian or Chinese of being an agent of international communism simply because racially he belongs to a people who have instituted a communist regime in their own country and seek to forcibly impose their cruel reign on the entire world. In contrast to this logical and humane approach which is applied to other peoples, the Jewish people, as a whole, on account of the deeds of a few Jewish apostates, is libeled as being an adherent of communism. We have still not been cleared of this libel.

Again, the various explanations of this phenomenon offered by scholars are unsatisfying. It makes no difference if the root of the problem is assigned to the psychic-conative sphere or the political-historical sphere. Such scientific classification is of no value; the phenomenon remains opaque and mysterious. For us, as religious Jews, there is only one answer to this enigma: it is the hand of the covenant of fate that was made in Egypt regarding the absolute uniqueness of the Jewish people which manifests itself through this otherwise incomprehensible reality.

The commandment of the sanctification of the divine Name and the prohibition against the desecration of the divine Name[15] can be explained very well in the light of this principle of shared responsibility and liability. The actions of the individual are charged to the account of the community. Any sin he commits besmirches the name of Israel in the world. The individual, therefore, must answer not only to his own personal conscience but also to the collective conscience of the people. If he behaves properly, he sanctifies the name of Israel and the Name of the God of Israel; if he sins, he casts shame and disgrace on the people and desecrates the Name of its God.

Fourth, shared historical circumstances give rise to shared activity. The obligation to give charity and perform deeds of lovingkindness derives its force from the all-penetrating and all-encompassing experience of brotherhood. The Torah, in laying down these commandments, uses the term *aḥ,* "brother," instead of *re'a,* "fellow." "And if thy brother be waxen poor . . . then thou shalt uphold him . . . and he shall live with thee" (Leviticus 25:35). "Thou shalt not harden thy heart, nor shut thy hand from thy needy brother. . . . Thou shalt surely open thy hand unto thy poor and needy brother in thy land" (Deuteronomy 15:7, 11). The confrontation with the people's strange and unusual fate-laden existence endows the Jew with a unifying consciousness in the field of social action. The common situation of all Jews without distinction—whether manifested on the objective level as shared historical circumstances or on the subjective level as shared suffering—opens up founts of mercy and lovingkindness in the heart of the individual on behalf of his brethren in trouble, which indirectly affects him as well. Maimonides formulated this idea in his unique style, at once highly concise and overflowing with ideas:

> All Israelites and those who have attached themselves to them are to each other like brothers, as it is said, "Ye are the children of the Lord your God" (Deuteronomy 14:1). If brother shows no compassion to brother, who will show compassion to him? And unto whom shall the poor of Israel raise their eyes? Unto the heathens, who hate them and persecute them? Their eyes are therefore uplifted solely to their brethren.[16]

We have stated that it is the consciousness of the fate imposed upon the people against their will and of their terrible isolation that is the source of the people's unity, of their togetherness. It is precisely this consciousness as the source of the people's togetherness that gives rise to the attribute of *hesed,* which summons and stirs the community of fate to achieve a positive mode of togetherness through ongoing, joint participation in its own historical circumstances, in its suffering, conscience, and acts of mutual aid. The lonely Jew finds consolation in breaking down the existential barriers of egoism and alienation, joining himself to his fellow and actively connecting himself with the community. The oppressive sense of fate undergoes a positive transformation when individual-personal existences blend together to form a new unit—a people. The obligation to love one another stems from the consciousness of this people of fate, this lonely people that inquires into the meaning of its own uniqueness. It is this obligation of love that stands at the very heart of the covenant made in Egypt.

THE COVENANT OF DESTINY

What is the nature of the covenant of destiny? Destiny in the life of a people, as in the life of an individual, signifies a deliberate and conscious existence that the people has chosen out of its own free will and in which it finds the full realization of its historical being. Its existence, in place of simply being the experience of an unalterable reality into which the people has been thrust, now appears as the experience of an act possessing teleological dimensions, replete with movement, ascent, striving, and attaining. The people is embedded in its destiny as a result of its longing for a refined, substantive, and purposeful existence. Destiny is the flowing spring of the people's unique exaltation: it is the unceasing stream of supernal influence that will never dry up as long as the people charts its path in accordance with the divine Law. A life of destiny is a life with direction; it is the fruit of cognitive readiness and free choice.

The covenant in Egypt was made against the Israelites' will. God took them unto Himself for a people without consulting them beforehand, as the verse states: "And I will take you to Me for a people" (Exodus 6:7). The covenant at Sinai, in contrast, was first presented to the Israelites before it was made. God sent Moses to the Israelites to bring them His word, and Moses returned to God with their response. The halakhah views the covenant at Sinai as a contract that can only be drawn up with the knowledge and consent of the party assuming obligations for the future, in this instance the community of Israel. The proclamation "We will do and obey" (Exodus 24:7) constitutes the foundation of the acceptance of the Torah.[17]

What is the content of the covenant at Sinai? It consists in a special way of life which directs man's existence toward attaining a single goal, a goal beyond the reach of the man of fate, namely, man's imitation of his Creator through an act of self-transcendence. The creative activity which suffuses the covenant of destiny flows from a source unknown to the man of fate. It derives from man's rebellion against a life of sheer facticity, from the desire pulsating within him for more exalted, more supernal modes of being. The deeds of lovingkindness and brotherhood which are interwoven into the covenant at Sinai have as their motivating force not the Jew's strange sense of isolation, but rather his experience of the unity of a people forever betrothed to the one true God. The absolute unity of God is reflected in the unity of the people bound to Him eternally. "Thou art One and Thy Name is One, and who is like unto Thy people, Israel, one nation on earth?" Jewish fellowship in this dimension is a result of the special filial relationship the members of this people enjoy with God. "We are Thy children and Thou art our Father." (Maimonides emphasized this motif in the passage we cited earlier.) At Sinai, God raised on high the covenant of fate which He made with a community which, against its will, finds itself alone, a community the members of which perform deeds of lovingkindness on behalf of one another as a result of this externally imposed isolation and separateness, and transformed the covenant of fate into a covenant of destiny which He made with a community possessing will and desire, a community sanctifying itself and directing itself toward encountering God. The "people," lacking direction and purpose (the Hebrew word for "people," *am,* as we have already noted, is related to the word *im,* "with"), became a "nation," which signifies a community possessing a distinct communal countenance and collective physiognomy (the Hebrew word for "nation" is *goy,* which is related to the word *geviyah,* "body").[18] The *am-ḥesed,* the people of lovingkindness, was raised on high and became a *goy kadosh,* a holy nation.[19] Holiness, which expresses itself in the form of an authentic mode of being, is the very foundation of the shared destiny of the nation.[20]

When the man of destiny confronts God he beholds the God of Israel, who reveals Himself to man only with His consent and at His invitation. The God of Israel enters into a relationship with finite, creaturely man only after the latter has sanctified himself and purified himself from all uncleanliness and pollution, and awaits, with passion and longing, this wondrous encounter. The revelation of the God of Israel does not take place under all circumstances and conditions. Such a revelation demands a special spiritual state, as set forth in the divine command, "Be ready for the third day" (Exodus 19:11). Without such preparation, such readiness on the part of man, the God of Israel will not just randomly and casually reveal

Himself. The God of Israel does not take man by surprise. Rather, He responds to man's fervid plea. However, the God of Israel takes no interest in the person who does not passionately yearn for Him with a longing that expresses itself in and takes the form of concrete actions. While the God of the Hebrews pursues man against his will and takes no heed of his opinions or wishes, the God of Israel consults with man prior to the encounter. Already in Egypt the Almighty revealed Himself to Moses not only as the God of the Hebrews but also as the God of Israel, who awaits man and invites him to serve Him. "Thus saith the Lord, God of Israel: Let My people go, that they may hold a feast unto Me in the wilderness" (Exodus 5:1).

CAMP AND CONGREGATION

In order to explain the difference between the people of fate and the nation of destiny, it is worth taking note of another antithesis, namely, the antithesis between camp (*mahaneh*) and congregation (*edah*). The Torah has used both terms together in speaking of the Israelites. "Make thee two trumpets of silver, of beaten work shalt thou make them; and they shall be unto thee for the calling of the congregation and for causing the camp to set forward" (Numbers 10:2).

Camp and congregation constitute two distinct sociological phenomena, two separate groups lacking any common features, devoid of any symbiotic relationship. The camp is created as a result of the desire for self-defense and is nurtured by a sense of fear; the congregation is created as a result of the longing for the realization of an exalted ethical idea and is nurtured by the sentiment of love. Fate reigns, in unbounded fashion, in the camp; destiny reigns in the congregation. The camp constitutes a particular stage in the historical development of the people, while the existence of the nation is identical with that of the congregation.

The camp, by its nature, does not constitute a distinctly human phenomenon. In the animal kingdom as well, we can already discern the glimmers of this phenomenon. There, too, the camp serves as protection against harm. Let flocks of sheep and cattle suddenly sense that danger is lurking somewhere, and, overcome by panic, they will confusedly stream down from every green mountain and high pasture and hastily herd together, interlock their horns, and press their heads one against the other. Fear finds its instinctive mechanical expression in the quest for survival through sheer physical contiguity. The primitive urge for individual mute creatures to come together in face of opposition and danger and form one camp is a basic feature of the animal instinct.

In the human realm as well, the camp is created only as a result of fear. When a person is terror-stricken by his involuntary fate-laden existence, he grasps his own helplessness and joins with his fellows both for protection from and victory over the enemy. The organization of a camp serves as a military tactic. Consider the phraseology used by the Torah: "When thou goest forth in camp against thine enemies" (Deuteronomy 23:10). The camp is born out of the dread of extinction and annihilation, out of the fear imposed upon it by fate. From the camp there emerges the people. The Israelites in Egypt were a camp to begin with; when God freed them they attained the rank of a people.

However, the congregation constitutes a distinctive human phenomenon; it is an expression of man's powerful spirit. The congregation is a typically human creation, a creation imbued with the splendor of the human personality. The congregation is created not as a result of negative factors, as a result of the fear of fate that pursues the man who senses his misery and weakness, but as a result of positive drives. The foundation of the congregation is destiny. A congregation is a group of individuals possessing a common past, a common future, common goals and desires, a common aspiration for a world which is wholly good and beautiful, and a common, unique, and unified destiny. The beginning of the congregation is grounded in the traditions of the Patriarchs, in the people's heritage, reaching back to its obscure dawn, while its end is rooted in a shared eschatological vision. The Hebrew word for "congregation," *edah,* is related to the Hebrew word for "witness," *ed.* The members of the congregation are witnesses.[21] And to what do they bear witness if not to events that are long since past, and to a wondrous future that has not yet arrived? The congregation encompasses not only the individuals living in the here-and-now but all who have lived and all who will live, from time immemorial until the eschaton. The dead, who have long since passed away, continue to abide in the realm of the congregation; and those who are yet to be born are already living in its domain. The congregation is a holy nation that has no fear of fate and is not compelled to live against its will. It believes in its own destiny, and it dedicates itself, out of its own free will, to the realization of that destiny. The covenant in Egypt was made with a people born from a camp; the covenant at Sinai was made with a holy nation.

CONVERSION THROUGH CIRCUMCISION AND IMMERSION

The individual's participation in the fate and the destiny of the chosen people-nation, and his experience of belonging to Keneset Israel, the Jewish community, as a complete entity which actualizes, through its historical existence, the two ideas of *ḥesed,* lovingkindness, and *kedushah,* holiness, together—such participation and such an experience of belonging are indissoluble and indivisible. The covenant at Sinai consummated the covenant in Egypt. Destiny attached itself to fate; both became one distinct covenantal unit. It is impossible to formulate a world-view that opposes the unity of the people of lovingkindness and the holy nation; that which belongs together cannot be sundered. A Jew who participates in his people's suffering and fate but does not bind himself to its destiny, which expresses itself in a life of Torah and mitzvot, violates a fundamental principle of Judaism and impairs his own singularity. Conversely, a Jew who does not grieve over the afflictions of his people, but seeks to separate himself from the Jewish fate, desecrates the holiness of Israel, even if he observes the commandments.[22]

Therefore, a Gentile who comes to attach himself to the Jewish community must accept upon himself the yoke of both covenants. He must enter into the magic circle of Jewish fate and, in a spirit of holiness, dedicate himself to Jewish destiny. Conversion consists in a person's joining himself to both the people formed by the covenant in Egypt and the holy nation formed by the covenant at Sinai. Take heed of a fundamental principle: There can be no partial conversion, and one cannot relinquish even the slightest iota of either of the two covenants. The devotion to Keneset Israel, both as a people whom God, with a strong hand, took unto Himself in Egypt, a people with its own history, suffering, sense of mutual responsibility, and commitment to deeds of mutual aid, and as a holy nation, committed, heart and soul, to the God of Israel and to His ethico-halakhic demands—this dual yet unified devotion is the most basic foundation of Judaism and the most fundamental feature of undergoing conversion.

Therefore, the halakhah has ruled that a convert who is circumcised but does not immerse himself, or immerses himself but is not circumcised, is not a proper convert until he is both circumcised and immerses himself. The act of circumcision (*milah*) was the charge given to Abraham the Hebrew, *Avraham ha–ivri,* the father of Jewish fate; it was performed by the Israelites in Egypt prior to their sacrificing and eating the paschal lamb, the symbol of the redemption from Egypt. For this reason it signifies the people's special fate, its isolation and its involuntary singularity. Circumcision is the *ot,* the sign incised in the very physical being of the Jew. It is a permanent sign between the God of the Hebrews and His people, a sign that cannot be effaced. If the flesh does not have the covenant of fate impressed upon it, then the singularity of the people is missing and the Gentile remains outside the bounds of the covenant in Egypt.

The act of immersion (*tevilah*), in contrast to that of circumcision, denotes the integration of a person in a great destiny and his entry into the covenant at Sinai. The Jews were charged with the commandment of immersion prior to the revelation of the Law at Sinai.[23] Immersion signifies purification and ascension from the profane to the sacred, from an ordinary, prosaic life to a life replete with an exalted vision. When the convert arises from his immersion, a spiritual reality suffused with destiny is newly formed within him, and he becomes sanctified with the holiness of Israel. It is not for naught that the act of acceptance of the yoke of the commandments is linked with the act of immersion.[24] For immersion, at its core, has as its sole purpose the representation of the experience of the revelation of the Law and of the ascension of a people, through a freely assumed obligation to perform the divine command, to the rank of a holy nation. If a Gentile was circumcised but did not immerse himself, he lacks that personal bond to Jewish destiny. Such a Gentile has disassociated himself from the covenant at Sinai and from an ethico-halakhic identification with the holy nation. In the conversion formula to be found in the Book of Ruth, both these aspects are set forth, and their gist is succinctly expressed in its last two phrases; "Thy people shall be my people, and thy God, my God" (Ruth 1:16).

MELANCHOLY REFLECTIONS AND CONFESSIONS

Let us ask a simple question: Have we not sinned against the covenant of fate, the covenant made with a camp-people? Have we not transgressed against our obligation to participate in the suffering of the people, to witness and feel its burdens, as the verse states, "and he [Moses] witnessed their burdens" (Exodus 2:11, and cf. Rashi ad loc.)? Let us be frank: During the terrible Holocaust, when European Jewry was being systematically exterminated in the ovens and crematoria, the American Jewish community did not rise to the challenge, did not act as Jews possessing a properly developed consciousness of our shared fate and shared suffering, as well as the obligation of shared action that follows therefrom, ought to have acted. We did not sufficiently emphathize with the anguish of the people and did very little to save our afflicted brethren. It is hard to know how much we might have accomplished had we tried harder. Personally, I think that we might have been able to save many. There is no doubt, however, that had we properly grieved over the afflictions of our brothers, had we raised our voices and forcefully demanded that Roosevelt issue a sharp protest-warning, backed by concrete actions, we could have substantially slowed the process of mass murder. We were witnesses to the greatest and most terrible tragedy in our history and we were silent. I do not wish to enter here into a discussion of details. This is a very sad and disturbing chapter in our history. But we all sinned by our silence in the face of the murder of millions. Have we not been summoned before the divine judgment seat to answer for our terrible transgression against the prohibition "Thou shalt not stand idly by the blood of thy fellow" (Leviticus 19:16), particularly when we stood idly by not just the blood of our *fellow,* but the blood of our *fellows,* in their millions! And when I say "we," I mean all of us—myself included—rabbis and laymen, Orthodox and freethinkers, the entire spectrum of Jewish political organizations: "your heads, your tribes, your elders, and your officers, even all the men of Israel . . . from the hewer of thy wood unto the drawer of thy water" (Deuteronomy 29:9–10). Do you know why we were so indifferent? Because our sense of people-hood was flawed. We did not properly grasp the whole concept of shared fate and what it means to be a people. We lacked, as did Job to begin with, the attribute of *ḥesed.* It was because Job did not possess the sense of shared historical circumstances and shared suffering that he did not know how to pray on behalf of his friends. He was concerned only for his own well-being and for that of his family. In us, as well, the experience of a camp-people was absent. Therefore, we failed to offer up prayers on behalf of our brothers, both prayers of the heart and prayers consisting of vigorous deeds of rescue.

Divine providence is testing us once again via the crisis that has overtaken the land of Israel. Let it be clearly stated: the matter does not just affect the political future of the land of Israel. The designs of the Arabs are directed not just against the political sovereignty of the State of Israel but against the very existence of the *Yishuv* in the land of Israel. They wish to destroy, heaven forbid, the entire community, "both men and women, infant and suckling, ox and sheep" (1 Samuel 15:3). At a Mizrachi convention I cited the view expressed by my father and master [R. Moses Soloveitchik] of blessed memory, that the proclamation, "The Lord will have war with Amalek from generation to generation" (Exodus 17:16) does not only translate into the communal exercise of waging obligatory war against a specific race, but includes as well the obligation to rise up as a community against any people or group that, filled with maniacal hatred, directs its enmity against Keneset Israel. When a people emblazons on its banner, "Come, and let us cut them off from being a nation; that the name of Israel may be no more in remembrance" (Psalms 83:5) it becomes, thereby, Amalek.[25] In the 1930s and 1940s the Nazis, with Hitler at their head, filled this role. They were the Amalekites, the standard-bearers of insane hatred and enmity during the era just past. Today their place has been taken over by the mobs of Nasser and the Mufti. If we are silent now as well, I know not the verdict that will be issued against us by the God of justice. Do not rely on the "liberal" world's sense of equity. Those same righteous liberals were around fifteen years ago, and they looked with indifference upon the extermination of millions of people; they did not even lift a finger. If, heaven forbid, yet a second spectacle of blood were to take place before their very eyes, it is likely that they would not even lose a night's sleep over it.

Let us, like Job, learn to pray on behalf of our friends. Let us feel the pain of the *Yishuv*. We must understand *that the fate of the Yishuv in the land of Israel is our fate as well*. The Arabs have declared war not only against the State of Israel but against all of Keneset Israel. They now are the leaders of the international anti-Semitic movement and are among its main financial supporters, lavishing vast sums upon it. Let us overcome that foolish and unworthy fear of "dual loyalty" that our enemies have managed to infect us with. First, we will never be able to acquit ourselves in the eyes of anti-Semites, and whatever we do will not satisfy them. Second, as was stated above, this is not just a matter of ensuring the existence of the State but involves coming to the rescue, the physical rescue, of masses of Jews. Is it not our sacred obligation to come to their aid? Are we to be forbidden to demand that the *Yishuv* be properly defended? We find ourselves confronted with the very same type of test that confronted Job—the need to offer prayer on behalf of one's friends, prayer comprised of deeds and self-sacrifice. And in our case, *our* friends are the entire *Yishuv* in the land of Israel. We have to do but one thing—open the door to the Beloved who is knocking—and immediately all the dangers will cease.

THE VISION OF THE RELIGIOUS "SHIVAT ZIYYON" MOVEMENT: ISOLATION AND SOLITUDE

What attitude ought the religious *shivat ziyyon* movement adopt vis-à-vis secular Zionism? It seems to me that political, nonreligious Zionism has committed one grave and fundamental error, an error based upon a false premise that secular Zionism introduced into the concept of the covenant in Egypt, the covenant of fate. With the establishment of the State of Israel, secular Zionism declares, we have become a people like all peoples, and the notion of "a people that dwells alone" (Numbers 23:29) has lost its validity. The extremists in the movement even wish to undermine the idea of one common fate—the fate of the camp-people—shared by the Jews in the Diaspora and the Jews in the land of Israel. This entire line of thought is not just a philosophical-historical error but also a practical mistake. Under the influence of this spirit of indiscriminate amity, this doctrine of the sameness of all peoples, the representatives of the State of Israel have oftentimes displayed an embarrassing naivete, improperly evaluated particular circumstances and situations, and failed to discern the hidden intentions of certain individuals. As a result of their childlike innocence, they trust the promises of people who promptly proceed to betray us and are overly impressed by flattery and blandishments. It appears to me that on a number of occasions the foreign policy of the State of Israel has manifested an absence of a sense of honor, of national pride, of caution, and of the fortitude to staunchly maintain one's own position.

All these mistakes flow from the initial error committed by secular Zionism when it sought to erase the sense of isolation and perhaps even the phenomenon of shared suffering from the book of our history. The voice of the Beloved knocking ought to open the eyes of all of us, even the most avowed secularists among us. The State of Israel has not been able and will not be able to abrogate the force of the covenant, "And I will take you to Me for a people" (Exodus 6:7), and to liquidate the shared fate that is the source of Jewish isolation. The State of Israel today is isolated in precisely the same manner that the Jewish people has been isolated during the thousands of years of its history. If anything, the isolation of the State today is even more striking than the isolation of the Jewish people in the past, for the present-day isolation manifests itself in the international arena. "They hold crafty converse against Thy people, and take counsel against Thy treasured ones. They have said: 'Come and let us cut them off from being a nation; that the name of Israel may be no more in remembrance.' For they have consulted together with one consent; against Thee do they make a covenant; the tents of Edom and the Ishmaelites; Moab and the Hagrites; Gebol and Ammon and Amalek; Philistia with the inhabants of Tyre; Assyria is also joined with them. They have been an arm to the children of Lot. Selah" (Psalms 83:4–9). Communist Russia together with the Catholic Vatican; Nehru, the disciple of Gandhi, together with the devout Catholic, Franco; the British Foreign office together with Chiang Kai Shek—all have banded together in the attempt to isolate the State of Israel, and they are assisted in their attempt by our enemies in other lands. This conspiracy has taken place after the establishment of the State, during a time when many of its leaders thought that the State had solved the Jewish problem, that it had brought Jewish isolation to an end and had introduced normalcy into our existence. The premise that the State has weakened anti-Semitism is simply wrong. On the contrary, anti-Semitism has grown in strength and now, as part of its war against us, makes use of false libels against the State of Israel. Who can foresee the outcome of this anti-Semitic hatred? The validity of the covenant in Egypt cannot be abrogated by human hands. We continue to be a nation, scattered and dispersed, but, at the same time, bound up with one another. *Our fate is the fate of the Yishuv, and vice versa: The fate of the Yishuv is our fate.* Let no part of the Jewish people delude itself into vainly seeking "to escape in the king's house, more than all the Jews" (Esther 4:13). Each and every one of us is obliged to pray on behalf of his fellow. The Jews of America are forbidden to be quiet or to relax as long as the danger confronting the State of Israel persists. Nor can the inhabitants of the Holy Land prattle on about such nonsense as "the new type of Jew" being created there who has nothing in common with the diaspora Jew. All of us are obliged to attend to "the voice of my Beloved that knocketh."

However, the error of secular Zionism is more serious than its simply not understanding the true meaning of the covenant in Egypt, the covenant of a camp-people, which takes the form of shared fate and involuntary isolation. Secular Zionism has sinned as well against the covenant at Sinai, the covenant made with a holy congregation-nation, which finds its expression in the shared destiny of a sanctified existence. Only the religious *shivat ziyyon* movement, with its traditional and authentic approach, has the capacity to rectify these distortions. If you were to ask me: What is the task of the State of Israel? I would answer: The mission of the State of Israel is neither the termination of the unique isolation of the Jewish people nor the abrogation of its unique fate—in this it will not succeed!—but the elevation of a camp-people to the rank of a holy congregation-nation and the transformation of shared fate to shared destiny. We must remember, as was emphasized earlier, that fate expresses itself primarily in an existence of necessity, in the inability to escape from Judaism, in the compulsion to suffer as a Jew. However, this is not the Torah's goal, nor is it the ideal set forth by our world-view. Our sense of unity with Keneset Israel, according to the authentic view of Judaism, must remain incomplete as long as it derives from the covenant of fate made with a camp-people living an existence of compulsion, a covenant to which we are bound by external constraints; it can only be complete if it derives from the covenant made with a holy congregation-nation, from the covenant of shared destiny. An existence of fate cannot satisfy man. On the contrary, it only inflicts pain upon him. The sense of isolation is highly destructive. It can crush man, both body and spirit, can paralyze his faculties, can stop up the flowing well-spring of personal creativity. In particular, this sense weighs heavily on man because isolation per se lacks meaning and purpose. The lonely, isolated sufferer wonders: wherefore and why? This isolation, which pursues man like a shadow, dulls his powers, his sense of awareness. Not so is the existence of destiny based upon the covenant made at Mount Sinai! Through this covenant, the "people"—a concept signifying subjection to the decree of an existence of necessity, participation in blind suffering, and the sensation of meaningless isolation—becomes transformed into a "holy nation" and attains the exalted rank of an ethico-religious congregation. From the depths of the consciousness of destiny a person can draw vigor and strength, creative powers, and the bliss of a renewed, free, and vibrant existence.

Let us review yet once again what was stated earlier. How do fate and destiny differ? In two ways. First, fate entails an existence of necessity; destiny is a freely willed existence, created by man himself as he chooses and charts his own path in life. Second, fate expresses itself in a bare, teleologically blank existence; destiny possesses both significance and purpose. A shared fate is simply the inability to rebel against fate; it is the tragic, Jonah-like incapacity to flee from before the God of the Hebrews. "But the Lord hurled a great wind into the sea so that the ship was like to be broken" (Jonah 1:4). A shared destiny means the unconstrained ability of the will to strive toward a goal; it means the free decision to devote oneself to an ideal; it means yearning for God. Jonah, in the end, cast off the blind fate pursuing him and chose the exalted destiny of the God of Israel. "I am a Hebrew and I fear the Lord, the God of heaven" (Jonah 1:9).

To be sure, there is an element of separation present even in the experience of a shared destiny; however, the separation entailed by destiny differs completely from that entailed by fate. It is not the negative feeling described in the prophetic vision of Balaam, "Lo, it is a people that shall dwell alone" (Numbers 23:9), but rather a unique consciousness vouchsafed by Moses, in the last hours before his death, to Keneset Israel, "And Israel dwelleth in security, alone the fountain of Jacob" (Deuteronomy 33:28). In truth, this separation is naught but the solitude of a pure and holy, splendid and glorious existence. It is the solitude that finds its expression in a person's uniqueness, in his divine image, and in his existential "I" experience. It is the solitude of the soul that dwells in concealment, in the depths of being; it is the solitude that is to be identified with a person's spirituality and individuality; it is the solitude that makes manifest man's dignity and freedom; it is the solitude of Moses, whose great spirit and exalted vision were beyond the people's comprehension; it is the solitude of Elijah and the rest of the prophets; it is the solitude concerning which Abraham spoke when he told his young men, "Abide ye here with the ass, and I and the lad will go yonder; and we will worship" (Genesis 22:5). While isolation involves harmful inferiority feelings deriving from self-negation, a person's solitude testifies to both his greatness and his sanctity, the greatness that is contained within his private domain and the sanctity that permeates the inner recesses of his unique consciousness. Loneliness robs man of his tranquility; solitude bestows upon him security, worth, and dignity—"security, alone."

Judaism has always believed, as we emphasized at the beginning of our remarks, that a person has the ability to take his fate in his hands and to mold it into destiny, into a life of freedom, meaning, and joy, that he has the power to transform isolation into solitude, a sense of inferiority into a feeling of worth. It is for this reason that Judaism has emphasized the importance of the principle of free will;

it is for this reason that it has attached such great value to human reason, which enables man to liberate himself from subjugation to nature and rule over his environment and subject it to his will. The Jewish community is obliged to utilize its free will in all areas of life in general, but in particular on behalf of the welfare of the State of Israel. If secular Zionism should finally realize that the State of Israel cannot terminate the paradoxical fate of Jewish isolation—that, to the contrary, the incomprehensible isolation of "And I will take you to Me for a people" (Exodus 6:7) has become even more pronounced in the international arena—then it must put to itself the ancient query: "What is thine occupation? and whence comest thou? and of what people art thou?" (Jonah 1:8). This question will be asked of us one way or another. If we do not ask it of ourselves, then the non-Jew will put it to us; and we must answer proudly, "I fear the Lord, the God of Heaven" (Jonah 1:9). Our historic obligation, today, is to raise ourselves from a people to a holy nation, from the covenant of Egypt to the covenant at Sinai, from an existence of necessity to an authentic way of life suffused with eternal ethical and religious values, from a camp to a congregation. The task confronting the religious *shivat ziyyon* movement is to achieve that great union of the two covenants—Egypt and Sinai, fate and destiny, isolation and solitude. This task embraces utilizing our afflictions to improve ourselves, and it involves spinning a web of *hesed* that will bind together all the parts of the people and blend them into one congregation, "one nation in the land"; and the readiness to pray for one's fellow, and empathy with his joy and grief. As the end result of this self-improvement we will achieve the holiness conferred by an existence of destiny and will ascend the mountain of the Lord. One great goal unites us all, one exalted vision sets all our hearts aflame. One Torah—the Written Torah and the Oral Torah—directs all of us toward one unified end: the realization of the vision of solitude, the vision of a camp-people that has ascended to the rank of a holy congregation-nation, bound together its fate with its destiny, and proclaims to the entire world, in the words of our ancient father, Abraham: "And I and the lad will go yonder, and we will worship and we will return to you" (Genesis 22:5).

—Translated from the Hebrew by Lawrence Kaplan

Rabbi Soloveitchik's essay was originally delivered as an address at a public assembly on Yom Ha-Aẓma'ut at Yeshivat Rabbenu Yitzḥak Elḥanan of Yeshiva University in New York City, 1956.

NOTES

1. See Berakhot 7a. According to R. Meir, Moses did not receive a reply to his request to comprehend the problem of suffering in the world—the righteous man who is in adversity and the wicked man who prospers. R. Yoḥanan in the name of R. Yose disagrees. Maimonides, in the *Guide of the Perplexed,* adopts the view of R. Yoḥanan in the name of R. Yose and asserts that God enlightened Moses regarding the governance of the totality of existence. See *Guide* 1:54: "This dictum—'All My goodness' (Exodus 33:19)—alludes to the display to him [Moses] of all existing things . . . that is, he has grasped the existence of all My world with a true and firmly established understanding."

2. The medieval authorities (*rishonim*) already discussed the issue of a man being deprived of choice because of his being extremely steeped in sin. See Maimonides, Laws of Repentance 6:3; and Nahmanides' *Commentary on the Torah* to Exodus 7:3, 9:12.

3. The connection between trouble and repentance finds its expression in the commandment to cry out and sound the alarm with trumpets whenever trouble befalls the community. Maimonides, in Laws of Fast Days 1:1–4, states: "It is a positive scriptural commandment to cry out and sound the alarm with trumpets whenever trouble befalls the community, as it is said, 'against the adversary that oppresseth you, then ye shall sound the alarm with the trumpets' (Numbers 10:9), that is to say: whatever is oppressing you, whether it be famine, pestilence, locusts, or the like, cry out over them and sound the trumpets. This procedure is one of the paths of repentance, for when trouble occurs and they cry out over it and sound the trumpets, everyone will know that evil has come upon them because of their evil

deeds. . . . On the authority of the scribes, fasting is prescribed whenever trouble befalls a community until mercy is vouchsafed to it from heaven."

There are two distinct commandments: (1) There is a positive commandment of repentance and confession for any sin that a person commits. This commandment is set forth in Numbers 5:6–7, "When a man or a woman commits any sin . . . then they shall confess their sin which they have done," and Maimonides, in his *Book of Knowledge,* devoted an entire section, The Laws of Repentance, comprising ten chapters, to it. (2) There is a specific obligation of repentance during a time of trouble, as set forth in Numbers 10:9, "And when ye go forth to war in your land against the adversary that oppresseth you, then ye shall sound an alarm with the trumpets; and ye shall be remembered before the Lord your God." In terms of concrete practice, this obligation of repentance, on a scriptural level, assumes the form of sounding the trumpets, and on a scribal level, the form of fasting.

Essentially the obligation of repentance in time of trouble is connected with the suffering of the community, as the Mishnah very precisely states, "for every trouble that befalls a community—may it not happen!" (Ta'anit 19a), and as Maimonides emphasizes in the text we cited just above. However, the obligation of an individual in trouble to return to God also stems from this Biblical passage. The fact that the halakhah accords recognition to a fast undertaken by an individual demonstrates that there is an obligation of repentance devolving upon the individual who finds himself in difficult circumstances. According to Maimonides, there is no such thing as a fast devoid of repentance. Maimonides, in Laws of Fast Days 1:9, states: "Just as a community must fast when in trouble, so an individual must fast when in trouble." Similarly, the baraita states: "Our rabbis have taught: If a city is surrounded by [hostile] Gentiles or threatened with inundation by a river, or if a ship is foundering in the sea, or if an individual is pursued by Gentiles or by robbers or by an evil spirit, [the alarm is sounded even on the Sabbah]" (Ta'anit 22b). [The bracketed phrase at the end of the quotation is the correct reading of the text, according to the Rif, Rambam, Rosh, Maharshah, and others. *Translator*] In all of these instances, then, it is permitted to sound the alarm (only verbally) on the Sabbath. This is also the ruling of Maimonides, as set forth in Laws of Fast Days 1:6. It follows from this that the obligation to cry out applies equally to the individual and the community. And of what value is crying out, if the cry does not issue forth from a soul that repents its sins? (It is understood that there is no law to sound the alarm *with trumpets,* even on a weekday, for an individual in trouble. One sounds the alarm with trumpets only for trouble which befalls a community. There are many laws, both in chapter 3 of Mishnah Ta'anit and in chapter 2 of Maimonides' Laws of Fast Days, establishing the nature of communal trouble, and none of these laws includes the individual in trouble. The only point of the baraita cited above is that an individual in trouble may cry out [according to Maimonides' explanation] even on the Sabbath.)

The difference between the general commandment of repentance and the specific obligation of repentance in time of trouble exhausts itself in one detail. Repentance for a sin is bound up with knowledge of the sin. As long as an individual is not aware of having committed any sin, he has no obligation to repent. One cannot oblige a person to seek atonement without knowledge of a sin, as it is said, "or if his sin be known to him wherein he hath sinned" (Leviticus 4:23). It is knowledge of a sin that obliges a person to bring a sin-offering. The same holds true for repentance. A person is not obliged to repent for concealed sins but only for revealed sins. However, in a time of trouble, the sufferer must examine his actions and search out his sins so that he may be able to repent for them. The very fact of suffering indicates the presence of sin and it commands a person: Find your sins and return to your Creator. This scrutinizing of one's deeds is a characteristic feature of the obligation of repentance bound up with suffering. We know that on fast days the courts would meet in session and examine the actions of the townspeople. The Talmud states: "In the morning of fast days there is a public assembly . . . and they examine the affairs of the town" (Megillah 30b). Similarly, Maimonides, in Laws of Fast Days 1:17, sets it down as a firmly established ruling that "on each fast day undertaken by a community beset by trouble, the court and the elders should meet in session at the synagogue and examine the deeds of the townspeople. . . . They should remove all of the obstacles [to righteous living] provided by transgressors and should carefully search and inquire of the extortioners and other criminals," (See Eruvin 13b: "and now that he [man] is created, let him scrutinize his [past] actions; and there are those who say: 'let him be careful about his [future] actions!'"). This obligation to scrutinize one's actions refers to a time of trouble. It would seem that the special commandment of repentance on the Day of Atonement (as set forth by Maimonides in Laws of Repentance 2:7, and by Rabbenu Jonah in *Gates of Repentance* 2:14 and 4:17) also involves, according to the ruling of the halakhah, a special requirement of repentance for concealed sins and the obligation to scrutinize one's deeds in order to uncover and bring to the surface the degrading underside of a person's life. In this respect, the obligation of repentance on the Day of Atonement is identical with the obligation of repentance in a time of suffering. And it is with reference to such occasions that the verse states: "Let us search and try our ways, and return to the Lord" (Lamentations 3:40). [Cf. *Shi'urim le-Zekher Abba Mari Z"L*, vol. 1 (Jerusalem, 1983), pp. 190–192. *Translator.*]

4. The following remarks are based on the talmudic discussion in Bava Batra 15a–b, which cites the views of several sages who differ as to when and in which generation Job lived.

5. Sanhedrin 94a.

6. See Maimonides, Laws of Kings and Their Wars 1:9 and the critical gloss of the Rabad ad loc. However, even Maimonides' view refers only to the situation as it existed once the kingship had been given to David and does not apply to any king

who reigned before him. See 1 Samuel 13:13–14. Already, at that moment, the divesting of the kingship from Saul's descendants had begun. There, as well, Saul could have mended his sin through repentance.

7.   This concept is expressed by Rava in Sanhedrin 72a: "Rava said: 'What is the reason for the [law of the thief] breaking into a house? Because it is certain that no man is inactive where his property is concerned. Therefore . . .'"

8.   Maimonides, in Laws of the Temple 6:16, states almost explicitly that the fact that the second sanctification, wrought by Ezra, remains in effect for its time and for eternity is grounded in the same reason he uses to explain why the holiness of the Temple precincts was not nullified. Physical destruction cannot expel the divine presence from the heap of ruins. [Cf. P. Peli, ed., *Al ha-Teshuvah* (Jerusalem, 1975), pp. 300–308; and *Shi'urim le-Zekher Abba Mari Z"L,* vol. 1, pp. 169–175. *Translator*]

9.   Judah Halevi, *Kuzari* 2:24.

10.   See *Yalkut Shimoni* on Deuteronomy 29:11, s.v. *shalosh beritot;* Berakhot 48b: "It [the Torah] was given with three covenants," and Rashi ad loc.

11.   Genesis Rabbah 42:8.

12.   See R. David Kimḥi, *Book of Roots,* s.v. *im:* "This word refers to joining and cleaving. And the word *am* [people] is derived from it because an assembly of individuals and their joining together with one another is termed an *am* [people]." See, as well, Gesenius, *Hebrew Lexicon,* s.v. *am.*

13.   See Tosafot, Menaḥot 37a, s.v. *O kum gali;* and *Shitah Mekubbeẓet* ad loc., par. 18.

14.   Sotah 37b; Sanhedrin 43b; and Rashi on Deuteronomy 29:28.

15.   See Maimonides, Laws of the Foundations of the Torah 5:11.

16.   Maimonides, Laws of Gifts to the Poor 10:2.

17.   The talmudic opinion that "the Holy One, blessed be He, overturned the mountain upon them like an [inverted] cask" (Shabbat 88a) expresses the idea that the Almighty suggested to the Israelites that they accept the Torah and devote themselves to Him of their own freewill in order, thereby, to live as a holy nation, instead of living an involuntary, fate-laden existence that might be compared to having a mountain overturned upon one like an inverted cask. See Tosafot ad loc., s.v. *kafah* and *moda'ah.* [See "The Lonely Man of Faith," *Tradition* (Spring 1965), p. 28, note **, for a different approach. *Translator.*]

18.   See R. Jonah ibn Janaḥ, *Book of Roots* (translated from the Arabic into Hebrew by R. Judah ibn Tibbon and edited by Wilhelm Bacher, Berlin, 1896), s.v. *goy.* See, as well, R. David Kimhi, *Book of Roots,* s.v. *goy:* "R. Johan [ibn Janaḥ] states that the word *goy* can refer to an individual: for example, in the verse 'Wilt Thou slay a person [*goy*] even if he be righteous?' (Genesis 20:4)." [See *Sefer ha-Rikmah,* translated from the Arabic into Hebrew by R. Judah ibn Tibbon and edited by Michael Wilenski (Berlin, 1929), chap. 28 (27), p. 307. *Translator.*] See also Solomon Mandelkorn, *Concordance, s.v. goy:* "It refers to individuals, members of one people,

who have become, as it were, one body." See, as well, Gesenius, *Hebrew Lexicon,* s.v. *goy.* There are times, however, when we find the word *goy* used to describe a herd of animals: for example, "For a nation (*goy*) is come up upon my land" (Joel 1:6, referring to a plague of locusts). It is understood that in referring to animals the word is being used in a derivative sense. See Radak and Rashi ad loc. See, as well, the commentary of the Gaon of Vilna to Isaiah 1:4, "Ah, sinful nation, a people laden with iniquity," where the Gaon states: "The word *am* refers to a group of many people, a multitude . . . while the word *goy* refers to those who adhere to a code of behavior. . . . And this is what our sages said [in the Haggadah] in commenting on the verse 'And he became there a great . . . nation' (Deuteronomy 26:5): 'This teaches that the Israelites were distinctive there.'"

19. The phrase "a holy people" (*am kadosh*) signifies a community that has elevated its peoplehood to the rank of holiness; it is, therefore, identical in meaning with the term "holy nation" (*goy kadosh*).

20. Jewish uniqueness began to be forged in the Egyptian crucible of affliction. This historical suffering fashioned the image of the community as a nation possessing a distinctive character and its own individual countenance, and, thereby, prepared it for that great and exalted moment when God made a covenant of destiny with it at Sinai. The verse "The Aramean [Laban] sought to destroy my father [Jacob], and he [Jacob] went down into Egypt, and he became there a great . . . nation" (Deuteronomy 26:5) testifies to the birth of Jewish uniqueness in Egypt. How fine is the interpretation of this verse offered by our sages: "This teaches that the Israelites were distinctive there." Nationhood and distinctiveness as a special well-defined entity are one and the same. In truth, the entire purpose of the bondage in Egypt was to create this people-nation of Israel. The Israelites went down into Egypt as the sons of Jacob but went up from there as a people bound to God and as a nation ready for the revelation of the divine presence and for God's making a covenant of destiny with them at Sinai. "When God wanted to make his [Abraham's] descendants a unique people, a perfect people, and to draw them near to Him, had they not first gone down into Egypt and been refined there, they would not have been His special people" (*Zohar* I, 83a). "However, until they went down into Egypt they were not yet a nation. . . . It is written, 'as a rose among the thorns, so is my love among the daughters' (Song of Songs 2:2). The Holy One, blessed be He, desired to make Israel according to the supernal pattern, so that there should be one rose on earth, even as it is on high. Now the rose that gives out a sweet aroma and is conspicuous among all other roses is the one that grows among the thorns" (*Zohar* II, 189b).

21. A congregation can also signify devotion to a destructive ideology by individuals who are plotting evil: for example, "this evil congregation" (Numbers 14:35) and "that he fare not as Korah and his congregation" (Numbers 17:5).

22. See Maimonides, Laws of Repentance 3:11. "One who separates himself

from the ways of the community, even if he does not commit transgressions, but disassociates himself from the congregation of Israel and does not perform commandments in their midst and does not share in their troubles and does not observe their fasts, but goes his own way as one of the Gentiles and as if he were not one of them—such a person has no share in the world-to-come."

23. Maimonides, Laws of Forbidden Intercourse 13:1–3, basing himself upon the baraita in Keritot 9a, states clearly that there was no immersion in Egypt and conversion took effect through circumcision alone, and that it was at Sinai that the Jews were commanded for the first time to immerse themselves in order to undergo conversion. Maimonides states: "Israel entered into the covenant by way of three rites—circumcision, immersion, and sacrifice. Circumcision took place in Egypt, as it is said, 'but no uncircumcised person shall eat thereof' (Exodus 12:48). Our master, Moses, circumcised the people. . . . Immersion took place in the wilderness before the revelation of the Torah, as it is said, 'and sanctify them today and tomorrow, and let them wash their garments'" (Exodus 19:10). Maimonides explains the statement in the sugya in Yevamot 71a ("But in truth [the text 'A sojourner and a hired servant shall not eat thereof' (Exodus 12:45)] comes to include a convert who was circumcised but did not immerse himself") as referring to the Passover offering in all generations subsequent to the Exodus but not to the Passover celebrated in Egypt itself, for in Egypt, according to all opinions, conversion was effected, fully and completely, by circumcision alone. Similarly, Maimonides interprets the statement of R. Joshua in Yevamot 46b ("Our forefathers also underwent immersion") as referring to immersion at the time of the revelation of the Torah, as the plain meaning of the verses cited in the sugya seems to indicate. However, Maimonides would admit that the "mothers," i.e., the women, immersed themselves even in Egypt, as stated clearly in the sugya there. For one cannot say that the women immersed themselves only prior to the revelation of the Torah and not in Egypt. Such an assertion would run up against an insuperable objection, already raised and emphasized by Rashi in his commentary ad loc., s.v. *be-imahot:* "And their wives immersed themselves, as the gemara explains later on; for if they did not immerse themselves, then through what [act] did they enter under the wings of the divine presence?" To paraphrase Rashi, some act is required for conversion to be effected. Similarly, the Tosefta, Pesaḥim 8:18, states that those handmaidens in Egypt who did not immerse themselves could not eat of the Passover offering. This holds true according to the first anonymous tannaitic view cited in the Tosefta as well as according to the view of R. Eliezer b. Yaakov. See Rabad, critical gloss to Maimonides, Laws of the Passover Offering 5:5. In truth, we could claim that even the males immersed themselves in Egypt, in addition to being circumcised, and that at Sinai they were commanded to undergo a new, second immersion necessitated by the revelation of the Torah, which conferred an added measure of holiness upon them. According to this view, every act of conversion, including the conversion which took place in Egypt, requires immersion. In support of this view, one may

adduce the position of many *Rishonim,* including Maimonides (Laws of Forbidden Intercourse 13:12), that the second immersion of a slave—the immersion after he has been freed—is a scriptural requirement, inasmuch as he is acquiring an added measure of holiness, and now, as a free person, is attaining the complete measure of the holiness of Israel. It is understandable, then, that the Jews at Sinai, upon entering into the covenant of the Torah and the commandments, required an additional immersion, over and above the immersion that had taken place in Egypt. One could argue that even the *Nimmukei Yosef* [see *Nimmukei Yosef* on the Rif, Yevamot 16b, s.v. *kiddushav kiddushin*], who states that the immersion of the slave after he has been freed is only a rabbinic requirement, would concede that the Israelites were required to immerse themselves at Sinai. One can distinguish between the case of the slave who already [upon becoming a slave] had been converted through circumcision and immersion, and via these rites had entered into the covenant, and the case of the Israelites at Sinai, who had to acquire an added measure of holiness, since they were entering into a second covenant. With reference to a slave, the view of the *Nimmukei Yosef* is that his being emancipated does not confer an additional measure of holiness upon him but, rather, removes a legal impediment. The slave's holiness is complete upon his undergoing circumcision and immersion. However, as long as he is a slave his servitude prevents him from being obliged to observe the positive time-bound commandments and forbids him to marry an Israelite woman. However, if the servitude is nullified through his being set free, then he is lacking nothing. It is for this reason that there is no scriptural requirement of immersion upon his emancipation. However, the Israelites at Sinai acquired a new level of holiness, a level of holiness that did not exist beforehand. Therefore, they required a second conversion rite and consequently a second immersion.

One may ask: Why didn't the Israelites require the symbolic letting of the blood of the covenant (*hatafat dam berit*) at Sinai as well? The following answer may be suggested. Circumcision, which always precedes immersion and by itself does not confer the holiness of Israel upon an individual, need not be undergone a second time (through the symbolic letting of the blood) when an additional measure of holiness is conferred upon a person. All we require is that an individual have had a proper circumcision for the sake of conversion; and if such a circumcision took place, then, even though at that time he only attained a lesser measure of holiness, he need not undergo the symbolic letting of blood when he attains a greater measure of holiness. Similarly, the slave who is freed does not undergo the symbolic letting of blood, even though he is now obliged to perform new commandments and is acquiring a greater measure of holiness, inasmuch as, to begin with, he underwent a proper circumcision for the sake of the conversion of servitude. However, immersion, which completes the act of conversion and gives rise to the holiness of Israel, has to be undergone a second time when the convert ascends from a lesser level of holiness to a greater level.

We are, however, confronted with a problem on examining the view of Naḥmanides. Naḥmanides, in his *Hiddushim* (Novellae) on Yevamot 47b, s.v. *nitrapeh*, states that if a convert first immersed himself and then was circumcised, the conversion is valid. According to this view, then, there can be times when circumcision comes at the conclusion of the conversion process. If that is so, we should reverse matters and require the symbolic letting of blood and not immersion in a case where the person is acquiring a greater measure of holiness.

In order to answer this problem we must examine another statement of Naḥmanides. In his *Hiddushim* on Yevamot 46a, s.v. *sheken maẓinu*, Naḥmanides is of the view that the Levites, who had been circumcised prior to the Exodus for the sake of fulfilling the commandments and not for the sake of conversion, did not require the symbolic letting of blood. Naḥmanides states: "This being so [that the Levites had been circumcised beforehand], how did they enter under the wings of the divine presence? But they underwent the symbolic letting of blood. It would appear to me, however, that in terms of the law requiring circumcision [for the purpose of conversion], the Levites did not require the symbolic letting of blood, for they were already circumcised. Nor may they be compared to a circumcised Arab or a circumcised Gibeonite [who does require the symbolic letting of blood if he is being converted]. For since he [the Arab or the Gibeonite] never received a command of circumcision, it is as if he is not circumcised at all." It is clear from Naḥmanides' statement that circumcision, unlike immersion, is not an integral part of the conversion process. Rather, its purpose is to divest the convert of his status as an *arel* (one who is uncircumcised). If the convert was not circumcised, he cannot acquire the holiness of Israel, for a person who is an *arel* cannot enter into the covenant. Therefore, if a person is converting and he has already been circumcised, he can [forgo the symbolic letting of blood and] immerse himself for the purpose of conversion. A circumcised Arab, since he was not circumcised for the purpose of conversion, is regarded as an *arel,* as is stated in Nedarim 31b, Yevamot 71a, and Avodah Zarah 27a. Therefore, when he converts he must undergo the symbolic letting of blood. However, the Levites, who were descendants of Abraham and were circumcised in accordance with God's commandment to their father Abraham, did not require the symbolic letting of blood.

In light of this premise we may now answer our question as to why, according to Naḥmanides who is of the opinion that at times conversion is concluded by the act of circumcision, we should not require circumcision [or, to be more precise, the symbolic letting of blood] for the sake of acquiring a greater measure of holiness.

We have seen that circumcision does not really belong to the conversion procedure; its whole purpose is exhausted in divesting a person of his status as an *arel*. It is for this reason that a person who is already circumcised and is consequently not an *arel* need not undergo the symbolic letting of blood when he ascends from a lesser level of holiness to a greater level. Immersion differs fundamentally from circumcision, for immersion is an act which gives rise to the holiness of Israel and constitutes an integral part of the conversion procedure. Therefore, in order for a person to acquire a greater measure of holiness, immersion is required, but not the symbolic letting of blood. Naḥmanides, however, [despite his agreement with the above] is of the opinion that immersion can take place before circumcision, for even though the convert does not become an Israelite immediately upon emerging from his immersion, the immersion, nevertheless, is effective for the future. Once he is circumcised and not an *arel,* the immersion that took place prior to the circumcision effects the conversion and gives rise to his status as an Israelite.

The question as to whether circumcision is part of the conversion procedure or whether it serves only to divest the Gentile of his status as an *arel,* which status interposes between him and the holiness of Israel, is dependent on a dispute between the *Rishonim* as to whether the presence of a court is required when the convert is undergoing circumcision.

From certain statements of Maimonides (Laws of Forbidden Intercourse 13:6, 14:5–6), it would appear that his view is that the presence of a court is required only for immersion. Therefore, it would seem that according to Maimonides, circumcision serves only to remove the Gentile's status as an *arel,* which status serves as a legal impediment to conversion. [The presence of a court is required for the conversion procedure. Since a court is not required for circumcision, it is evidently not part of the conversion procedure. *Translator.*]

The *Tur* (Yoreh De'ah: Laws of Converts 268) and the *Shulḥan Arukh* (Yoreh De'ah: Laws of Converts 268:3), on the other hand, require the presence of a court for circumcision as well as for immersion. [This would indicate that circumcision is part of the conversion procedure. *Translator.*] Moreover, the very same view is set forth explicitly by Naḥmanides in his *Hiddushim* on Yevamot 45b, s.v. *mi lo tavlah.* This would appear to controvert our assumption that the sole purpose of circumcision, according to Naḥmanides, is to divest the convert of his status as an *arel.* The very fact that Naḥmanides requires the presence of a court during circumcision indicates that the act of circumcision is an act which effects conversion and therefore must be an act of the court. Our original question arises anew. Why didn't the Levites undergo the symbolic letting of blood at Sinai since their circumcision, to begin with, was not undergone for the sake of conversion?

(To be sure, Naḥmanides in his *Hiddushim* on Yevamot 45b, s.v. *mi lo,* agrees with the view of the Tosafot, Yevamot 45b, s.v. *mi lo,* that immersion and circumcision, if done for the sake of performing a commandment, are sufficient [for conversion, even if they were not performed for the sake of conversion]. In support of his view, Naḥmanides cites a statement from the Palestinian Talmud, Kiddushin 3:12. However, this view of Naḥmanides would still not serve to resolve our problem. Circumcision and immersion for the sake of performing a commandment can qualify as valid elements in the conversion procedure only after the laws of conversion were revealed and the ruling was established that conversion takes place through circumcision and immersion. In such a context, circumcision and immersion effect conversion even if they were done for the sake of performing commandments and not for the sake of conversion. Included in the intent of the commandment is the commandment as an act effecting conversion. However, the Levites were circumcised in Egypt before the Israelites were commanded to circumcise themselves for the purpose of conversion, of entering under the wings of the divine presence. This being the case, their circumcision could not have constituted an act of conversion, since the Israelites were only charged with circumcision for the sake of conversion afterwards.)

It would appear that Naḥmanides is of the opinion that circumcision constitutes an integral part of the conversion procedure only as long as the convert has not already performed the commandment of circumcision properly. But once he has performed the commandment, it would not be part of the procedure. Circumcision, as an act of conversion, only takes effect when the individual is lacking in the performance of the commandment of circumcision. Therefore, a circumcised Arab who converts requires the symbolic letting of blood because his circumcision is of no value, and through the symbolic letting of blood he will fulfill the commandment of entering into the covenant of our father Abraham, which is an inextricable part of the commandment of circumcision. However, the Levites, as descendants of Abraham, had already fulfilled the commandment of circumcision in all its fine details, and had completely discharged their obligation. Therefore, they did not require the symbolic letting of blood. For what would they accomplish thereby? It follows that their conversion was effected by immersion alone, as is the case with women or with one whose male organ has been cut off. Thus Naḥmanides, at the conclusion of his discussion of the Levites, states: "Therefore, the Levites are adjudged as women, so that they would enter under the wings of the divine presence through immersion." Therefore, when a convert ascends from a lesser to a greater holiness he does not require the symbolic letting of blood, for he completely fulfilled the commandment of circumcision previously. In contrast to circumcision, immersion is part of the conversion prodecure not because one is fulfilling a commandment or discharging an obligation through its performance. For immersion, aside from its significance as an act effecting conversion, does not constitute any type of legal performance. Therefore, immersion, in terms of its conferring upon one the holiness of Israel, can be undergone many times, and every time one acquires a greater measure of holiness, one requires immersion.

24. That the acceptance of the yoke of the commandments accompanies immersion, inasmuch as immersion gives rise to the status of one's being an Israelite, is almost a truism. This view is set forth in the sugya in Yevamot 47a–b and seems to be implied as well by Maimonides' statements in Laws of Forbidden Intercourse 13:12 and 14:6 (the latter ruling being based on the above sugya). Rashi, in his commentary on the sugya, s.v. *u-modi'in oto,* makes the point explicitly: "Since

he acquires the status of a convert through immersion, therefore, when he under-goes the obligatory immersion he must accept upon himself the yoke of command-ments." However, the Tosafot, Yevamot 45b, s.v. *mi lo tavlah,* states that the accep-tance of the yoke of the commandments can precede immersion.

Maimonides, in Laws of Forbidden Intercourse 13:17, states: "A convert who was not examined or who was not informed about the commandments and the punishments [for transgressing them], but was circumcised and immersed in the presence of three laymen, is deemed a [valid] convert." I once heard from my father and master [R. Moses Soloveitchik] of blessed memory, that Maimonides does not mean to say that a person who converted with the intention of not observing the commandments is deemed a valid convert. Such a notion would subvert the entire concept of conversion and the holiness of Israel, which exhausts itself in our obliga-tion to fulfill God's commandments. Maimonides' position is that the acceptance of the commandments, unlike immersion, does not constitute a distinct act in the pro-cess of conversion that would require the presence of a court. Rather, acceptance of the commandments is a defining feature of the conversion process that must be undergone for the sake of fulfilling the commandments. Therefore, if we know that the convert, at the time of immersion, is willing to accept the yoke of the command-ments, the immersion effects conversion even though there was no special act of informing the convert about the commandments and his consenting to fulfill them, since the convert intends to live the holy life of an observant Jew. It would appear, however, that the view of the Tosafot, cited earlier, is that the acceptance of the commandments is a distinct element in the conversion process and, consequently, that the law necessitating the presence of a court refers to the court's presence at the act of acceptance. Only this act of acceptance—and not immersion—requires the presence of the court.

Nahmanides, in his *Hiddushim* on Yevamot 45b, s.v. *mi lo tavlah,* states: "Even a male convert who accepted [the commandments] upon himself prior to his being circumcised must once again accept [them] upon himself when he immerses him-self." It would seem, at first glance, that according to Nahmanides there is an act of acceptance of the commandments which takes place at the time of circumcision. However, one might suggest that Nahmanides is not referring to a special act of acceptance of the commandments at the time of circumcision, but, rather, is char-acterizing the general nature of circumcision. Circumcision must be undergone for the sake of obligating oneself to fulfill the commandments. This interpretation of Nahmanides' view is similar to the explanation offered earlier with respect to Mai-monides' position. Maimonides, however, is of the opinion that the absence of a distinct act of acceptance of the commandments does not constitute any legal impe-diment to the validity of the conversion. Nahmanides, on the other hand, agrees with the Tosafot that there is a distinct act of acceptance of the commandments and that it requires the presence of a court. However, Nahmanides believes that aside from the distinct act of acceptance, both circumcision and immersion must be undergone for the sake of being obliged to perform the commandments, that is to say, for the sake of conversion.

25. Maimonides, Laws of Kings and Their Wars 5:4, writes the following regarding the seven nations of Canaan: "It is a positive commandment to destroy the seven nations, as it is said: 'But thou shalt utterly destroy them' (Deuteronomy 20:17). If one does not kill any of them that falls into one's power, one transgresses a negative commandment, as it is said: 'Thou shalt save nothing that breatheth' (Deuteronomy 20:16). But their memory has long since perished." The Radbaz, in his commentary ad loc., notes that the source for Maimonides' concluding comment, "But their memory has long since perished," is the statement of Rabbi Joshua in Mishnah Yadayim 4:4: "Sennacherib, king of Assyria, came up and intermingled all the peoples."

It is, however, striking and passing strange that Maimonides, in setting forth the commandment to wipe out Amelek, does not add the concluding phrase, "But their memory has long since perished." Thus states Maimonides in Laws of Kings and Their Wars 5:5: "Similarly it is a positive commandment to destroy the remembrance of Amalek, as it is said: 'Thou shalt blot out the remembrance of Amalek' (Deuteronomy 25:19). It is also a positive commandment to remember always his evil deeds and the waylaying [he resorted to], so that we keep afresh the hatred manifested by him, as it is said: 'Remember what Amalek did unto thee' (Deuteronomy 25:17). The traditional interpretation of this injuction is: 'Remember,' by word of mouth; 'Do not forget,' out of mind, that it is forbidden to forget his hatred and enmity." It would appear from Maimonides' statements that Amalek is still in existence, while the seven nations have descended into the abyss of oblivion.

One may query: Why didn't Maimonides apply R. Joshua's principle that "Sennacherib, king of Assyria, came up and intermingled all the peoples" to Amalek as he did to the seven nations? The answer to this question is very simple. Scripture testifies that Amalek is still in existence. Note what the Torah states: "The Lord will have war with Amalek from generation to generation" (Exodus 17:16). If that is the case, then it is impossible that Amalek be completely destroyed before the coming of the Messiah. As the sages state: "The [divine] throne will not be whole and the [divine] Name will not be whole until the descendants of Amelek are completely blotted out" (Midrash Tanḥuma on *Ki Teze,* end; and Rashi on Exodus 17:16). But—where is he? I once heard the following answer from my father and master [R. Moses Soloveitchik] of blessed memory, namely, that any nation that conspires to destroy Keneset Israel becomes, according to the halakhah, Amalek. My father and master added: We have been charged with two commandments concerning Amalek. The first is the obligation to blot out his memory. This obligation devolves upon every person with reference to an individual Amalekite and is set forth in the verse "Thou shall blot out the remembrance of Amalek" (Deuteronomy 25:19). The second is the readiness to do battle as a community against the people Amalek. This requirement is set forth in the verse, "The Lord will have war with Amalek from generation to generation" (Exodus 17:16). Thus, if any people seeks to destroy us, we are commanded to do battle against it when it rises up against us, and this battle of ours is an obligatory war (*milhemet mizvah*) on the basis of the verse from Exodus, "The Lord will have war with Amalek from generation to generation." However, the obligation to wipe out individual Amalekites, as set forth in the verse from Deuteronomy, applies only to genealogical descendants of Amalek. Now it is true that Maimonides' ruling also includes the obligation to blot out individuals, an obligation which does not apply to any nation other than Amalek, even if that nation seeks to destroy the Jewish people [and this obligation is no longer in force, since there are no longer any identifiable genealogical descendants of Amalek]. Nevertheless, since the obligation to do battle against Amalek as a people would apply to such a nation, Maimonides did not use the phrase "But its [Amalek's] memory has long since perished." There still exists a category of Amalek [as a people] even now after the peoples have been intermingled [and there are no longer any individual Amalekites].

Perhaps the above is the basis for the ruling of Maimonides in Laws of Kings and Their Wars 5:1 that a defensive war waged by the Jewish people against an aggressor is an obligatory war. Such a war falls under the rubric of "The Lord will have war with Amalek from generation to generation." To be sure, Maimonides in his ruling singles out the war against Amalek for special mention [which would seem to indicate that the war against Amalek and a defensive war against an aggressor are two separate categories]. Nevertheless, one may maintain that a war waged by the Jewish people against an aggressor who seeks to destroy it still belongs to the category of the war against Amalek. Note carefully the sugya in Sotah 44b, s.v. *Amar R. Yohanan.*

The Face of God
Thoughts on the Holocaust

DR. NORMAN LAMM

I

In my attempt to formulate a Jewish approach to the Holocaust, it should not be expected that I will venture an answer to the ancient question of *zaddik ve-ra lo* ("the righteous whom evil befalls") the vexing problem of the suffering of the innocent and the prosperity of the wicked, one that puzzled such biblical giants as Samuel, David, and Jeremiah.

The problem of theodicy—"justifying" the ways of God to man, offering rational explanations for the ethical and philosophical dilemmas presented by the disjointedness and inappositeness of conduct and circumstance, the quality of one's moral life and his fortune or misfortune—has a long and honorable history. But there is no one theodicy in Judaism. From Job to the sages of the Talmud, from Maimonides to Luria to the Besht, there is only one constant, and that is the *question* of *zaddik ve-ra lo,* the righteous who is afflicted with evil. The number of *answers* varies with the number of interpreters. No one approach has official, authoritative, dogmatic sanction in Judaism, although each has something of value to contribute. And the question remains the Question of Questions for Judaism, as it does for every thinking, believing human being.

How, then, shall we approach the problem? Let us begin by dividing it into two parts: first, the universal problem of suffering, the cry of *zaddik ve-ra lo,* why should the innocent suffer, intensified in the Holocaust by its unprecedented magnitude and cruelty. In kind, the Holocaust mystery is a continuation of the ancient question of evil and suffering—more urgent perhaps, but essentially the same.

The second part is not universal-metaphysical but national-theological. The Holocaust is not only a human challenge to God's justice and goodness, but a Jewish challenge to His faithfulness and promise. The absolute novelty of the Holocaust lies in its threat to the continuity of the Jewish people as such. It not only outrages man's ethical sensibilities, but it throws into disarray most of our notions of the philosophy of Jewish history.

In other words, the novelty, the demonic novelty, of the Holocaust lies not so much in the murder of six million Jews as in the decimation of one third of the Jewish people and the trauma to the remaining two thirds.

II

In trying to come to grips with the Holocaust and to probe, haltingly but inevitably, for some scrap of understanding of this cataclysm, we are confronted with an immediate dilemma: the very relevance of "meaning" to the Holocaust. Can we hope to find even a shred of meaning in the "black hole" in Jewish history? If we maintain that we can, we are in effect asserting a *zidduk ha-din,* a justification for the death, torment, and suffering of one million children and five million adults. We shall come back to this later, but I will say now that the very idea is repugnant to me and bespeaks an insufferable insensitivity. Moreover, of the "meaning" we purport to discover does not measure up to the magnitude of the suffering, then we have not only erred, but we have profaned the memory of the martyrs. However, if we then pursue the other alternative, and declare that the Holocaust had no meaning, we seem to rob their deaths of any redeeming dimension and furthermore, appear to deny a great and abiding principle of Judaism, that of *hashgahah peratit,* divine providence over all human individuals.

Apparently, not everyone appreciates that a dilemma even exists.

Thus, almost all of those (few) Orthodox thinkers who have ventured into this area at all offer variations of the *mi-penei hata'einu* ("because of our sins") thesis, so-named from the initial words of the special Musaf section of the service for the new month and the festivals, declaring that we only *recite* the order of the sacrificial Temple service liturgically, but do not actually *make* the offerings, for the reason that the Temple was destroyed and we were exiled "because of our sins." They see the Holocaust as punishment for Israel's sins.

The late Satmarer Rebbe, Rabbi Yoel Moshe Teitelbaum, is clear and unambiguous. In his two books, *Va-Yoel Mosheh* and *Al ha-Ge'ulah ve-al ha-Temurah,* he decides that the Zionists were responsible for the tragedy of the six million. The arrogance of nationalistic self-determination in trying to build a Jewish state caused the great destruction. The fact that so many Zionists were secularists, nonbelievers, only made matters worse. They violated the injunction to remain passive, refrain from interfering in the divinely preordained plans of redemption, and to await the miraculous coming of the Messiah. Hence, the Zionists are guilty, and all the Jewish people suffered because of their sins. This theme is interwoven with another, and both recur throughout the Satmarer's writings: the power of Samael, the archdemon, to test and seduce Israel into sin. These cruel tests with which Samael accosts us, often with the help of miracles, are characteristic of our pre-messianic tribulations. Of course, it does not occur to the Satmarer or his followers, in their anti-Zionist demonological interpretation of history, that the reverse might be true: that the Holocuast was the bitter test, and the "miracles" of statehood and military triumph and national survival were and are the reward for our sufferings and anguish.

A less well known figure (Rabbi Emanuel Hartom, writing in the Israeli journal *De'ot* a few years ago), takes the opposite view of the Satmarer: The Holocaust is the punishment for our neglect of Erez Israel. Our failure to participate en masse in the Return to Zion indicated a tragic defection from Judaism, a betrayal of the Promise to Abraham, and hence the unprecedented punishment we call the

Shoah. That at least a portion of our people was spared is in itself a tribute to divine compassion for, having chosen to remain in exile, we implied our readiness to assimilate and thus turn our backs on God. One wonders what this particular rabbi would answer to the criticism, leveled at him in a later issue of the same journal, that it certainly is odd that the Holocaust struck first and hardest at those very centers of Jewish life that were most intensively Jewish, pro-Eretz Israel, and anti-assimilationist.

There is a third variation of the *mi-penei ḥata'einu* thesis, this time by an American (Rabbi Avigdor Miller), a mashgiah, or spiritual supervisor, at a Brooklyn yeshiva. Let me quote a few of his precious lines: "Because of the upsurge of the greatest defection from Torah in history, which was expressed in Poland by materialism, virulent anti-nationalism, and Bundism (radical anti religious socialism), God's plan finally relieved them of all freewill and sent Hitler's demons to end the existence of the communities. (*Rejoice, O Youth*, pp. 278–289). One wonders at the statement that Polish Jewry experienced the greatest defection from Torah in history: more than in the days of the prophet Elijah? Isaiah? worse than German Jewry? American Jewry?

But let us not quibble about such trivial matters as facts. Is there any validity to the *mi-penei ḥata'einu*, the Holocaust-as-punishment explanation on which the various responses we have mentioned are based?

Of course there is. The thesis is a corollary of the whole principle of *sakhar ve-onesh*, reward and punishment. It is a theme found throughout the Prophets and the Talmud.

And yet—I reject the cavalier invocation of this theme as a way of "explaining" the Holocaust. Indeed, in these special circumstances of such unprecedented butchery and unequaled suffering and unimaginable danger to our survival, recourse to *mi-penei ḥata'einu* is massively irrelevant, impudent, and insensitive.

Why so? First, there are many approaches to suffering, as I indicated at the outset, and sin is not the only one. Indeed, the whole brunt of the Book of Job is to reject the simplistic recourse to *mi-*

penei hata'einu in any and all circumstances: Job was not guilty of any sin—that is the premise of the whole book—and yet he suffered. It was the friends of Job, who insisted he must be guilty of some hidden sin, who were rebuked by God. Hence, for us who live in comfort and security years after the event to point an accusing finger at European Jewry—probably one of the greatest and most creative and most beautiful in all Jewish history—and castigate them for shortcomings of one kind or another ostensibly deserving of such horrendous suffering, is an unparalleled instance of criminal arrogance and brutal insensitivity. How dare anyone even suggest that any "sin" committed by any significant faction of European Jewry was worthy of all the pain and anguish and death visited upon them by Hitler's sadistic butchers? How dare anyone, sitting in the American or British or Israeli Paradise, indict the martyrs who were consumed in the European Hell?

Second, whoever undertakes to expound the thesis of *mi-penei hata'einu* for any specific event, in the gory detail we mentioned earlier, risks violating a most heinous sin of his own—that of *zidduk ha-din,* justifying the punishment and travail of the people of Israel. The sages did not take to this too kindly.

According to the rabbis, Moses himself was punished for making offensive statements about his people. Moses told the Israelites: "Listen, ye rebels" (Numbers 20:10). His punishment: ". . . you shall not bring this assembly into the land which I have given them" (ibid v. 12). Elijah complained to God that "the children of Israel have forsaken Thy convenant" (1 Kings 19:10). Shortly thereafter, we read of God's command to appoint a successor, Elisha, in his place. Isaiah, too, used offensive language. In the course of a prophetic revelation, he confessed his feeling of worthlessness by saying: "Woe is me, for I am undone; because I am a man of unclean lips." But he erred by adding the significant words: "and I dwell in the midst of a people of unclean lips" (Isaiah 6:5). Soon afterwards we read of how one of the angels of God, "with a glowing coal in his hand, which he had taken with the tongs from off the altar," touched the mouth of the prophet and said: "Lo, this hath touched

thy lips and thine iniquity is taken away, and thy sin expiated"
(Isaiah 6:7). According to a Midrash, this was in atonement for the
sin of criticizing his fellow Jews as "people of unclean lips" (*Yalkut
Shimoni,* Isaiah chap. 6). The Talmud tells us that King Manasseh
killed Isaiah, who died when the sword reached his mouth—which
had uttered the defamation of Israel (Yevamot 49b).

The sages' aversion to condemning one's fellow Jews and justifying their suffering, no matter how terrible their behavior, is taught
in a famous tale of two great amoraim (Midrash Shir ha-Shirim 1):
R. Abbahu and R. Simeon ben Lakish entered the city of Caesarea.
R. Abbahu said to R. Simeon: "Why did we come here, into this
country of abusers and blasphemers?" Whereupon R. Simeon
dismounted from his donkey, took some sand in his hand, and
pushed it into R. Abbahu's mouth. "What is this?" asked R. Abbahu. R. Simeon replied: "The Holy One does not approve of one
who slanders Israel." (I am indebted to Prof. Eliezer Berkovits for
this reference.)

So let all those who are quick to interpret the Holocaust as punishment for Jewish sins be warned that they risk running afoul of the
sages' anger at whoever undertakes the sordid task of blaming his
fellow Jews—and especially if such accusations are unjust.

Third, I am also troubled by a certain moral deficiency in those
who seek to apply the *mi-penei hata'einu* philosophy to the Holocaust, and that is—their sense of utter self-confidence, their dogmatic infallibility. They *know* that six million Jews were killed because
there were Zionists among them, or because there were non-Zionists
among them, or because there were assimilationists or *apikorsim* or
whatever among them. While the rest of us poor benighted souls
cannot begin to fathom, today, some forty years after the event, *that*
it happened, *how* humankind could have degenerated so as to permit
it, *what* all this pain and torture did to the martyrs and to their
survivors—all this while, these smug interpreters of the Holocaust
have no questions, no doubts, no problems, no uncertainties. They
just know everything about the Sho'ah, especially *why* it happened.
The enormity of this callousness, the outrageousness of such insen-

sitive arrogance in elaborating this *zidduk ha-din* is mind-boggling. It is, to my mind, unforgivable.

One last comment about the advocates of applying *mi-penei ḥata'einu* to the Holocaust: this is the first time in Jewish history, to my knowledge, that supposedly pious and learned Jews—a rebbe, a rav, a mashgiach—have made so colossal an error in elementary grammar. They use the words *u-mi-penei ḥata'einu,* "because of *our* sins," when they really mean to say *u-mi-penei ḥatae'ihem,* "because of *their* sins"! In the past, every case of interpreting a disaster as the result of sin was one in which the interpreter included himself in the group that was guilty; it was "our sins," not anyone else's, that caused us to be exiled from our land. Today, in trying to explain the greatest of all disasters ever to befall us, small-minded people blame others, not themselves. The anti-Zionists blame the Zionists, the Zionists blame the anti-Zionists, the secularists blame the Orthodox rabbis who did not encourage emigration, and the Orthodox blame the assimilationists and the socialists and everyone else not in our camp. This last point alone is enough to disqualify the whole line of reasoning from being applicable to the Shoah.

In sum, if we ask, if we may resort to the *mi-penei ḥata'einu* rationale for the Holocaust, my answer is a resounding no—indeed, six million times no!

III

But if we cannot find meaning in the Holocaust as a sign of divine displeasure with Zionism or with anti-Zionism or with defection from Torah, what then was it all about? Is it possible that this was the way divine providence arranged to bring about the creation of the State of Israel?

Such an argument deserves no less contempt than the three Holocaust-as-punishment theories I mentioned above. It is incredible and unconscionable even to entertain the thought that a God who is just would ever indulge in such a cruel calculus as permitting

the torturing, gassing, and burning to death of six million innocent
victims in order to bring about the creation of a Jewish commonwealth and the apparatus of statehood. Only the most devious
mentality could long maintain such an obtuse notion. I would not
want to be guilty of burdening every Israeli child, living or unborn,
with the knowledge that his freedom was acquired at the expense of
who knows how many other children who were tossed alive into the
raging flames of the crematoria to make place for him in a Jewish
state. Enough said about this.

But does all this mean that there is no meaning to the Holocaust? And is meaninglessness an adequate alternative? Does it not
deny the principle of *hashgaḥah peratit,* of divine providence?

I cannot offer any pat answers for the enormous questions of the
Holocaust. Short of the renewal of prophecy in Israel, I will challenge any interpretation which pretends to more than the human
mind can undertake or more than the truly human heart can bear.
What I would like to do is to explore this question of meaning—
meaningfulness or meaninglessness—as it applies to the Shoah, in
the hope of providing a *framework* rather than a solution. If I am
right, and convincing, then in this framework, about which I have
thought and brooded for a long time, we may begin to grope for the
formulation of our own responses, and perhaps, include other
major historical events since the Shoah.

The conceptual framework I offer is that of *Hester Panim,* the
"hiding of the face," as the term is used both in Scripture and the
Talmud.

IV

All of the Bible is the record of the dialogue between God and
Israel. From the moment we were chosen—whether one dates that
from the revelation to Abraham or to Moses at Sinai—we have been
inextricably bound up with Him, never to be disentangled one from
the other. Now, the fortunes of this dialogue are described by two
terms: *Hester Panim,* the "hiding of the face," and *Nesiat Panim,* the

"lifting of the face." When two people love each other, they face each other, they look adoringly at each other. This mutuality in love is the essence of the dialogue; whatever "words" flow from it, whether narrative or normative, are significant but secondary. But when one party is disloyal to the other, when he sins against the other, then that other turns his face away, he refuses to gaze at the one who wrongfully injured him. As a consequence, the party who first sinned turns his face away. Their relationship thus sustains a blow. Should they feel a need or desire to reestablish relations as of old, then one of them will slowly lift up and turn his face to the other and await the reciprocal turning of the other's face as a gesture of reconciliation.

Now, the beginning of the rupture of the dialogue is *Hester Panim,* the initial turning away of the face by the one sinned against. The beginning of reconciliation takes place with *Nesiat Panim,* when the first effort is made to face one another in love and devotion, and to forgive past sins. In terms of the God-Israel dialogue, *Hester Panim* denotes God's self-removal from the context of Israel's company into His transcendence and remoteness, and *Nesiat Panim* denotes the reverse. This is the meaning of the verse in the threefold priestly blessing, "May the Lord lift up His face unto thee" (Numbers 6:26).

What causes *Hester Panim* and *Nesiat Panim* to take place? Sin brings in its wake punishment, the acme of which is *Hester Panim;* the turning aside of God's face is worse than any punishment He metes out to us directly. *Teshuvah,* repentance, is generally the precipitating factor in the era of *Nesiat Panim.* But that is not always so. Sometimes it is God who initiates the process of *Nesiat Panim* by turning to us, in a special historic act of compassion and pity—what the Kabbalah calls *itaruta dileila,* "the arousal from Above."

V

What, however, does *Hester Panim* imply for a national collectivity, for *Am Yisrael?* It is clear that for an entire people, the concept of

Hester Panim makes no sense unless they were previously in a state of dialogue or mutuality with God. If the people had not been originally engaged with the Divine, *Hester Panim* would simply be irrelevant. Indeed, that is what the Talmud teaches us only Israel can experience *Hester Panim,* for only Israel has the kind of special relationship with God that makes for the vicissitudes of *Hester Panim* and *Nesiat Panim* in history (Ḥagigah 5b).

Let us therefore explore further the nature of this historical *Hester Panim,* the one that refers to the whole people of Israel. There are two verses in Va-Yelekh:

> Then my anger shall be kindled against them in that day, and I will forsake them and I will hide My face from them,and they shall be devoured, and many evils and troubles shall come upon them, so that they will say in that day: Are not these evils come upon us because our God is not among us? And I will surely hide My face in that day for all the evil which they have wrought, in that they turned to other gods. (Deuteronomy 31:17–18)

Some commentators see this as representing two levels or a two-step process; so, for instance, Ramban and the Neẓiv. Maimonides (in both the *Yad* and the *Guide*) tells us that in both cases, that of the individual and that of the nation, the removal of the Shekhinah, which is equivalent to *Hester Panim,* implies the end of divine protection. *Hester Panim* means that one is exposed to all dangers and becomes the butt of all fortuitous circumstances.

This is how Maimonides puts it:

> His fortune and misfortune depend upon chance. Alas! How terrible a threat! . . . Hence, it may occur that the good man at times suffers, whilst no evil befalls those who are wicked; in these cases, what happens to them is due to chance. This principle I find also expressed in the Torah: "And I will hide My face from them, and they shall be devoured, and many evils and troubles shall befall them; so that they will say on that day, Are not these evils come upon us, because our God is not among us?" (Deuteronomy 31:17). It is clear that we

ourselves are the cause of this hiding of the face, and that the screen that separates us from God is of our own creation. This is the meaning of the words: "And I will surely hide My face in that day, for all the evils which they shall have wrought" (Ibid., v. 18). There is undoubtedly no difference in this regard between one single person and a whole community. It is now clearly established that the cause of our being exposed to chance, and abandoned to destruction like cattle, is to be found in our separation from God. (*Guide* 3:51)

For Maimonides, then, the dynamic of *Hester Panim* is as follows: first there is sin, and then there is divine retribution. This punishment is *part* of divine providence. Man, however, misinterprets the nature of the punishment, and repudiates the dialogue altogether, holding that his misfortune signifies the absence of God, not just His displeasure, and therefore the unhappy events are interpreted by him not as punishment, but as chance occurrences precisely because God is either "absent" or indifferent to man. This is, in essence, a denial of God's providence, and the punishment (for this consequent theological rather than original behavioral sin) is ironically appropriate: the true denial to man of divine providence, i.e., *Hester Panim*. In this state of alienation, Israel becomes a derelict people, left by God to its own resources and to the mercy of both nature and history.

At this point, we must ask some pointed questions about this thesis of *Hester Panim*. If *Hester Panim* means, in the ultimate, death, then how do we explain the survival of Israel even from as massively convulsive an event as the Shoah? Even more, how explain such happy events as the restoration of Jewish independence in 1948 and the Six-Day War in 1967? Of course, according to the scheme I have elaborated, it is logically possible to attribute these national triumphs as well to divine indifference, in which luck and Jewish brains played a major role. But can we, realistically and not just logically, say that these too were "chance" events played out by conflicting vectors in a meaningless historical continuum under the cloak of *Hester Panim?*

I do not believe so. It taxes credulity too much to accept that such extraordinary occurrences are the result of mere chance, of a throw of the dice on the stage of history. My critical faculties refuse to assent to such events at such a time as the result of mere randomness. And yet I do believe we are in a state of *Hester Panim* which, existentially, implies meaninglessness. How, then, do I explain this?

The Talmud records the following two opinions: "Rava said: 'The Holy One said, Even though I have hidden My face from them, "in a dream do I speak to him" (Numbers 12:6).' R. Joseph said: 'His hand is stretched forth over us.'" (Ḥagigah 5a).

I suggest that what we have here is not a classical *maḥloket,* rather a delineation of two levels of *Hester Panim,* yielding four separate stages in the dialogue between God and man:

1. Absolute *Hester Panim*
2. A survival *Hester Panim*
3. An intermediate *Hester Panim*
4. *Nesiat Panim*

The first or lowest level, that of absolute *Hester Panim,* applies to individuals only. In its last stages it results in the death of the individual separated from his Creator.

Now, this category does not apply to the people of Israel. It is a fundamental principle of Judaism that the Jews will survive and, through them, all of mankind will be redeemed. The covenant will never be revoked; the *berit* will endure. God may "hide His face" from us and abandon us to historical causality, to the fate of the deterministic laws that guide all mankind, but never will He allow us to be swallowed up forever in the eternal night of total extinction. Under *Hester Panim,* as the prophet Jeremiah said, we are "like" a widow—but never actually a widow, forever forsaken. In Hosea's metaphor, God may have banished us as punishment for acting the harlot and being disloyal, but never does He send us an actual divorce. Our chosenness in the first place was not based on our merit, and hence our demerits do not cancel our election. Our transgressions of the terms of the covenant are punished, but the covenant remains intact.

That is what is implied in R. Joseph's characterization of the second category: "His [divine] hand is stretched over us." His eyes may be averted from us, His face turned away in anger or disappointment, leaving us subject to all the twists and turns, all the tortuous torments of an aimless path in history—but His hand covers us and prevents our total extinction.

It is, indeed, the pit, the nethermost level of Israel's broken dialogue with God. Unlike individual man, for whom *Hester Panim* can result in death, for Israel it can never lead to extinction. But it remains indeed the worst of all suffering. So do we read in the Jerusalem Talmud (Sanhedrin 10:2):

> There is no more difficult hour in the world than that hour in which the Holy One said to Moses, "And I will surely hide My face in that day" (Deuteronomy 31:17). From that time on—"And I will wait for the Lord who hideth His face from the house of Jacob, and I will hope for Him"—for He said at Sinai, "for [My covenant] shall not be forgotten by their seed" (Deuteronomy 31:21).

The Yerushalmi seems to imply, first, that *Hester Panim* is the most dreadful and terrible of all punishments and, second, that even during *Hester Panim* there is no *total* abandonment, so that the prophet can still hope for a renewal of relationship, and can still point to the Sinaitic promise of *Hester Panim* never being taken to its final conclusion.

However, other than the sheer physical survival of the people, in however pitiable a condition, this state of *Hester Panim* is one of a total eclipse of the divine in our national life; its terrors are awesome. God remains inaccessible through prophecy. Our prosperity or adversity are the products of chance and effort—but not ordained by divine destiny. During an extended period of historical national *Hester Panim,* we are given over to the uncertainties of nature and history, where we can be raised by the tides of time and circumstance to the crest of the world's waves—or hurled pitilessly into the fierce troughs of life. Neither our success nor our failure means anything during *this* stage of *Hester Panim.*

I would venture that this period began at about the time of the destruction of the Second Temple, and extended to its nadir, the Shoah. Hence, before we entered the state of full-fledged *Hester Panim,* one could still say *mi-penei hata'einu,* for "meaning" could still be attributed to our predicament, and exile as punishment made sense in a context of meaningfulness. But this is no longer relevant or permissible in a state of intensive *Hester Panim.*

VI

Such was the period of the Holocaust. It was the ultimate expression of meaninglessness, and that was, perhaps the ultimate blow to its victims—and we are all its victims, those who survived and those who did not.The extent of the tragedy cannot be conveyed in any matrix of meaning. Indeed, any ascription of meaning to the Holocaust comes close to blasphemy. Only a humble confession of intellectual and spiritual surrender in the search for meaning, uttered in shame and futility, can prevent the memory of the martyrs from being disgraced.

This is, I confess, a bold assertion: that other than God's role in preserving us, there is no clear "sense" or "meaning" in Jewish history since the destruction of the Second Temple. I agree that this is a worrisome proposition. But our sacred sources not only support it, they point to it. We are in a state of *keri,* of hapless aimlessness. We are, as the sages put it in the Talmud, excommunicated by Heaven.

Now, when I say that *Hester Panim* is a period of meaninglessness, I of course do not intend automatically to nullify all meaning in Jewish history. (I am not of the Ben-Gurion school, which denies any significance or value to Diaspora history.) Rather, what I mean is that the *totality* of Jewish history, from the beginning to the messianic end point, is the highest form of meaning, in that it represents the engagement of man with God; and by "meaning," I intend nothing less than the universal redemptive design of history. However, *within* this process of meaning there exists a hiatus, a blank, an empty space, a "bubble," in which meaninglessness pervades. In this period, which is the epoch of *Hester Panim,* the history of the people as such makes no sense; that is, this period taken by *itself,* other than the sheer survival of Israel, shows no specific responsiveness to a divine plan. It is thus, in a manner of speaking, a period of "meaningful meaninglessness."

This does not, however, imply that in the period of *Hester Panim* individuals can find no meaning in their lives. On the contrary, such an assertion constitutes a morally weak submission to *Hester Panim.* The period of God's hiding of His face is meant not only as punishment but also as challenge (see the Hasidic parable at the end of these remarks). During this period, we are called upon to break the vicious cycle of mutual turning and hiding from each other. It may be more difficult to pray, but pray we must. It may seem impossible to feel His presence, but feel we must as we bend all our energies and innermost emotions to His service. We must, indeed, storm the very gates of Heaven, hurling ourselves against the barred windows, demanding entrance, loving despite distance, trusting—against all the puny logic of mere philosophers—that our Creator is there, listening to us, beckoning to us, waiting for us, and ready to respond. Yes, life is difficult under *Hester Panim*—but it is not impossible. There is a mysterious economy of meaning, whereby individuals may find meaning in their engagement with God while the people as a whole suffers meaninglessness—even as it is quite conceivable that individuals should be lost in a *Hester Panim* of meaninglessness while the people as a whole rises to new levels of meaningfulness.

VII

I could conclude here, but both our Talmud text and the context of Holocaust Remembrance Day, followed soon thereafter by Israel Independence Day, make it imperative that I add a few comments for the sake of at least minimal comprehensiveness.

There is a third stage of *Hester Panim,* above R. Joseph's stage of sheer survival, and just below *Nesiat Panim,* and that is Rava's category of the "dream state" in which the ancient dialogue is resumed. I refer to this as the intermediate stage, one which may or may not lead to *Nesiat Panim* and the ultimate redemption.

This "dream state" is one in which Israel can detect the first hints of a change in its fortunes. There is a whisper, a faint allusion, a rumor of divine reconciliation. There occur events which imply that, more than God's hand covering us, there is also the very beginning of a resumed dialogue, the barely perceptible turning of God's face to us. The dialogue is not yet by any means direct, as between two friends in a state of wakefulness. There is no eye contact, *ayin be-ayin nirah,* there is just a hazy sequence of events—a daydream that begs interpretation, that urges us to explore latent possibilities, that encourages us to decipher the symbols of the dream. This is a somnambulistic *Hester Panim* which presents us with the suggestion of grand, new historic opportunities. If both partners "play it right," their eyes will meet if only fleetingly, the old yearnings may yet be aroused, the embers of an ancient love yet be stirred up from the millennial abyss into which they had fallen, encrusted with ages upon ages of indifference and apathy and solitude.

Such a state may have occurred during the Purim episode for Persian Jewry. The very name Esther (Heb. *ester*) was held by the sages to symbolize a state of *Hester Panim* (Hullin 139a). The redemption took place, but God's name was not mentioned in the Megillah. There was not yet *Nesiat Panim,* but it certainly seemed like more than the survivalist stage of *Hester Panim.* The late Zvi Singer (Yaron) has suggested that the Book of Esther's self-description as "words of peace and truth" refers to the fact that the narrative can be read as a straightforward diplomatic success story—"words of peace"—in which Ahasuerus and Mordecai and Esther are the heroes, especially the Persian king; or as "words of truth": the hidden direction of all the events by the Creator of the world, who is also the Redeemer of Israel. The Purim miracle could be interpreted naturally or supernaturally, secularly or religiously, as would a pagan or a believer. They were in a dream state, the intermediate *Hester Panim* of the third stage. The results were felicitous; the reaction of acceptance by the Jews, according to the well-known passage in the Talmud, not only referred to the festival of Purim, but to the reconsecration of all Israel to the covenant of the Torah itself. The dialogue was resumed, and *Nesiat Panim* took place.

It is my belief that after the dreadful period of *Hester Panim* of the survivalist variety, we have, since the Holocaust, been presented with the possibilities inherent in the intermediate state. The Jewish state has been restored, and has in turn restored dignity to our people. Israel has demonstrated the kind of might and resolve that has won the begrudging admiration of the nations of the world. Jerusalem has been returned to us, the Kotel liberated.

"When the Lord restored the captivity of Zion, we were as dreamers" (Psalms 126). We are in a dreamlike trance. We have experienced the first stirrings of reconciliation, of "the arousal from Above." God is turning His face toward us.

We have the choice, as did Jewry in the days of Mordecai and Esther. We can ignore the hints, attributing the victories either to our own military strength and diplomatic skill or to sheer luck, or recognize in them the first rays of *Nesiat Panim*. We can, by failing to respond to the divine initiative with our own corresponding "arousal from below," forfeit our historic opportunities; or we can seize upon them so as to usher in a new age in Jewish history—one in which both success and failure will make sense, in which both national prosperity and adversity will be graced with meaning.

Which will it be? In the earlier years of the state, through the Six-Day War and the euphoria that followed it, I was truly optimistic. I thought that a genuine shudder of *teshuvah* had been experienced by *all* our people, that the great Jewish renaissance had begun.

But then we settled into a routine, and now—now I am less optimistic, although I have not despaired. If there is any *mi-penei hata'einu* to be recited, it is ours—Orthodox Jews who love Israel. It is we who have so far failed to seize the historic opportunities—

there, here, everywhere. We have failed to show our fellow Jews the beauty of Torah. We have alienated them instead of attracting them. We have managed to make them hate us rather than love what we stand for. We have pushed them instead of pulling them, not only turning our faces from them, but our backs to them. We have been busy with building careers instead of studying and teaching Torah—the sina qua non for moving on to *Nesiat Panim*. We have been distracted by our pursuit of middle-class luxuries, instead of dedicating our lives to sanctifying the divine Name demonstrating Torah's loveliness to all Jews, in Israel and Diaspora alike, in fulfillment of the rabbinic injunction to "love people and bring them close to Torah" (Avot 1:12). We have not loved them enough, and we have not brought them close enough.

But history proceeds in long strides, not in short steps. We still have the opportunity to return God's glance, to fill our lives with meaning and not emptiness, with providence and not chance, with destiny and not fate.

The Rebbe of Mezhibozh commented on the verse in Jeremiah: "My soul—says God—weeps in secret places." This can be explained, said the Rebbe, by what happened to me and my grandchild. He asked me to play hide-and-seek with him and I agreed. I closed my eyes and counted, and he went to hide. I was suddenly distracted by a friend and forgot all about the child. Soon I heard him crying from his hiding place, "No one has come to look for me."

So does God cry in His secret place: "No one comes to look for Me."

The Ribbono Shel Olam is waiting for us to seek Him out. He is now more accessible than He was in the last two thousand years.

Let us search for Him—together.

"The Face of God" was originally delivered as an address at Yeshiva University on Yom ha-Shoah, May 6, 1986, and was subsequently published as a pamphlet by Yeshiva University's Department of Holocaust Studies.

The Holocaust and the State of Israel: Are They Related?

Rabbi Abraham R. Besdin

The events of the Holocaust and the birth of the State of Israel both intrigue the mind and defy comprehension. They are anti-thetical in nature, yet are bafflingly interrelated. This essay will distill from numerous studies and symposia apocalyptic and redemptive implications of these two traumatic experiences.[1]

Historically, the Jewish people always blamed itself for all its misfortunes and credited God for its moments of fulfillment. Our sages inculcated this attitude as not only theologically valid, but also as pedagogically calculated to spur the people on toward introspective self-examination, thus leading toward improvement. "Because of our sins we were exiled," the Jew says in his prayers, which precludes self-pity, rebelliousness, or melancholy. It induces a determination to rectify one's waywardness and to get on with ones' destiny. God expects more from Israel, for they exist as the embodiment of His teachings and as the mentor of all mankind. Their deviation does not concern them alone but, rather, frustrates the divine plan for all mankind. Their leadership role entails greater resposibilities, which, in turn makes failure more censurable.

These rationales of Israel's tragic experiences hardly seem adequate in face of the magnitude and demonic fury of the Holocaust. An entire continent became engulfed in unmitigated evil, involving the complicity of religious, cultural, and scientific elements of society. The primary victim was the Jew, who suffered a brutal decimation of his ranks. This is an unparalleled experience even for Israel, which suggests messianic overtones even in its incomprehensibility. Elie Wiesel expressed his stupefaction: "To me the whole event remains a question mark. I still don't know how man could have chosen cruelty. I still don't know how God could have allowed him such a choice. I still don't know why Jews kept silent. In fact, I know nothing. And frankly, I don't know how one can talk about it."[2] We stand muted into silence, unable to apply the usual standards of evaluating Jewish suffering and unwilling, as well, to suggest that the victims were deserving of their fate. This represents the great agony of our contemporary Jewish experience.

Matching the Holocaust in power and mystery is the reconstitution of the State of Israel in May of 1948. Only a dogmatic agnostic would fail to see the transcendental overtones of this sudden transformation of Jewish dignity and hope. The unprecedented concurrence of support for Jewish statehood by Joseph Stalin and Harry Truman at the height of the Cold War, the dramatic military victories of the few over the many, the engagement of the mighty British navy by the scarred remnants of the concentration camp who penetrated the determined blockade in cattle boats and rickety freighters—these logistical improbables bespeak the supernatural and the messianic. The Six-Day War, which restored Jewish sovereignty to our holiest sites and gave the state viability, also involved the remarkable concurrence of remote coincidences, all converging toward a particular end. Here, too, as with the Holocaust, we perceive the transcendental even as we are baffled by its deeper implication.

II

Are the two events related messianically and not merely in proximity of time? An attempt to link them seems to diminish the import of both. Israel cannot be the answer for the Holocaust. There cannot be any answer, explanation, of restitiution for a tragedy of such dimensions. No divine favor can undo unspeakable pain. The Holocaust stands in all its inexplicable horror, and to suggest a redeeming aftermath of causal explanations is to reduce the unfathomable to human categories. Similarly, the State of Israel is a divine gift of such generous magnanimity, whose splendor would be dissipated by defining it as a reward for a previous deprivation, and intended balancing out of the scale of justice.[3]

Even as we deny their interrelatedness, we are, nevertheless, compelled to associate them because we experienced them together, sequentially, one seemingly growing out of the other. In a practical sense, the Holocaust created the uprooted remnant which could not return to its previous habitation. Psychologically, it fired a determination amongst the survivors and, vicariously, amongst world Jewry not to accept the tragedy in its brutal finality but, rather, to appropriate at least a small portion of triumph. The Holocaust also created feelings of remorse and a softening of the heart amongst many in the Christian world who realized the full immensity of the crime which their civilization had perpetrated and who were, consequently, more amenable to the idea of Jewish statehood.

In any case, the linking of tragedy and redemption is basic biblical teaching. Isaiah and other prophets related destruction and consolation, the eclipse and sunrise, the *toḥaḥah*—the terrifying admonitions which Moses directed at the Israelites—were inevitably followed by words of comfort and promises of restoration. Our sages conveyed this pithily with the words,[4] "On the day the Temple was destroyed, the Messiah was born." This much is certain, that the anger, frustration, and sense of revenge of the survivors were sublimated and galvanized toward a restorative goal. Its potentially explosive and destructive fury was transmuted into a burst of creativity and will-to-live.

III

The theological problem posed by the Holocaust is deserving of more serious consideration. It was David Hume, the British empiricist, who formulated the dilemma as follows: "If God wants to prevent evil but is unable, then he is impotent; if He is able but is not willing, then He is wicked; if He is both able and willing, why then evil?''

The Torah's answer is that God is able to avert apparent evil, is certainly willing to do so, but will, at times, choose not to do so. His decision may be dictated by broader considerations of moral import which are not discernible to us. An act is good or evil, not in fragmentary isolation but rather in its contextual frame of reference. Killing is reprehensible but not in *milḥemet miẓvah* or in an execution duly decreed by a Jewish court. An amputation to further life and health is similarly not evil. This argument essentially bids us to accept His justice on faith in acknowledgment of man's limited ken of judgment.

Jewish mysticism speaks of God's "self-constriction" (*sod ha-ẓimẓum*) whereby He circumscribes the all-pervading impact of His will, in order to allow room for man's freewill to operate.[6] God limits His own freedom to intercede, lest it destroy the full range of man's options. If man is to retain his singular status as a being "in the image of God" and not merely an automaton, he must be allowed to rebel against God Himself. The inevitable consequences of such a condition are human suffering and seeming or actual injustice, but it cannot be otherwise. Our sages undoubtedly appreciated this point when they spoke of God's personal commiseration. "When man suffers, what does the Divine Glory say? My head and arm are heavy (with anguish)."[7] Anthropomorphically, He laments the necessity of sorrow as an inescapable accompaniment to man's glory as a singular being.

The questing human spirit is hardly assuaged, however, by the above rationales. They may be adequate for life's daily situations, which are not cataclysmic in their impact and scope. They seem hollow, however, when we deal with a catastrophe which scourged one third of His people with unparalleled brutality. Does not the Torah tell us that He does and has intervened redemptively, and especially so when it affects the destiny of His chosen people? Is not our calendar filled with festal moments commemorating His intrusion into history? If so, why was this period of horror deemed unworthy of His redemption? Would the unique gift of man's freedom have been nullified in its innumerable areas of option if the tyrant's nefarious scheme had been blunted in a manner reminiscent of Purim?

IV

There is another principle which, perhaps, most saliently comes to grips with our dilemma. One of the direst of the imprecations mentioned in the Bible is the threat that "I will surely hide My face in that day for all the evil which they have wrought" (Deuteronomy 31:18; see also 31:17 and 32:20). This suggests a suspension of the divine covenantal dialogue with Israel and a withdrawal of His constant surveillance over its welfare. Israel is left to the turbulence of chance, the accidents of nature, and the caprices of history as is purgative in intent. The covenant, however, dormantly remains in effect, with the assurance that He will not allow Israel's extinction. "Even when they are in the lands of their enemies, I will not reject them, neither will I abhor them, to destroy them utterly and to break My covenant with them, for I am the Lord" (Leviticus 26:44).[8] This principle of retribution involving an estrangement from His presence is also operable with individuals, as we note in the psalmist's desperate plea, "How long, O Lord, will you forget me forever, how long will you hide your face from me?" (Psalms 13:2).

The opposite pole of God's noninvolvement is the reassuring principle of *nesiat kapayim* (turning His face unto thee), as clearly stated in the Kohanite blessing, "May the Lord lift up His countenance upon you and give you peace" (Numbers 6:26). Here we have the active relationship restored and His participation in human history with Israel as His agency. While the Holocaust represents Israel cast adrift, the State of Israel suggests the beginnings of a resumption of the old dialogue, a fraternal partnership in the effectuation of God's purpose in creation. We perceive His closeness in recent events, as if in a dreamlike trance, unsure of its reality and fearful for its enduring character.[9] We alternate between exhilaration at the prospects which seem to be unfolding and the fear that if we do not respond appropriately to the spiritual opportunities opening to us, we may frustrate their development through our unworthiness. The Divine role of either withdrawal or involvement is, in itself, a moral posture whose meaningfulness we can only discern in broad outlines.

The Book of Job was included in the Bible canon in order to help us cope with this most difficult theosophical problem. The Talmud even questions the historicity of Job, but the basic quandary of justifying God's ways is rooted in daily reality. Why, asks Job, is he subjected to such torment, since he has lived righteously. His friends suggest that it is undoubtedly a just retribution for clandestine sins. God suddenly appears, rebukes the friends, and upholds Job's righteousness. No explanation for his suffering is given; puny man is challenged by God for his presumptuousness in seeking to understand His inscrutable judgment. Can man otherwise encompass in his intellect the mysteries of cosmic creation? Job is comforted and consoled, not by any explanation but by God's reassuring closeness, that He is near once again. Martin Buber explains: "The true answer that Job receives is God's appearance only, only that distance turns to nearness, that 'his eyes sees Him,' that He knows him again. Nothing is explained, nothing adjusted; wrong has not become right, nor cruelty kindness. Nothing has happened but that man again hears God's address."[10]

A great Hasidic saint, Levi Isaac of Berdichev, said: "I do not ask, O Lord of the world, to reveal to me the secrets of Thy ways. I could not comprehend them. I do not ask to know why I suffer but only this: Do I suffer for Thy sake?"

In the final analysis, the Holocaust remains an enigma whose meaning eludes us. From the depths of our faith, we are reconciled to its metaphysical significance. We fervently pray, however, that "it be for Thy sake," that out of its agony there will truly emerge the ecstasy testifying that once again His countenance is "lifted up" to us.

NOTES

1. *Judaism,* Summer 1967, Symposium on "Jewish Values in the Post-Holocaust Future": participants, Emil Fackenheim, Richard Popkin, George Steiner, and Elie Wiesel; *Tradition,* Winter 1965–Spring 1966, "Representative Works of the Holocaust Literature" by Ben Eilbott, a review of six works; *Tradition,* Summer 1968, "The Religious Meaning of the Six-Day War": participants, S.Y. Cohen, N. Lamm, P. Peli, W. Wurzburger, M. Wyschogrod.

2. *Judaism,* Summer 1967.

3. Emil L. Fackenheim, "Jewish Faith and the Holocaust," *Commentary,* August 1968, grapples essentially with this dilemma.

4. Numbers *Rabbah* 13. Similarly R. Akiba was cheered when he saw jackels in the ruins of the Temple because now that the prophecy of doom had been fulfilled, the prophecies of consolation and restoration must follow (Talmud Makkot 246).

5. "Dialogues concerning National Religion," quoted by C.W. Hendel in *Hume Selections* (New York, Scribner's, 1927), p. 365.

6. See Gershom G. Scholem, *Major Trends in Jewish Mysticism* (New York: Schocken Books, 1941), pp. 260–265. *Zimzum* originally meant "concentration" or "contraction," but if used in the kabbalistic parlance it is best translated by "withdrawal" or "retreat."

7. Mishnah Sanhedrin 6:5.

8. See also Yalkut 83, "For no nation will be able to utterly prevail over them."

9. See Norman Lamm in *Tradition,* vol. 10, no. 1, p. 8. "There is a sudden, dreamlike, almost unreal and uncertain confrontation in which the two partners have caught a glimpse of each other's faces and acknowledge each other's faces."

10. Martin Buber, *At the Turning* (New York: Farer, Straus & Young, 1952), pp. 61–62.

Thoughts on the Holocaust

Rabbi Emanuel Rackman

Christians and Jews alike honor Elie Wiesel for many reasons, but not the least of them is the way he—like a prophet of old—has forced philosophers and theologians to ponder the impact of the Holocaust on their conceptions of God and human nature. He is not so presumptuous as to claim that he has answers to the mind-boggling questions. I certainly do not have them either, but I do want to put an end to what I consider truly sophomoric efforts by others to illuminate a darkness that is simply impenetrable.

I should say at the very outset that whenever I write about the Holocaust, I do so with fear and trepidation. For me it is like writing about the unknowable. People who experienced its horrors have a right to relate the facts, what they saw and heard, what they did, how they felt, how they reacted. They may also indulge in generalizations about the behavior of fellow victims and about what they think precipitated the indescribable tragedy. I indulge them even the right to curse or bless God.

What I cannot tolerate are attempts by historians to be judgmental about the martyrs and to decide whether their behavior was saintly or villainous. When these historians also are ignorant of the nature of Jewish life in the countries of Jewish suffering and of the content of the Jewish tradition throughout the ages, they articulate views that I often find offensive. And when anyone tries to explain why God permitted it to happen, I virtually scream. I respect the drive of those who believe in God to discover why God behaved as He did. Yet I would much rather submit that the answer is beyond man and leave it at that. Intellectual honesty sometimes demands that we admit that we cannot know what will never be known until God Himself tells us.

Why God acted or failed to act as He did is beyond us. But certainly it was not our sins that caused the Holocaust. Only non-Jews caused it. Our sin, if any, was our blindness in not anticipating it and our inertia and silence while it was happening.

True, we may have sinned as a people and as individuals. But is the punishment commensurate with the gravity or heinousness of the sin? We would resent a human judge who acted in this way. Can we not, therefore, ask whether the Judge of all the earth should not be at least as just as a human judge?

I know many a colleague who still maintains that God punished us. I wish they would shut their mouths once and for all. Not only are they talking nonsense but they are also relieving the Christian and Moslem worlds of guilt. And they are justifying another Holocaust, for we are less righteous now than we ever were. (Even as I write this I feel myself screaming within me.)

For Jewish philosophers of all ages the problem of evil generally was one with which they could hardly cope. And there are some today who superficially or with depth still write on the subject, which is given the impressive name "the problem of the theodicy." Somehow, prior to World War II the answers may not have satisfied but we could live with the paradox that a benign God might create evil for a purpose known to Him, and we tolerated its continuance at least until the end of days. Most of the rationalization was ridden with doubt, but somehow religious faith was not shaken massively.

However, the death of six million Jews—and millions of others—because of the indescribable bestiality of Hitler was too tragic a phenomenon not to upset all prior views. One simply could not believe that God would not intercede to save. The result was either a denial of God or total resignation to Him, because any hypothesis other than His existence made life meaningless. One chose God because it was the only viable alternative.

I wish that I had the infinite wisdon necessary to give a satisfactory answer. I shall delude neither myself nor anyone else by suggesting that I am even close to an explanation. If I did, I could make myself immortal—nay, I would be as immortal as the Infinite because I fathomed His ways. But one explanation I must reject, and from that rejection perhaps one will discover a ray of light that will ennoble our lives and experiences.

The one explanation, which I first heard from the lips of Martin Buber, and thereafter from many Jewish thinkers, traditional and nontraditional, is that the period of the Holocaust was a period of *Hester Panim* for God. He simply hid His face—He turned away from man, and man and his id ran amok, with the resulting devastation. The notion is suggested in Deuteronomy. At times God, so to speak, withdraws from His preoccupation with His covenanted people and havoc follows.

I do not know how I had the hutzpah thirty years ago to argue with Martin Buber. But I did, and now that I am older, I can be even more daring.

I cannot accept the idea that an omniscient, omnipotent God would ever make Himself unaware of what is happening on earth. Perforce He must know everything at all times. To take literaly the biblical expression that God hides His face is to make too anthropomorphic a judgment. A God who is so petty as to yield to pique is too ignoble a God for man to worship! The verses in Deuteronomy that suggest the notion must mean something else.

I cannot imagine that Martin Buber was a literalist with regard to other anthropomorphic passages in the Bible. Would he be so literalist with regard to Moses' wish to see God's face and God's reply that only His back could be seen? Maimonides gives this passage a magnificent allegorical interpretation. Why then must we moderns become literal with regard to similar passages of the Bible and portray God as playing "hide-and-seek" with us?

If we are unequivocal in our commitment to the idea that God knows all and can do all because He is omniscient and omnipotent, then we must assume that He knew what was happening but intentionally did not act. And why He did not act is simply beyond us. Perhaps from His not acting we may learn something about His refusal to interfere with the freedom of will of even maniacs like Hitler, but then we would have to admit that He sets a bad example for me. He ordered us not to stand by idly when innocent blood is shed. Why did He? I repeat—Job's answer is still the best. It is a no answer. We do not know, but "though He slay me, I still trust in Him."

Yet does the phrase "hiding the face" have no meaning for us? Of course it does, but not to provide the reason for God's behavior during the Holocaust.

If we bear in mind one profound insight of Hirsch's and Heschel's, we will find meaning in the phrase. They suggested that the Bible is not a book to be used by humans primarily to arrive at an understanding of God.

It is not a textbook of man's theology. It is rather a textbook of God's anthropology. It tells us how God sees man. Thus, for example, we do not really know why God denied Adam the right to eat from one specific tree in the Garden of Eden, but we know how Adam defied God. We do not know why God favored Abel's offering and not Cain's, but we know how Cain reacted. We do not have much detail about the sins of humanity before the Flood, but we know with what arrogance new generations conspired to frustrate God. Similarly, the sins of Sodom and Gomorrah are only subtly suggested, but the response of Abraham when told about God's plan became a model for all mankind. That is what one means when one speaks of the Bible as a guidebook not to help us fathom God but rather to see ourselves—how we are and how we ought be.

With this as our premise, it is not unreasonable that God tells us, in the Bible, what He will do under certain circumstances—not because it accords with His Being or His Justice but rather to help us see ourselves as if in a mirror.

Therefore, He told us that the day would come when we would betray Him and ignore His law. We would be punished, but even the punishment would not make us fully aware of our guilt. We would not fathom the meaning of our suffering, or sense our guilt, or take the steps necessary to achieve true penitence and a return to Him. We will hide. We will fail to see and to hear. Our hearts will be obtuse; our eyes blind and our ears deaf. And God's hiding from us will mirror our hiding from Him. Perhaps that will help us to visualize the character of our own performance and we shall be stimulated to make amends.

That is what the text tells us. God said that even when Jews reflect in their misery upon the cause of all their suffering, they will not blame themselves, but rather God, His absence, His neglect (Deuteronomy 31:17). How else could God teach them to reflect more profoundly, the better to discern their existential situation, than to hide Himself, which He does (ibid, v. 18). Perhaps as He hides, we will recognize that this is what we are doing, and we will open our ears to hear, and our eyes to see.

Now, that is precisely what happened in our lifetime and is continuing to happen. God did not hide. It was, rather, we who had lost our capacity to hear. Our self-centeredness prompted us to hear only what we wanted to hear, and God's hiding mirrored our behavior in the hope that we would see ourselves as we are and change our ways.

Were our ears not deaf during the Holocaust? We refused to listen to reports that were being transmitted to us, in ways direct and indirect, that Hitler had become the greatest human butcher in world history. We now know so much more about our deafness at that time.

First we doubted the veracity of the reports. Then we assured ourselves that we could do nothing. Lastly we even weighed—with unforgivable self-centeredness—the price of rescue against the cost of prolonging the war. We were so coldly calculating instead of hearing—simply hearing the flames of the crematoria. It was not God who hid His face but we who had hidden ours.

But it did not start with World War II. Why didn't Jews hear what was happening all about them in eastern and central Europe from almost the beginning of this century, and why were they deaf to the call of Zionism and its messianic implication? Why did they cling to the fleshpots and decline to act as the situation warranted—with emigration to Israel and the development of the land? Why did they wait so long before realizing how vicious was the voice of the anti-

Semite all about them? And indeed, are we not listening to that same voice today, or are we not hiding from it?

Similarly, the United Nations, which was born as a result of World War II, has overwhelming evidence that a large bloc of its members seek the genocide of Jews again. Yet has it the capacity to listen? It does not hear or fathom anything but that which it wants to hear.

All of the resolutions of its Security Council with regard to Israel are so indescribably vile that the mere thought of them makes the heart sick.

If we had listened in the United States to the calls of distress that were coming from the ghettos for more than a generation, we might have solved our urban problems long ago.

If university administrators and faculty had listened to the complaints of students when they were first expressed, we would not have had the avalanche of campus upheavals.

If parents had listened to their own children in their teens and shared their concerns and forebodings, we would not now have hundreds of thousands in revolt against our every cherished value and institution.

The truth is that even husbands and wives do not listen to each other—each hears and knows only what he or she craves, and without the art of listening to each other, their marriages must end in divorce.

As a matter of fact, how can we ever ask God to listen to us when we do not hear Him when He speaks to us! All that is happening in and to Israel may very well be His address to us, inviting us to recognize His role in our redemption, and cautioning the rest of humanity not to permit continuing injustice to the Jew to catapult the world into another global war and the annihilation of all mankind!

All of us must learn to listen. God does not hide His face. Rather does He mirror our hiding—our burying of our heads in the sand like ostriches.

If we are to save ourselves and all mankind, we must open our ears and our eyes. If God hides His face, it is because He wants to remind us that we are hiding ours!

That also describes how I felt when I recently read a volume edited and published by Prof. Geoffrey Hartman of Yale. It is entitled *Bitburg in Moral and Political Perspectives.* As I reflect on what happened, I fault myself for not having been more articulate and more indignant than I was about that which the President of the United States said and did. I must have hidden my face to the horrendous implications of any attempt to "bury the hatchet" or to "come to terms with the past."

Suddenly I experienced a déjà vu. In 1985 I accepted the President's explanation that forty years after the war, the time might have come for a reconciliation with the enemy, precisely as forty-odd years earlier I accepted President Roosevelt's explanation that to save the victims of Nazi tyranny would prolong the war and victimize many innocent American soldiers. I said to myself: "How many times must it happen before I detect the sham and stop hiding my face?"

It has been said that one of the deepest moral quandaries of modern times is the tension between world Judaism's need to remember the crimes of the Holocaust and post-Nazi Germany's need to forget. Bitburg represented the President's surrender to the latter need, while everything that he is now doing to meet the former need will hardly help Germans to remember.

For Elie Wiesel's role in the matter, Jewry must be everlastingly grateful. And we must also thank God that, in this instance, Wiesel did not have to stand alone. Christians and Jews proved equal to the challenge with him, and Prof. Hartman's book attests to the pluses and minuses of a historic affair called Bitburg.

In any event, we have nothing more to say other than that God's ways are unknown to man. We will never be able to explain why He permitted the Holocaust to happen. Those who think that they have an explanation only make Him look worse, and I would rather plead ignorance of His ways than blaspheme Him. All I do know is that He wishes me to live righteously. His command that I be righteous must ever be the lodestar of my existence, even if I cannot account for or justify or rationalize His inscrutable behavior during the Holocaust.

Yet what does one do with the countless references in our sacred literature and our liturgy to the fact that disobedience to Him is the cause of disaster befalling us? And were we not promised that we would be rewarded of our righteousness? Was that not God's commitment in the covenant—His side of the "bargain"?

How does one reconcile these facts with my rejection of any explanation for God's behavior during the Holocaust? I am sure that the question is still better than any answer one will receive. Yet reply I must, but with caution that in this connection too, I have no completely satisfactory rationalizations.

Many of our sages resolved the dilemma by saying that the reward for obedience and the punishment for sin are otherworldly. In another realm of existence God will fulfill His word. This view became especially central in Christian thought. Other sages did not deny the validity of this approach, but since the Bible speaks of this-worldly rewards and punishments, and not of otherworldly ones, one has reason to ask why one cannot see any connection on earth between virtue and God's bounty, on the one hand, and vice and God's wrath, on the other.

With the biblical statements which affirm the connection one can make one's peace and say that the blessings and the curses are meant for the group. If Jewish society and the Jewish state, and not only single individuals, fulfill God's will, then there will be peace and plenty. Otherwise, the consequences will be unbearable.

A basic truth is contained in this caveat—and even if the biblical language is hyperbolic, nonetheless the powerful language was intended to make Jews realize that only a just society can long endure, while a corrupt one must disintegrate. History has proven this to be generally true. Therefore, if one is not too strict a literalist, one can discern a message of lasting significance in the Torah.

This would certainly apply to the second paragraph of the Shema (Deuteronomy 11:13–17). In it the Jewish people were told that if they obeyed the Law, God would do everything necessary to make their sojourn in the Promised Land a blissful one. For failure to obey the Law, however, they would perish. This promise and warning were addressed to the group—the people—the state and society.

Professor Lenn Goodman of the University of Hawaii has suggested that there is no promise in this passage that God will reward the people for obedience to His Law. All that is said is that if they obey the Law, and if God rewards them, then they should be careful not to become smug because of their bliss and forget the Lord who made it possible. Otherwise they will be punished. His suggestion makes good sense, but there are other passages which definitely make the promise to reward obedience.

One possible answer to our question is to say that to an immature people God had to speak as one does to children. For a mature people, however, the obedience itself is its own reward, as the verse in Leviticus expresses it: "I will be your God, and you will be my people" (Leviticus 26:12). The thought of a mutual love affair for profit is horrendous to sensitive people, and, therefore, for the truly mature, the service of God for a promised benefit is equally unthinkable. "We must not serve God in order to receive a reward," said our sages in Ethics of the Fathers.

But what about the emphasis in our prayers on the connection between our sins and our exile, which incidentally encouraged our persecutors in the last two thousand years to do what they did? They said that they were simply fulfilling God's wish. This was widely held Christian doctrine.

To this I give what may appear to be the view of a schizoid person. I do not see that on earth the righteous are rewarded and the wicked punished, but I do believe that it is excellent exercise for a religious person to practice introspection and ponder that perhaps, when he is made to suffer, God is trying to teach him something that will make him an even better servant of man and God than he presently is. Yet, while he may think well of himself, he may never attribute other people's misfortunes to their sinfulness.

Especially troublesome is the High Holy Days prayer that tells us—on the basis of a talmudic text—that the days of judgment are the occasion for our being sentenced, "Who will live and who will die." We find it impossible to reconcile our overwhelming experience with the literal interpretation of that prayer. We discover that the most righteous are not sentenced to life and the most wicked do survive to the following year. God's ways remain inscrutable. Then why utter a prayer with whose literal meaning we cannot identify?

Needless to say, we forget that the prayerbook was never intended to be a textbook in systematic philosophy or theology. Prayer is generally in the category of poetry—not logic. It is very much the product of moods, and logical coherence is not its hallmark. But so many thoughts are suggested by the prayer that who would dare to excise it!

It teaches us how flitting life is—how frail we are—how many are the threats to our existence. Then why not make the years and the days count!

It teaches us that our deeds do make a difference. One added good deed by one person can swing the balance of the survival of humanity and not only for the individual self.

It teaches us that in the imponderable "bang" of the universe, a still small voice can still be heard.

It communicates a sense of awe and trepidation, which in the modern age we need badly to reduce our arrogance and our self-assurance that we are the complete masters of our fate and captains of our destiny.

It induces a sense of solidarity with all mankind, the creatures of one Creator, who must one day account to Him for that which they did with the gift of life.

For centuries that prayer did all of this—and not only for Jews to whom its imagery was real but even for those who saw in it only the multiple meanings and reminders.

One last word. As the Bible still inspires those who take it literally as well as those who see in it much allegory, so the liturgy can inspire those who take it literally and those who see more than words in the text but also spirit, awe, adoration, commitment, and solidarity with fellow Jews in the service of God and man.

The Hatred and the Fear

Rabbi Eliezer Berkovits

I

Our main preoccupation with the Holocaust has been under the aspect of the problems of faith with which this latest of the European catastrophes of the Jewish people has presented the Jew. It is possible that because of this we have neglected to pay adequate attention to a fuller understanding of the reasons for the tragedy. In particular, we have not probed with sufficient intensity into the causes of Nazi Germany's hatred for and fear of the Jews. How could what happened have happened? How is a human being capable of such satanic hatred as that of the German Nazis and their international allies? How was such ingeniously conceived cruelty possible? How could human beings intentionally lower themselves to a level of inhumanity that could be called beastly only by insulting the wildest animals of prey? Secondly, how is the fear to be explained? At the beginning of the Second World War, Nazi Germany was one of the greatest military powers on earth, yet it was afraid of the Jews. When they delaimed, "The Jews are our misfortune," and indeed that of all mankind, they really believed it. The fear was honest, real, oppressive. How is it to be understood? Finally, how may we explain the encouraging indifference of the Western world toward the foulest crime in history? And far beyond such participatory indifference, the chances of Jews escaping from the ghettos and the death camps were reduced to an intolerable minimum by the actual cooperation of large sections of the European population, whose own countries were crushed and plundered by the Germans. How are we to explain such eager cooperation between

the oppressed and the oppressor in the planned destruction of the
Jewish people?

II

Camus, in his book *The Rebel,* attempts to analyze the terrorism
practiced by nazified Germany. In this connection, he quotes the
words of one Ernst Junger, whom he describes as the only person of
higher culture who gave Nazism the semblance of philosophy.
Camus quotes Junger, who wrote: "The best answer to the betrayal
of the body of life by the spirit is the betrayal of the spirit by the
spirit, and one of the great and cruel pleasures of our times is to
participate in the work of destruction."

Far from seeing in this statement only a semblance of philosophy, we recognize in it the very essence of Nazism. Two basic concepts appear in it: the betrayal of the body of life by the spirit, and,
as a response to it, the betrayal of the spirit by the spirit. It would
seem to us that the idea of the betrayal of the body of life by the
spirit adjudges the realm of the spiritual as the enemy of life. The
spirit affirms freedom as the sole means by which man is able to
accept responsibility for his deeds. It demands moral discipline
from man, and it prescribes a way of life in loyalty to values whose
origin is in a transcendental dimension. All this is a betrayal of life,
which is then understood as purely biological, the life of the instincts
and of the natural drives. It is possible to deny the values and the
authority of the spirit. This, however, would not yet be the betrayal
of the spirit by the spirit. The spirit betrays the spirit when the denial
becomes an ideology, when the satisfaction of the instincts and
primitive appetites is elevated to "religious" ritual. It is the "sanctification" of the barbarous, inhuman, demonic in human nature. It
is the planned desecration of all spiritual values. Nazism is not a
political movement, but—as the spirit's betrayal of the spirit—it is
essentially a nihilistic spiritual movement.

The confrontation with Judaism is natural. In Judaism the highest commandment is *Kiddush ha-Shem,* the sanctification of God's name; in Nazism, it is—as one might say—the sanctification of the Satanic. The hatred is understandable; its limitless cruelty is due to the fear that this kind of nihilistic betrayal of the spirit has of Judaism and the Jewish people. It is the Jewish opposition to the "holy" betrayal of the spirit that is feared. However, it is not fear of the teachings of Judaism. A great military power like Nazi Germany would not be afraid of teachings alone. It was not because of the Ten Commandments or "Thou shalt love thy neighbor as thyself" or the faith in the One God that the Jewish people were singled out for destruction by the rebellion against the world of the spirit. Other religions, too, affirm such principles and believe in God in a similar manner. However, other major religions were overtaken by major spiritual disasters, i.e., too much this worldly success in the domain of Caesar, in the materialistic kingdom of world history. Half a billion and many millions more of believers prove nothing in the dominion of the spirit, they prove nothing of the presence of God, of the power of their commitments to the ideals they profess. Principles of faith may have their psychological significance for the individual believer. However, in the context of world history, many millions of believers, who rule over vast countries, are in possession of rich natural resources, live within their own natural boundaries, and may rely on their own vast armies, do not represent any kind of spiritual force in the world. They exist, survive, and rule thanks to the material might in their possession. They could not serve as objects for attack by the spirit's betrayal of the spirit. There was no need for Nazism to plan "final solutions" for them. The attack on their material power bases, victory in battle was sufficient.

Judaism and the Jewish people alone are a serious threat to the betrayal of the spirit; not because of their teachings, but because of the unique nature of the power that they represent in the history of mankind. We are not thinking here of Judaism as the mother of Christianity, nor of its influence in the rise of Islam; but of the power of Judaism as Judaism and of the Jewish people as formed and sustained by Judaism. Of course, the Jewish people lacked the kind of power that alone counts in the history of the other nations. But therein, exactly, lies the cause of the fear of the Jews. Jewish survival, based on the spiritual values of Judaism, the continuity of Jewish existence over thousands of years, is the great mystery for the nations; it has no explanation according to their categories of interpretation. This people of the Jews has survived and continues to exist in spite of the fact that it lacks the entire materialistic power base that alone seems to guarantee national suvivial. The very fact that this people has been able to maintain itself against all the barbarous attacks that intended to destroy it, is witness to the presence in history of a power source entirely different from the one that normally grants life and survival to nations. The ability of the Jewish people to continuously renew itself after the kinds of disasters that have eliminated mighty nations and vast empires from the world is witness to the influx of some secret energy whose source is the reality of a spiritual dimension. The betrayal of the spirit is a rebellion against the spiritual force that makes itself manifest only in the life and the continuity of existence of the Jewish people. Thus, the more radical the spirit's betrayal of the spirit is, the more intensely wild and cruel is the hatred for the Jews, a hatred which is richly fed by the fear of him. The fear is genuine, it is honest and is not just the child of some mental delusion. The fear of the spirit that betrays the spirit is justified; it has its basis in historic experience.

The "final solution" aimed, beyond the destruction of the Jewish people, at bringing about the final defeat of that spiritual force against which were directed all the hatred and energies of Nazism's betrayal of the spirit. They were right in thinking that if they do not succeed in uprooting the "Jewish influence" in history through the destruction of the Jewish people, they will also fail in their plans of world conquest. They were sensing correctly that "the Jewish influence" was holding the secret presence of "the hiding God" in the history of man. That "influence" was indeed the danger that threatened the course of that nihilistic rebellion whose mad ambition was not only world conquest but also intended to poison the soul of mankind and to trample under foot all the values of the spirit.

III

Nazi Germany's challenge to mankind was a spiritual one. However, specifically that kind of a challenge Western civilization was unable to meet. Nazism is the legitimate offspring of Western civilization that was, to a large extent, shaped in the Christian image. There exists an intimate linkage between the hatred and fear of Nazism and the hatred of Christianity for the Jews and the fear of them. The all-too-eager supporters of the Jewish-Christian dialogue pay too much attention to theology, as if the problem of Christian-Jewish relationships was due to differences of tenets of faith and religious affirmations. The supporters of the dialogue thus far were lacking in moral courage and ethical honesty to face the truth that emerges clearly from the Christian behavior towards the Jewish people ever since Christianity, as the result of the mightiness of the sword of Constantine became the ruling religion in the Western world. Untold masses of human beings do not oppress, persecute, murder men, women and children with consistent cruelty through many centuries for theological reasons. The Christian cruelty, too, had had its demonic component. It has been wild and barbarous in a manner not unlike that of the Nazis and their numerous international supporters. The reason for it is well indicated by what we have heard to be defined as the spirit's betrayal of the body of life. In the history of Western civilization, Christianity represents the element of this betrayal. A great deal of modern psychological insight, and the importance that the concept of repression received in it, is due to this element. Christianity's evaluation of the body is negative. It found its classical expression in the statement of Jesus when he declared that his kingdom was not of this world. It was more popularly formulated in the dictum of the Christian apostle Paul who said: "It is better to marry than to burn." The body is seen as the ass of burden, the seat of evil. With its idealistic teachings, love for one's enemy, "resist ye no evil," "turn the other cheek," sustained by its other-worldliness, Christianity was the suppressor of the claims of natural needs of the bodily drives. It was an unnatural oppressive burden on the biological and instinctual parts of human existence. Christianity was the cause of everpresent tension within the masses of its adherents, who were told that they were saved from their corrupt nature and fall, their sins were forgiven, and they themselves redeemed by their faith. Thus they were expected to behave in a manner that contradicted their natural condition. That was the betrayal of the body of life by the spirit.

The tension was seeking release; the suppression, liberation. They were found in primitive and cruel instinctual outbursts and rebellion against the imposed values of the spirit. However, the rebellion could not be directed against Christianity itself. On the conscious level of their extremely limited self-understanding, the masses were professors of the Christian faith. In their eyes the cause of all their troubles were the Jews and Judaism. They were told that they were the new Israel. The Christian hatred of the Jew is the answer of the repressed instincts to the spirit's betrayal of the body of life that Christianity turned out to be. In essence Christian Jew hatred is the Christian's rebellion against Christianity.

The cruelty of this rebellion that has been poured out over the Jews through the ages is intensified by the Christian fear of the Jew. Christianity has been unable to find a positive function in history for the continued existence of the Jewish people. In the Christian world view, the survival of the Jewish people represents a serious problem. Christianity took over the vocation of the Jewish people in an improved form. If it was the true Israel what need was there for Judaism? How come the Jews did not disappear? Thus, Christianity conceived an ingenious answer: *testes iniquitatis suae et veritatis nostrae.* Old Israel still had a function in history: "They are witnessing to their iniquity and to our own truth." They testified to all that by their degraded condition, by the suffering that was inflicted upon them by the Christian world. The explanation, served a very useful purpose. It was able to pacify an occasionally disturbed Christian conscience. It made the persecutors the self-appointed interpreters and executors of the mysterious divine will. It rendered genocide practiced through centuries a God-pleasing act. More significant, however, is the fact that the explanation for the embarrassing continued existence of the Jewish people reveals the Christian fear of the Jews. Christianity has been extremely successful. It conquered the entire Western world; it was spreading its branches most impressively into all the continents and still it needed reassurance. In spite of its great success, it still needed Jewish suffering in order to prove how right it was and how wrong the Jews were. The primitivity of the proof and, even more, the need for it only prove one thing: the inner insecurity of the Christian about his own truth and serious doubts regarding their valuation of the place and the truth of Judaism in the world. If only those Jews would have disappeared for good, everything would be so much simpler. But the Jews did not disappear in spite of all the hatred and persecution. Their unexplicable very existence was the challenge, it was the threat. It was feeding mightily the cruelty with which the rebellion of the instincts took revenge on the spirits for its demands.

Ernst Junger called the spirit's betrayal of the spirit the "best answer." The betrayal of the spirit by instinctual rebellion is the other, according to Nazism, not the best answer. Nazism elevated the instinctual betrayal from the level of primitive inhumanity to the level of ideological barbarism. The response of the primitively demonic was transformed into the sophisticated betrayal of the spirit by the spirit. Thus, Nazism is a legitimate development of Western civilization. The West's encouraging and, often, participating indifference towards the greatest and most inhuman crime in history is understandable.

IV

To understand the nature of the hatred and the causes of the fear is important for the self-understanding of the Jewish people. It is important for understanding our place in the history of mankind, our task and the unique nature of our strength.

The Holocaust was history's great challenge to the conscience of man. Its outcome was to decide the entire course of human history for generations to come. It was a challenge to international conscience to make a stand on behalf of humanity and justice, compassion and love. Mankind reached one of the major crossroads of history and chose the path of the betrayal of the spirit through indifference. Now it is well on the road to spiritual decadence and moral degeneration. The entire dismal course of history since the beginning of the Second World War to this day is the necessary consequence of the moral bankruptcy of Western civilization in failing to meet the spiritual and moral challenge of Nazism. Christianity called the Jews witnesses according to their understanding. Witnesses we are according to the words of Isiah:

> "Ye are My witnesses, says the Eternal, that you may know and trust in Me and understand that I am He. Before Me there existed no God, nor will there be one after Me."(43,10).

The *Sifrei* comments on this by saying: When you are my witnesses, I am God, when you are not my witnesses, I am not.I doubt whether at any time in the past these words were as applicable as today. At this hour the Jewish people are the only one through whose ever-uncertain destiny God may reveal his presence in world history. This defines the place of the Jew, his importance, his task and responsibility under the darkening skies of man's future.

In our days radically revolutionary changes occurred in the history of the Jewish people. From the hell of the spirit's betrayal of the spirit, Israel emerged into the fulfilling promise of its return to the land of its fathers. What are the consequences of this new situation of the Jewish people for Jewish existence in the light of the new self-understanding? This is the challenge of all challenges by which all Israel is being tested in this hour. On our response to the betrayal of the spirit that today threatens to engulf all mankind depends not only our own destiny; but it will have its influence on the future of all men.

Different Paths, Common Thrust: The "Shoalogy" of Berkovits and Frankl

Rabbi Reuven P. Bulka

The direction of Jewish thought has taken a dramatic shift in the past two decades with the most significant impact of this shift being felt in the past few years.

In general, perhaps overgeneral terms, the focus has shifted from "the promise of the future" to "the persecution of the past." The promise of the future was intertwined with the birth and growth of the State of Israel, a development which engendered great excitement and augered well for the future of Jews and Judaism. Excitement about Israel understandably abated with time. Internal and external issues betrayed the stunning reality that Israel's existence created many new problems even as it solved more crucial ones.

Matters linked to the Jewish identity controversy, the relation of Israel to the Diaspora, and lately, the debate over the right of Jews outside Israel to publicly criticize Israel's policies, have almost, obscured the fact of Israel as a haven from oppression. In our minds, Israel's existence is so secure we may even contemplate public disagreements concerning Israel's government. It says something of the collective Jewish psyche that it could adjust to this new phenomenon so quickly, perhaps too quickly.

At the same time those expressions concerning Israel became characterized by diminished excitement and increasing critique, a new focus of concern appeared on the scene, the Holocaust. The term "Holocaust" to describe the Nazi mass murder and attempted genocide of the Jews only came into vogue in the early 1960s.

At that time, a man who was destined to become intimately involved, even a catalyst, for the proliferating study of the Holocaust, offered to give a course on that topic but was turned down by the dean of his faculty.[1] This reflected quite accurately the position occupied by the Holocaust in the minds of the Jewish public at that time.

Since then, most notably in the past few years, this has changed dramatically. One can safely say that if a university were contemplating offering just one course of a Jewish nature, the odds are quite high that it would offer a course about the Holocaust.

Holocaust-related courses are offered in nearly one hundred American and Canadian universities, with the number reaching into the several hundreds if one includes the American institutions of higher learning with Holocaust-related courses in their catalogues.

I

To what can this most radical change be attributed? Probably not to any single factor, but to a host of factors and conditions which have converged to thrust the Holocaust into the forefront of Jewish thinking. The Eichmann trial was a definite consciousness-raiser. The pre–Six-Day War crisis of 1967 threatened the existence of Israel, resurrecting memories of a similar attempt to extinguish Jewish existence. The Yom Kippur War in 1973 drove home this very possibility with an even greater impact because Israel, between 1967 and 1973, was becoming increasingly isolated in the world community, a process which has accelerated ever since. Oil and soil, the issues of energy and territory, are dominant factors in Israel's pariahlike position in the community of nations. While it is obvious, it nevertheless bears mentioning that reporting reality does not imply agreeing with its presumptions. The rejection of Israel and the reasons behind it are at the very least lamentable, and all too often, despicable.

The plight of Soviet Jewry, which only became a major issue for the American Jewish community in the late 1960s, also evoked fears of a cultural genocide, a suffocating of Jews by erasing Judaism. "Never again," the slogan which captured the public mind on this issue, was a direct reference to the Holocaust and the resolve that such a disaster would never again befall the Jewish people.

As the global reality brought the repressed memory of the Holocaust to the fore, the private realities of families who suffered from Nazi inhumanity were being affected. It was slowly becoming evident that a post-Holocaust trauma existed which had repercussions on the survivors and their offspring. This, combined with the escalating desire of many children to know more of what their parents had gone through, forced the incredible horrors of the victims and survivor-victims to slowly become public conversation. Clinically, the assumption that repression is unhealthy and may affect relationships led many who had remained silent about their torture to be more open. Meta-clinically, in a parallelism, repression denied a basic, though distasteful component of Jewish history to a generation reared in abundance, relatively free from *existence anxiety*. What is repressed comes out clinically in speech; meta-clinically it comes out in speech, poetry, articles, books, films, and the like. Thus, the literal glut of the past decade has served as a catharsis even as it has radically altered the focus of our collective attention.

Today there is hardly a respected journal of Jewish thought which does not include numerous articles on the Holocaust. Also, the psychological journals devote increasing attention to the effects of the Holocaust,[2] with third-generation implications the latest development on the scene.

Other factors, such as the new ethnicity, the focus on one's past, in the mode of *Roots,* have encouraged the Jewish search for its immediate past, leading to the mass-media showing of *Holocaust* in 1978, an event which Neusner has called the "Jewish *Roots.*"

II

Whatever the reasons, it is evident that the Holocaust is "here to stay." That it should occupy our attention is a different matter. The controversy which is rapidly developing on the role of the Holocaust in Jewish life centers on two vital areas, politics and theology. In politics the major concern is what the place of the Holocaust should be in American foreign policy, most specifically with regard to Israel.[3]

This presentation is concerned with the other vital area on which the Holocaust has an impact, the area of theology. The position of the Holocaust in Jewish thought has become such an overwhelming issue that it has become a self-contained branch of its own, what I choose to call "Shoalogy" (*Shoah* is the Hebrew term for "Holocaust"). However one responds to the theological challenge of the Holocaust, one *must* address the issue, whether it be in the form of a new theology or in the reaffirmation of the old theology. It rightly heads the list of theological issues which must be confronted as Judaism endeavors to forge its destiny in the next critical decade.

Theological reactions to the Holocaust have ranged the full gamut of intellectual diversity. On the one extreme, Richard Rubenstein in *After Auschwitz,* declares that it is *now* impossible to believe in divine providence. Schlesinger effectively points out an essential flaw in Rubenstein's argument.[4] The Holocaust was not the first instance of Jewish suffering; it followed centuries of inquisitions, pogroms, crusades. If the suffering up to the Holocaust did not render belief in divine providence impossible, what is there about the Holocaust that changes this? Quantity or quality of suffering is not the issue; suffering itself is the issue. And that issue has plagued Jewish thinking from the beginning of exile.

On the other side of the spectrum, Emil Fackenheim stands out as the leading thinker among those who would make of the Holocaust the central motif of Jewish affirmation. Fackenheim's reaction is an all-embracing Shoalogy which beckons all Jews to listen to the commanding voice from Auschwitz, a voice which implores them to persist as Jews lest they grant Hitler a posthumous victory. Fackenheim espouses a 614th commandment which in effect is the first commandment of a new theology.

While Fackeheim's impassioned directive has undoubtedly found a receptive ear among many whose reaction to the Holocaust expressed itself in some form of eternal spiritual resistance—"you want to get rid of the Jews, we'll show you; just to spite you we will live on!"—the school of Shoalogy he represents, which sees the Holocaust as the dominant theme in Jewish thought, has been questioned, even challenged by those who fear that such a focus distorts Judaism, dooms Judaism to continually approach life mired in melancholy, and deflects from the positive affirmations and futuristic Torah-imbued meanings which speak to Jews in a spirit of optimism.[5]

Amidst these two extremes, between the Holocaust signifying the end of the Jewish mission under divine guidance and the Holocaust as the impetus for a spiritual rebirth as resistance, one encounters various differing Shoalogies. The writings of Eliezer Berkovits and Viktor Frankl place them in this category. Both approach the Holocaust from different vantage points. Berkovits is a Jewish philosopher and Frankl is a philosopher (aside from being a psychiatrist) who is Jewish. Berkovits writes of the Holocaust as an insider to Jewish destiny but as an outsider to the actual camp experience; Frankl writes as a survivor of four concentration camps but outside the framework of Jewish destiny. Their approaches reflect the differing parameters within which they operate, but at the same time their thrusts project an intriguing similarity. What follows is an examination of these two Shoalogies.

III

Eliezer Berkovits has written three books which relate to the theological riddle posed by the reality of suffering. The first, *God, Man and History: A Jewish Interpretation,* was written in 1959. It is a profound statement of Jewish philosophy, exacting and comprehensive, fusing the rational and the mystical, and offering a broad overview of the Jewish role in unfolding of universal destiny.[6] In this book Berkovits seriously examines the question of suffering, but at no time makes direct reference to the Holocaust. This is the same man who was destined to write two major books concerning the Holocaust. The reason for this omission is quite simple. In 1959, the Holocaust had not yet been catapulted beyond the framework of Jewish suffering throughout the ages into a unique, unprecedented brutality which demanded special examination.

His second book, *Faith After the Holocaust,* was published in 1973. The book was completed by 1972, though there is evidence within the text that its genesis was as early as the spring of 1967, before the Six-Day War.[7] Historically, one would be obliged to grant Berkovits some anticipatory sense that the Holocaust would become an issue, since the watershed, if one can pinpoint any, would have to be the June 1967 war. Even before that, to be sure, some articles on the destruction of European Jewry had appeared, but they were a trifle by any standard of measurement.[8] *Faith After the Holocaust* is the volume which contains Berkovits's Shoalogy, though the theology of suffering which is suggested in his earlier volume flows naturally into his wrestling with the Shoah.

The final work in the Berkovits trilogy, *With God in Hell: Judaism in the Ghettos and Deathcamps,* was completed in 1978 and published in 1979. In this work Berkovits painstakingly illustrates that the feeling of Judaism having died in the death camps is mistaken. Instead, the camps may be viewed as a spiritual Masada (before the final act) which reaffirmed Judaism in the worst hell and is thus instructive for a committed Judaism of today and tomorrow.

The three volumes follow an interesting progression, from focus on the past, the master plan, to concentration on a contemporay tragedy, to attention on the future in the light of this tragedy. This is Berkovits's framework, yet the essence of Berkovits's thinking in the sphere of Shoalogy cannot be divorced from the question of suffering itself. Thus, "the experience of God's 'absence' is not new: each generation had its Auschwitz problem."[9]

The reality of suffering for Berkovits, is a consequence of human freewill. In Berkovits's words:

But if man alone is the creator of values, one who strives for the realization of ideals, then he must have freedom of choice and freedom of decision. And his freedom must be respected by God himslef. God cannot as a rule intervene whenever man's use of freedom displeases him. It is true, if he did so the perpetration of evil would be rendered impossible, but so would the possibility for good also disappear. . . . If God did not respect man's freedom to choose his course in personal responsibility, not only would the moral good and evil be abolished from the earth, but man himself would go with them. For freedom and responsibility are of the very essence of man. Without them man is not human. If there is to be man, he must be allowed to make his choices in freedom. If he has such freedom, he will use it. Using it, he will often use it wrongly; he will decide for the wrong alternative. As he does so, there will be suffering for the innocent.[10]

God had to create the possibility of evil if there was to be the potentiality for its opposite, for goodness, for harmony, for love. Paradoxically, that which is good is so because of the possibility of evil; that which is evil is so because of the possibility for good.

The long-suffering of God, according to Berkovits, is directed to the wicked as well as to the righteous. For "man is to be, God must be long-suffering with him; he must suffer man. This is the inescapable paradox of divine providence."[11] The germ of this notion is already in evidence in Berkovits's earlier work where he asserts that in order to protect the individual's spiritual independence it is necessary for God to "hide."[12]

The world itself, were it perfect, would be indistinguishable from the Creator and would extinguish itself by tumbling back into God. God, as Creator of a dialogical world, was obliged to make it imperfect, to create darkness and evil.[13]

To the question of Jewish suffering Berkovits at times waxes universal. He writes:

However prominent and incomparable an example of underserved suffering the Galuth may be, it is not the only case of its kind. He who asks why God permits "the people of God" to be persecuted might as well ask why God allows any injustice to be inflicted on any of His children or creatures.[14]

This is the "earlier Berkovits" speaking. The "later Berkovits" does not renounce this seemingly out-of-place spate of universalism.

> Once the problem of evil is understood in its valid dimensions, the specific case of the Holocaust is not seen to be essentially different from the old problem of theodicy. . . . Understood in its vastest intellectual dimension and its radical ethical relevance, the question is not why the Holocaust, but why a world in which any amount of underserved suffering is extant.[15]

On a personal level, there is a positive value in suffering which, rightly endured, purifies and deepens the personality. It causes an orientation toward introspection, forgoing momentary pleasures in favor of the more enduring values of human existence, even the ultimate meaning in a realm beyond time and space.[16]

IV

With all this, questions remain. Firstly, even if God has granted, perforce, individual freedom, there must be a point where intervention becomes an imperative. God cannot allow villains to go unchecked in their pursuit of destruction. Granted that God must hide to protect human independence,[17] yet, as Berkovits posits, God must also be present. There must be a breaking point at which God enters the scene to prevent utter chaos and destruction. What is the point at which absence becomes a hopeless inaccessibility? And, most importantly, what can one say specifically of the Holocaust in this context?

To the first question, Berkovits states categorically that it is not for mortals to say when a situation has arisen that has to be salvaged by a miracle.[18] Yet all the theories of suffering, the necessity of God's hiding, cannot explain God's silence during the Holocaust, never mind justify it.[19] This is beyond our ken. The crucial question, for

Berkovits, is whether Judaism's faith in the God of history can still be maintained after the Holocaust.

In approaching this question, Berkovits rejects the argument from quantity. If one questions the Absolute God, it should not be on the basis of six million; rather, it should be on the assumption that with God the suffering of one ought to be as scandalous as the suffering of millions. While it is more human to question God's allowing the suffering of many, it is not more humane; it is more ethical to ground the query on the inability to fathom the agony of a single soul.[20]

For Berkovits, the Final Solution was an attempt to dethrone God. The presence of a God of history was the antithesis of the Nazi renunciation of universal human values. By eliminating God through destroying His people, the Nazis would have achieved the Final Solution.[21]

As far as Rubenstein is concerned, the Nazis succeeded, not so much by what they achieved, but by the way Rubenstein chooses to interpret their mass murder. For Berkovits, it is clear that the Germans failed.

> No, the Holocaust is not all of Jewish history, nor is it its final chapter. That it did not become the Final Solution as was planned by the powers of darkness enables the Jew who has known of the divine presence to discern intimations of familiar divine concern in the very midst of his abandonment.[22]

Berkovits, convinced as he is of Israel's place in God's master plan, cannot see how the Holocaust interferes with this cosmological design. Either God's encounters with Israel did or did not happen. If they did, Auschwitz does not transmute these encounters into fiction. If they did not occur, then they are delusions independent of Auschwitz.[23]

Ultimately, the difference between Rubenstein and Berkovits boils down to the matter of faith. A shaky faith can be easily knocked off its tenuous moorings by the Holocaust. A steadfast faith, à la Berkovits, remains stubbornly unshakable. Israel, reborn territorially after the Holocaust, remains poised to be the catalyst for the ultimate goal, "to establish the world in mankind as the Kingdom of God."[24]

The Holocaust proved not merely what man was capable of doing to the Jew. It proved what man is capable of doing to his fellow. The Holocaust demonstrated the moral feasibility of what the bomb has made into a realistic possibility, the premature end of the world and devastation of humanity.[25] Power, that ultimate weapon of history, has been rendered impotent by the megapower which can, with a finger's push, destroy the world. The State of Israel injects itself as the small but mighty ideological affirmation which can lead humankind back to its senses, and on the road to its ultimate destiny.[26]

For Berkovits, the cosmos begins to fall into shape. Though for the hatemongers the near-success of the Nazis may inspire further attempts to complete the job, in reality the Nazi failure is the ultimate lesson that Israel cannot be destroyed. However perilously close they came, they missed, as did those before them, though at a colossal cost. Israel moves on undeniably as the moral leader in the unfolding of God's master plan.

Thus, ultimately, the parochial and the universal merge, for Berkovits, in the eventual explication of the messianic ideal.

V

The approach of Viktor Frankl to the Holocaust cannot truly be termed a Shoalogy. The question of suffering, the question of the ultimate inhumanity, is approached by Frankl within the broader context of "meaning." Not, to be sure, the meaning of Israel; rather, the meaning of suffering against the backgrouund of the meaning of life and the ultimate cosmological meaning.

The Viktor Frankl who survived four concentration camps is the same Viktor Frankl who had the opportunity to escape Nazi tyranny for a position awaiting him in the United States. But, just before he was to leave, he came home one day and saw on the table a remnant from a Viennese synagogue that had been destroyed by the Nazis. As fate would have it, it was a broken-off stone of the Fifth Commandment which had adorned the synagogue, and which his father, who was killed by the Nazis along with most of Frankl's family, had brought home. For Frankl, there was a meaning to this; the meaning, as he saw it, was that he should remain with his parents, which he did.

Frankl came to the camp with his most treasured possession, the manuscript of what was to be his first book. But everything had to be surrendered when entering the camp. He was given the clothing of a dead prisoner and found in it a scrap of paper from a prayer book (siddur). That scrap contained the Shema, the affirmation of faith in God with all one's soul, which Frankl interpreted as the command to say yes to life in spite of suffering, even dying.[27]

As No. 119,104 Frankl was called upon to actualize the philosophy he had developed before he was incarcerated and which was to be confirmed, even reinforced, in the camp setting. That philosophy asserts that there is an unconditional meaningfulness to the world, in spite of suffering and death, a meaning which is there to be detected in any and all circumstances. The psychological side of this philosophical principle is expressed, simply but succinctly, in the assertion the "the striving to find a meaning in one's life is the primary motivational force in man."[28] Here, since the major issue is theological, attention will be given primarily to Frankl's philosophical-theological views.

Frankl, as one can sense, is a man of faith, imbued with an unconditional faith in God. The faith which he affirms in an ultimate meaning "is preceded by trust in an ultimate being, by trust in God."[29] Frankl, in answering a crucial theological problem concerning the dialectics of faith, proposes the following:

> I would say that God is not dead but silent. Silent, however, he has been all along. The "living" God has been a "hidden" God all along.

You must not expect him to answer your call. If you probe the depth
of the sea, you send off sound waves and wait for the echo from the
bottom of the sea. If God exists, however, he is infinite, and you wait
for an echo in vain. The fact that no answer comes back to you is
proof that your call has reached the addressee, the Infinite.[30]

There is a familiar ring to Frankl's view; it recalls Berkovits's
argument that God must absent himself, must be hidden. Yet Frankl
is more categorical in his assertion. According to Frankl, we do not,
we cannot have the answers to the meaning of the world. They are
beyond, they are in a different dimension. He states: "We can therefore at best grasp the meaning of the universe in the form of a super-
meaning, using the word to convey the idea that the meaning of the
whole is no longer comprehensible and goes beyond the comprehensible."[31]

There is more than a hint, in Frankl's writings, of an ultimate
cosmological meaning, a macro-meaning, onto which all the
micro-meanings of this world need to be latched for the micro-
meanings themselves to have ultimate significance.

Insofar as the subject of suffering is concerned, Frankl the thinker claims that it is impossible to explain the necessity of Godly intervention in terms of punishment, for no one can really know why
God has punished or why God was gracious in sparing punishment,
for God's reasons cannot be apprehended by mortals.[32] One recalls
Berkovits's comments about the inability of humans to judge when
it is necessary for God to inject onto the human scene.

The ultimate meaning of human suffering resides in the same
superworld as does the ultimate cosmological meaning: "Is it not
conceivable that there is still another dimension possible, a world
beyond man's world; a world in which the question of an ultimate
meaning of human suffering would find an answer?"[33] For Frankl,
the riddle of suffering and the riddle of life are one and the same.

On a more personal level, Frankl sees suffering as a guard
against psychic rigor mortis. The person who suffers remains psychi-
cally alive, mature, even grows because of the suffering.[34] Again

Berkovits's view of suffering as leading to a transcending of the material toward the more enduring values of human existence rings a familiar bell.

Life contains meaning even unto the very last breath. The act of dying is an act of living, not to be denied the human being.[35] This general statement of Frankl's is translated by Berkovits into a profound understanding of *kiddush ha-shem* as "not achieved in death, but in living out the meaning of one's life at its most intense level as a Jew facing death."[36] What for Berkovits is *kiddush ha-shem* (the sanctification of God) is for Frankl *kiddush ha-hayyim* (the sanctification of life). Again, the difference is contextual.

VI

What about Frankl's response to the Holocaust? His courageous personal response is already well-chronicled in his emotion-laden book, *Man's Search for Meaning.* Already there, and later in other places, Frankl throws in a paragraph or two on the implications of the Holocaust which, when added together, form an interesting picture.

In an earlier article, Frankl's response to the Holocaust was explored in the background of the optimistic streak and the abundant use of paradox that permeate Frankl's thinking.[37] Presently, Frankl's response is examined in the light of his views concerning the meaning of suffering, among other meanings. For Frankl, because the human being can be diabolically evil, the human being can also be virtuous. If one could do no evil, one's good deeds would be devoid of virtue. The price we pay for having freewill is that it comes with the potentiality for evil.

Again, the parallel with Berkovits is striking. One could almost interchange Frankl's view and Berkovits's insistence that if God did not respect the freedom to choose, moral good would disappear. With that freedom to choose, moral good would disappear. With that freedom goes the risk that it will be used wrongly, causing unnecessary suffering.[38] Frankl goes on to make a statement that only a survivor has the right to make:

> But I prefer to live in a world in which man has the right to make choices, albeit wrong choices, rather than a world in which no choice at all is left to him. In other words, I prefer a world in which, on the one hand, a phenomenon such as Adolph Hitler may occur, and, on the other hand, phenomenon such as the many saints who have lived."[39]

The rest is commentary.

Frankl's response echoes the response of Berkovits to the question, Can the Jew still believe in the God of history after the Holocaust? For Berkovits, that faith is unshakable and true, Auschwitz notwithstanding. For Frankl, either one believes in God unconditionally or one does not believe at all. If belief is unconditional, it will be able to withstand the fact that six million died in the Holocaust.[40] If it is not unconditional, it will collapse even at the death of one innocent child.[41]

Frankl, like Berkovits, rejects the quantity argument. It is absurd to bargain with God, to argue that six thousand or one million deaths are tolerable, but from one million and up, there is no more room for belief and it must be renounced.[42]

Before exploring the implications of the parallels in the works of Berkovits and Frankl, it should be noted that the similarities go beyond the particular area of the Holocaust. The broad cosmology, the emphasis on freedom, responsibility, and meaning, the use of paradox in developing ideas are just some points of similarity in the thoughts of Berkovits and Frankl. Besides the many meeting points, there are also differences, striking differences. However, exhausting the two systems in a comparative analysis must be left for some future occasion.

VII

For the record, in assessing the similarities and variances in the thought systems of Berkovits and Frankl relative to the Holocaust, it should be noted that Berkovits is quite familiar with Frankl and has read some of his works. However, there are no references at all to Frankl in the first two volumes of the Berkovits trilogy on suffering. The third book is a different story. There Berkovits makes repeated reference to Frankl and often quotes or paraphrases him at great length.

On the other hand, Frankl, himself, is not familiar with Berkovits' works. On one occasion I mentioned to Frankl that a noteworthy Jewish philosopher shows a great affinity with his thinking (referring, of course, to Berkovits). The response of Frankl, who at all times projects an intellectual curiosity, revealed a lack of familiarity with Berkovits. However, this apparent disparity does not slight Berkovits, for he and Frankl travel in different circles. Berkovits is a Jewish philosopher who travels primarily in Jewish circles; Frankl is a psychiatrist and the father of a school of psychotherapy known as logotherapy, whose locus of movement is more global and certainly not particularly Jewish. Berkovits's main preoccupation is with the unfolding of Jewish destiny; Frankl's is with injecting meaningfulness into life and lives. The two approaches may be destined to fuse, but at present they are different paths with a common thrust.

Frankl's classic work describing his camp experiences and his response, first appeared in English translation in 1959 under the title *From Death Camp to Existentialism*. Since then, the book's title has been changed to *Man's Search for Meaning*. Historically, his response came before the great surge of interest in the Holocaust. Yet, even though few people conversant with Holocaust literature have not read Frankl's classic or at least been exposed to it, his views have been almost totally ignored in anthologies or original works on the Holocaust. This ignoring of Frankl has been lamented in some relatively recent literature.[43] Judging by the present direction of Holocaust concern, the phenomenon is not without explanation.

The Holocaust has become intertwined with Jewish ethnicity, merged into what Neusner has described as the civil religion of Jews. The Holocaust belongs to the Jews; it is a uniquely Jewish tragedy. But Frankl's response, however consistent it may be with Jewish thought, is not perceived as a Jewish response; it is perceived as a "human" response.

Berkovits, himself, is instructive in this regard. In *With God in Hell*, where he repeatedly calls on Frankl for insightful comments on camp reality, one gets the feeling that Frankl is being used as the straight man to set up the Jewish contrast. This is not to say that Berkovits is unaware of Frankl's Jewishness; quite the contrary. However, Berkovits's moving volume gives the reader to believe that Berkovits has excluded Frankl from the honor roll of Jewish responses to Nazi brutality. Thus, for example, Berkovits contrasts Frankl's apparent difficulty in trying to strike out his former self (more precisely, to make a clean break with his whole former life), as he thought he had done upon entry, with Elie Cohen, who could accept his function as a "lavatory inspector."

For Berkovits, the distinction is clear. "Nothing that the Germans did to the authentic Jew hurt his self-respect."[44] Degrading behavior by the Nazis only convinced these Jews of the Nazis' spiritual pollution and reinforced their own sense of personal value. The assimilationist Jews were another story. Their self-respect was rooted in their having been recognized by the outside world, by the German or Austrian social structure. Suddenly, the carpet was thrust out from under them. The world in which they would have liked to feel at home betrayed its moral and spiritual disintegration. Berkovits writes:

> Frankl, the distinguished product of Western culture, was upset when the guard, instead of taking him seriously enough to punish him, just threw a stone at him to remind him of his status of a "domestic animal." Yizhak Katzenelson would not have paid any attention to an incident of this kind. In his eyes the ghetto and concentration camp guards were creatures with which you had so little in common that they could never insult you.[45]

This keen insight of Berkovits's may have some validity, but in the case of Frankl it seems at least slightly exaggerated. This is the same Frankl who remained with his parents because he found a remnant of the Fifth Commandment on the table; the same Frankl who was so deeply affected by the Shema he found in his prison uniform. To be sure, he was not then, nor is he now, what one could label *frum* (observant), but he did not compromise Jewish identity either before or during his stay in the camp. Frankl had not been schooled in talmudic tradition, but that he possesses a Jewish heart is beyond question. His lack of awareness of particular modes of Jewish expression explains why he did not march those exhausting treks studying Talmud,[46] but what he knew and mastered of Jewish tradition he did not stifle. Is it an assimilationist Jew who, a few days after liberation, walking in the country, in flowering meadows, with the larks in joyous song, falls to his knees and exclaims, " I called to the Lord from my narrow prison and He answered me in the freedom of space?"[47]

It is true that Frankl, in order to transcend the trivialities which camp conditions forced everyone to orient around, would imagine himself in a lecture hall addressing an attentive audience on the psychology of the concentration camp. In this way Frankl was periodically able to rise above camp conditions, to see them as belonging to the past. The authentic Jew, as Berkovits describes, did not escape. "They imposed another rhythm on that raw reality to which they were subjected and thus drew out its dehumanizing poison. They lived their lives as Jews."[48]

Is it wrong to suggest that Berkovits is hereby insinuating that Frankl did not live his camp life as a Jew? How can Frankl's heroic efforts to help fellow prisoners, his constant affirmation of faith in God, be ignored? These are vital Jewish categories, faith in God and sensitivity to fellow beings. Why can this not be incorporated among the Jewish responses? Berkovits has great respect for Frankl, but the respect is for Frankl the person, not Frankl the Jew.

Berkovits' attitude toward Frankl places into sharper focus the position of Frankl in the Shoalogy scheme. While others ignore Frankl, Berkovits is forthright enough to state exactly where he thinks Frankl fits in the broad spectrum of responses to the Holocaust.

Having questioned Berkovits's accuracy in this, I note, however, that were Frankl to rewrite his post-Holocaust affirmation today, the climate of ethnicity would not affect him, and if it did, it would only be in the direction of placing greater emphasis on the universal. For Frankl, the challenges of the Holocaust are global. The Jews were the targets, but all humankind are the victims, a view which Berkovits would be quite comfortable with. Frankl has forgiven, he has returned to Austria. He is at home there, but also ever conscious of who he is.

VIII

Even taking into account Berkovits's attempts to philosophically dissociate from Frankl, the common thrusts of both are too powerful to ignore. Both argue against holocaustopia, against a short-sighted vision of the future because of the Holocaust. For Berkovits, the God of history still lives; for Frankl, after Auschwitz God is not dead, and life's meaning is yet available. For both, evil is the price we pay for having freedom to choose. But even in the camps, some chose sainthood, transcending their predicament in heroic efforts on behalf of their faith or their brethren. Ample testimony for this is found in the works of Berkovits and Frankl.

The camps were a human (subhuman, to be more exact) creation. But saints such as the father who refrained from redeeming his son from certain death because he knew that by so doing some other innocent child would be gassed are the most powerful resisters, eternal models who say no to bestiality, yes to life.[49] As Frankl aptly puts it, man is that being who invented the gas chambers upright, with the Shema Yisrael on his lips.[50]

Realistically, even though the potential humanity of man remains a possibility, "we must not close our eyes to the fact that *humane* humans are, and probably will always remain, a minority. But it is precisely for this reason that each of us is challenged to *join* the minority."[51] Messianic hope rejects the view that humane

humans will remain a minority. It has faith that the process of joining the minority will eventually create a majority.

For Berkovits, the Holocaust should not sidetrack Jews from
their mission. The Holocaust should be evidence for the inexora-
bility of Jewish destiny, for establishing "the world in mankind as
the *Kingdom of God.*"[52]

For Frankl, the unconditional meaningfulness of life has not
been compromised by the Holocaust. The Holocaust has reempha-
sized the need for a world permeated with meaning. The world of
meaning, the *kingdom of ultimate meaning,* is, in Frankl's world-view,
inextricably linked to the source of ultimate meaning, God.

In sum, Berkovits and Frankl operate within differing frame-
works, but their ultimate visions are of global messianic proportions. The twain may yet meet.

This article originally appeared in *Tradition* 19, no. 4 (Winter 1981): 322–338.

NOTES

1. Paula E. Hyman, "New Debate on the Holocaust," *New York Times Magazine,*
Sept. 14, 1980, pp. 65, 67, 78, 80, 82, 86, and 109. The author reports this episode
involving Irving Greenberg, who is presently deeply involved in Holocaust-related
activities, including Zachor: The Holocaust Resource Center, which he founded
together with Elie Wiesel and which publishes *Shoah* magazine, the President's
Commission on the Holocaust, and numerous articles on this important topic
which he has authored.

2. The *Journal of Contemporary Psychotherapy* 11, no. 1 (Spring–Summer 1980), is
devoted entirely to psychological and social sequelae of the Holocaust. The *Journal
of Psychology and Judaism* 6, no. 1 (Fall–Winter 1981), devotes the entire issue to a
study of the Holocaust. These are just two notable examples of a pervasive phenomenon in psychological literature.

3. For a good overview of this topic, see Robert Alter's "Deformations of the
Holocaust," *Commentary* 71, no. 2 (February, 1981): 48–54.

4. George Natan Schlesinger, "Arguments from Despair," *Tradition* 17, no. 4
(Spring 1979): 15–26.

5. The articles by Hyman and Alter referred to in nos. 1 and 3 are good reviews of the debate. Additionally, *Moment* 6, nos. 3–4 (March–April 1981), carries a short symposium on this issue. Immanuel Jakobovits, in "A Memorial That Rebuilds: A Foundation That Lives," *Jewish Life* 3, no. 3 (Fall 1979): 18–31, argues that we should shift from preoccupation with the Holocaust, which has passed, to alarm over the present erosion of Jewish life, which threatens our future. A remarkably similar position to that advocated by Jakobovits is exposed by Jacob Neusner in "Beyond Catastrophe, Before Redemption," *Jewish Digest* 26, no. 8 (April 1981): 47–52, adapted from an article in the *Reconstructionist* 46, no. 2. Walter S. Wurzburger, in "Theological Issues Connected with Teaching the Holocaust," in *Teaching the Holocaust: An Exploration of the Problem,* Proceedings of a Colloquium, Stone-Sapirstein Center for Jewish Education (New York, 1976), pp. 24–32, argues for reasoned approach to the Holocaust which avoids extremes and orients toward the fulfillment of Jewish destiny, a theme which dominates the present thesis. Ismar Schorsch, in "The Holocaust and Jewish Survival," *Midstream* 27, no. 1 (January 1981): 38–42, suggests that Lurianic mysticism may be a useful frame for developing an optimistic model of Jewish thought in the post-Holocaust era. This is just a small sampling of diverse approaches within a common view that the Holocaust cannot be allowed to overtake Jewish thought and impose a negative, backward focus onto Judaism.

6. This book is continually confused with another book of a similar title, Dimont's *Jews, God, and History,* a popular and popularized scanning of Jewish history. If books can have identity crises or identity confusion, the volume of Berkovits makes for an excellent case study. A reissue of the book under a more differentiated title, such as "The Unfolding of Jewish Destiny," would be, at once, more appropriate and more likely to establish its distinctive quality.

7. In *Faith After the Holocaust* (New York: Ktav 1973), p. 144, Berkovits indicates that he decided to set down his thoughts on the problem of faith raised by the European Holocaust in the early spring of 1967.

8. The *Index to "Tradition"* for 1958–1969, published by the Rabbinical Council of America in 1970, and prepared by Micha Falk Oppenheim, shows no original articles on the Holocaust. The *Judaism: Twenty Years Cumulative Index, 1952–1971* (New York: American Jewish Congress, 1972) shows only three articles on the Holocaust before 1967. Study of the other journals would probably yield the same type of finding. All this has since changed drastically.

9. Berkovits, *Faith After the Holocaust,* p. 98.

10. Ibid., p. 105. A comparable position is already enunciated by Berkovits in his *God, Man and History: A Jewish Interpretation* (New York: Jonathan David, 1959), pp. 141–146.

11. Berkovits, *Faith After the Holocaust,* p. 106.

12. Berkovits, *God, Man and History,* p. 48. Here, Berkovits is concerned with

personal encounters, the individual's relationship with God. The overwhelming Presence would render true encounter impossible.

13. Ibid., pp. 76–77.

14. Ibid., p. 143.

15. Berkovits, *Faith After the Holocaust,* pp. 130–131.

16. Ibid., p. 121.

17. Schlesinger "Arguments from Despair," seemingly takes issue with this view. He points to Pharaoh and, in a later letter (*Tradition* 18, no. 3 [Fall 1981], p. 316), to Balaam as two instances of individuals who experienced the might and majesty of God, yet kept to their evil ways. Perhaps there is room for some compromise in that Berkovits is arguing not about a specific instance, but about a general, obvious cause-effect relationship which intervenes at all times to punish evil and reward the good. Such a dynamic would, in true Pavlovian fashion, program people for the reward. There might be the odd masochistic exception, but it would be the exception that proved the rule.

18. Berkovits, *God, Man and History,* p. 148.

19. Berkovits, *Faith After the Holocaust,* p. 128.

20. Ibid., pp. 129–130. See Schlesinger, "Arguments from Despair", where this point is similarly expanded.

21. Berkovits, *Faith After the Holocaust,* pp. 117–118. While one must admire Berkovits's almost poetic analysis, I sometimes find it hard to relate "profound diabolical thinking" to the Nazis. "Animals let loose from the cage" seems to be a more apt description of those monsters.

22. Berkovits, *Faith After the Holocaust,* p. 136.

23. Ibid., p. 135.

24. Berkovits, *God, Man and History,* p. 139.

25. Berkovits *Faith After the Holocaust,* p. 141.

26. Ibid., p. 143. Unfortunately, Berkovits's scenario has not yet unfolded. To this point in time, the desire of Israel's surrounding enemies to annihilate it, have put the country on constant alert; Israel's very existence is still at stake, and its power is a most vital component in the capacity to repel or discourage attack.

27. Duane Schultz, *Growth Psychology: Models of the Healthy Personality* (New York: Van Nostrand, 1977), p. 106, misconstrues Frankl on this. In reporting on Frankl's finding the Shema Yisrael, containing the imperative to "love thy God with all thy heart, and with all thy soul, and with all thy might," Schultz suggests that Frankl interpreted this *differently from the Orthodox religious meaning.* For him it became "the command to say yes to life despite whatever one has to face, be it suffering or even dying." But this is not different from the Orthodox religious meaning. In fact, it is remarkably reminiscent of Rabbi Akiva's derivation from this very verse that the obligation to affirm faith in God applies "even if He takes your soul" (Berakhot 661b).

This is not the only instance where Frankl posits a view which comes uncannily close to a talmudic proposition. For a more comprehensive study of this topic, see my *The Quest for Ultimate Meaning: Principles and Applications of Logotherapy* (New York: Philosophical Library, 1979).

28. Viktor E. Frankl, *Man's Search for Meaning: An Introduction to Logotherapy* (New York: Washington Square Press, 1963), p. 154.

29. Viktor E. Frankl, *The Will to Meaning: Foundations and Applications of Logotherapy* (New York: World Publishing, 1969), p. 145.

30. Frankl, *The Will to Meaning*, p. 154.

31. Viktor E. Frankl, *The Doctor and the Soul: From Psychotherapy to Logotherapy* (New York: Bantam Books, 1967) p. 25.

32. Frankl, quoted in Reuven P. Bulka, "Logotherapy and the Talmud on Suffering: Clinical and Meta-Clinical Persepectives," *Journal of Psychology and Judaism* 2, no. 1 (Fall 1977): 39.

33. Frankl, *Man's Search for Meaning*, p. 187.

34. Frankl, *The Doctor and the Soul*, p. 88.

35. Ibid., p. 37.

36. Eliezer Berkovits, *With God in Hell: Judaism in the Ghettos and Deathcamps* (New York: Sanhedrin Press, 1979), p. 109.

37. Reuven P. Bulka, "Logotherapy as a Response to the Holocaust," *Tradition* 15, nos. 1–2 (Spring–Summer 1975): 89–96.

38. Berkovits, *Faith After the Holocaust*, p. 105.

39. Viktor E. Frankl, "The Philosophical Foundations of Logotherapy," in *Phenomenology: Pure and Applied,* ed. Erwin W. Strauss (Pittsburgh: Duquesne University Press, 1961), p. 55.

40. Frankl here waxes unconsciously "Jewish." He refers to the six million even though, according to Simon Wiesenthal, there were eleven million victims. On the other hand, Yehuda Bauer, in "Whose Holocaust," *Midstream* 26, no. 9 (November 1980): 42–46, vehemently refutes Wiesenthal. The vast majority of Jews were killed in death installations, according to Bauer, not concentration camps. Outside of Jews and gypsies, the total number of people who died in the concentration camps was in the half-million range. Non-Jewish civilian casualties numbered between twenty and twenty-five million.

Statistics, however, as Bauer points out, miss the point. The point is that this was a *war against the Jews,* with the entire German machinery geared to the attempted genocide. There are six million witnesses in death to this. As such, Frankl and anyone else who refers to the "six million" is historically accurate.

41. Viktor E. Frankl, *The Unconscious God: Psychotherapy and Theology* (New York: Simon and Schuster, 1975) pp. 15–16.

42. Ibid., p. 16.

43. Reuven P. Bulka, "Logotherapy as a Response to the Holocaust." See also

Reuven P. Bulka, "Frankl's Impact on Jewish Life and Thought," *International Forum for Logotherapy* 3 (Spring 1980): 41–43.

44. Berkovits, *With God in Hell,* p. 58.

45. Ibid., p. 59. Aside from the comments in the text, it should also be clear that Frankl was psychologically analyzing the guard's behavior and found it a typical and deplorable attitude toward the prisoner. To suggest that Frankl's self-esteem depended on the guard's value system is far off the mark.

46. Ibid., pp. 64–65.

47. Frankl, *Man's Search for Meaning,* p. 142. The reference here is to the famous *Min ha-Mezar* (Psalms 118:5). It should be kept in mind that Frankl probably did not have a Book of Psalms with him at the time and was likely reciting the verse from memory. This beautiful application, worthy of a great homilist, reflects Frankl's familiarity with Psalms. To this day, he reads daily from the Psalms.

48. Berkovits, *With God in Hell,* p. 64.

49. Ibid., pp. 42–43.

50. Frankl, *Man's Search for Meaning,* pp. 213–214.

51. Frankl, *The Unconscious God,* p. 84.

52. Berkovits, *God, Man and History,* p. 139 (emphasis added).

Hashgaḥah Peratit

Rabbi Zevulun Charlop

I recently came upon a remarkable book called *Escape to Shanghai*.[1] It told the story of the escape of the Mirrer Yeshiva, one of the most prestigious yeshivot of Russia-Poland before World War II, from the deathly clutches of the Nazi Holocaust, almost in its entirety, together with scores of other *talmidei ḥakhamim* and religious luminaries. Much of the ferment for the revitalization of Jewish learning and tradition in the United States, Israel, and other parts of the world was due to this group. The saga of their escape is marked with so many absolutely unlikely and incredible happenings that one just has to acknowledge that miracles indeed still do happen. Moreover, that there is indubitably *hashgaḥah peratit,* that God watches over each and every one of us individually—that there is particular divine providence. An unlikely procession of events and places gives a keen imprimatur to the wondrous nature of their *yeẓiat mitzrayim,* their exodus.

1. The infamous Ribbentrop-Molotov pact between Hitler Germany and Stalin Russia stipulated, for some peculiar reason that still defies historical logic, that Lithuania was to maintain its independence after a fashion, and that Vilna, that premier city of Jewish life, was to be returned to an "autonomous" Lithuania. Because of this, for a year after the outbreak of World War II, Vilna became a haven of refuge for the leading yeshivot, and provided just enough breathing space for the ultimate escape.

2. It was at this time that Japan, suddenly, and for the first time, opened a consulate in Kovno, another Lithuanian center of Jewish activity, with full credentials to issue visas. The Japanese consul was Seji-Hara, who deserves an especially honored place in our historical record among the *ḥassidei umot ha-olam,* the righteous of the world. Why the Japanese chose that moment to open a consulate,

and precisely in Lithuania, remains a fortunate mystery to this day. Its whole duration was only nine months, but Hara, utilizing every means available to him, managed nonstop to stamp visas and unbelievably satisfy every single request for a transit permit to leave Europe, and to go wherever, through Japan.

3. After the Japanese consul left on the heels of the Soviet takeover of Lithuania at the end of 1940, the NKVD, the dreaded Russian secret police, incredibly opened two emigration offices, one in Vilna, and the other in Kovno. This was quite surprising, as Russia did not allow emigration. Nonetheless, they sold first-class train tickets to Vladivostock, on the Trans-Siberian Railroad, in heated coaches, amply stocked with food, for the ruble equivalent of twenty dollars.

4. The Japanese freighter that many of the Mirrer contingent boarded in Vladivostok on their journey to the land of the Rising Sun met up with the worst sea storm in the memory of its captain and crew. The captain lost control of the helm, and his S.O.S. signal went unanswered; but wondrously, the ship listed into port in Japan without the loss of a single life. Shortly thereafter it sank.

5. They landed in Kobe, Japan, and were startled to find a small, well-to-do Jewish community of twenty-five families, which had settled there only twenty or twenty-five years before, and yet was sufficiently able to house, clothe, and feed the hundreds of their guests. That they received any kind of hospitality at all in Japan was in itself remarkable, as the Japanese were under severe pressure from their Axis partners, the Germans, to adopt their infamous Jewish policy.

6. But probably the greatest miracle of all, certainly the most blatant, was manifest in Shanghai, their next stopping place after Japan, and which was to become their residence until the end of the war. When they reached that bustling and war-marked Chinese city, they had a right to wonder anxiously where in the world they would stay, and how they would survive.

Now our story has to backtrack about fifteen years. A Jew who had integrated himself entirely into Chinese society and had amassed a vast fortune was lying on his deathbed. One night he had an urgent and troubling dream about Jerusalem. He called in the rabbi of the city, who interpreted it to mean that Heaven was summoning this Jew to build a magnificent synagogue in the heart of Shanghai. In spite of the fact that there were practically no Jews living there at the time, and that they would be hard put to find a minyan for the Sabbath and holidays, the Jew accepted the rabbi's interpretation, to the consternation of many he allocated literally millions of dollars to build a huge sanctuary, as well as two large dining rooms and oversized kitchens fully equipped with every utensil, plate, and silverware, enough for hundreds of people. The most expensive and extravagant materials were used in the building of this synagogue compound, for it was enclosed by a large surrounding courtyard and lawn.

Believe it or not, for the fifteen years of its existence, until 1940, when these yeshiva *baḥurim* from Lithuania came to Shanghai, the dining rooms and the utensils had never been used. The synagogue itself was lucky when it could make a minyan. There was no logical reason for having a synagogue there, and certainly not such a grand one.

It was obvious that the shul had been waiting for fifteen years to fulfill the great, albeit brief destiny that was assigned to it. Can there be any doubt that the Chinese Jews' dream fifteen years before had one purpose only—which at the time could not even be glimpsed by the human mind—to serve as a temporary home in the Orient for this haggard and hounded and illustrious group. The presence of the synagogue enabled the continuation of the same intense measure of learning and devotion that had prevailed in Mir itself.

A similar and no less spectacular story unfolded half a world away, in the synagogue in Lourenço Marques, the chief city of Mozambique, East Africa, when it was a protectorate of Portugal. At the same time that the Mirrer Yeshiva found refuge in Shanghai, there was another band of Jews who just as miraculously found their way to Mozambique.

There were few if any Jews living then in Lourenço Marques.

Therefore, we can imagine the amazement of the refugees when they discovered a small but an absolutely gem of a shul—completely furnished with Ark and Torahs, table and benches. It seems that some years before, a lone Jewish business man had gotten it into his head that he had to build an entire synagogue for himself, with all its appurtenances, as if there were a Jewish community there, even though there was none. Again, an undeniable evidence of providence.

The famed Mirrer *mashgiah,* Rabbi Chazkel Levenstein, spiritual mentor of this group, whose every fiber pulsed with the zeal of faith, and who was vividly able to communicate his enthusiasm to his listeners, oftentimes would point to the Ramban's impassioned summation of the story of Passover to light up their own remarkable experience:

> Some . . . deny the principle of providence, "and make man as fish in the sea" (Habakkuk 1:14), believing that God does not watch over them . . . for they say, "The Eternal has forsaken the land" (Ezekiel 8:12). This is why Scripture says in connection with the wonders in Egypt . . . "That you, Pharaoh, may know that I am the Eternal in the midst of the earth" (Amos 8:18), which teaches us the principle of providence, that G-d has not abandoned the world to chance![2]

This crucial principle is illustrated by still another tale of Holocaust survival.

Rabbi Menachem Ziemba, one of the great rabbinic scholars of Poland before the war, became a chief spiritual force in the Warsaw ghetto. Jews of every stripe looked to him for religious guidance and also for balm to ease the awful wounds of body and annals of man's inhumanity to man. An authentic hero of the ghetto, he was a signal inspiration in the gallant uprising of the wretched few against the ruthless many, which has become memorialized in the consciousness of decent men everywhere, and in which he lost his life.

On the eve of the uprising, hours before the advent of Passover, word of a imminent Nazi assault, whose purpose was the final destruction of the ghetto, had reached its remnant population. The question was whether to mount resistance against the overwhelming might of the Wehrmacht or passively to be resigned to the inevitable.

In that critical juncture, Rabbi Ziemba, first of all, ordered every Jew to carry in his pocket the minimal amount of matzah required to fulfill the mitzvah of eating matzah on Passover, so that they could celebrate Israel's deliverance from bondage wherever they might happen to be, in makeshift bunkers or crouched on roofs as snipers, waiting for the impending German attack. This was the ultimate defiance! Then he exhorted them with a remarkable interpretation of a verse from Psalms that is at once an insight that lights up our understanding of Jewish survival and an unyielding credo by which to live: "For God knows the ways of the righteous, but the way of the wicked shall be lost" (Psalms 1:5). Rabbi Ziemba read the verse a little bit differently, but his reading, nonetheless, was fully legitimate within the constraints of Hebrew usage and excruciatingly appropriate for that dismal time and setting: " 'That God knows' is the way of the righteous, and that 'all is lost' is the way of the wicked." The righteous man, in every circumstance, even in the heart of incomprehensible depravity, proclaims, "God knows"; accounts are made, and there is a reckoning. To give up, even in the face of seemingly hopeless odds, is the way of the wicked.

Several months ago, a dear friend, Mr. Jacob Stransky, lay dying. He called me to his bedside, and with an incredible peace and presence of mind told me a story that vivified for me the idea of "God Knows!" Before the war, he had lived in a small town in Czechoslovakia. He was married and had five children. Every Friday morning, before coming to the synagogue for his daily prayers, he would go the river that bordered his town to catch some fish and bring them to his beloved rabbi for the Sabbath. From time to time he would take along his two oldest sons, and the rabbi would tell Mr. Stransky, "These boys are going to grow up to be great scholars in Israel."

However, Hitler m.h.b.r. came, and Mr. Stransky was the only survivor of his family. His wife and all his children were consumed in the relentless fire of the Holocaust. "I used to shout out," he told me, "Rabbi, what happened to your promises? Instead of scholars, I'm left only with the seared curse of children burnt to ashes!"

"After the war, I set out rebuilding a new home with a wonderful lady," and he pointed to Mrs. Stransky. "We came to America. Thank Heaven, she gave me three lovely daughters, may they live and be well, and lo and behold, raised in the Bronx, of all places, to the Holy One, blessed be He, in His amazing ways, found them three husbands from different parts of the world, and different vocations, who I can testify are no less committed to Torah and doing mitzvot than my pious townfolk in the old country. And now, *barukh Hashem,* I have grandchildren learning God's word in the finest yeshivot. So Rabbi, as I take leave of this world, it is with contentment and the grateful knowledge that somehow the rabbi's promise is being realized after all."

That God knows after all!

NOTES

1. Elchanan Yosef Hertsman, *Escape to Shanghai* (Moznaim Press, 1981).
2. Ramban's comment on Exodus 13:17.

A Halakhic Perspective on the Holocaust

RABBI DR. STANLEY BOYLAN

INTRODUCTION

The phenomenon of the Holocaust poses significant questions for
every morally sensitive human being and for committed Jews in
particular. As the events themselves grow more distant, their significance looms ever larger; time allows us the historical perspective to
begin to comprehend what transpired. While the Holocaust has
been analyzed historically and sociologically, we have not addressed
the Holocaust from a truly Jewish perspective, within a halakhic
framework. This article attempts to view the Holocaust, in classical
halakhic terms, as a confrontation with Amalek.

Maimonides, in both the *Sefer ha-Miẓvot* and the *Yad ha-Ḥazakah*,
contrasts the war against the Canaanites and the war against Amalek. The commandment of war against the Canaanites was fulfilled
and is no longer operative; the Canaanites have long since lost their
identity. The commandment of war against Amalek, however,
applies in every generation and awaits the Messiah for its comple-
tion.[1] Maimonides' ruling, while echoing the words of the Torah,
"A war of God against Amalek from generation to generation"
(Exodus 17:16) is troublesome. With the exception of the Jews, all
the ancient peoples of the Near East have disappeared as nations:
"Sennacherib has come and confused all the nationalities."[2]

Rabbi J.B. Soloveitchik, my revered rebbe, addresses this problem in a note in "Kol Dodi Dofek." Quoting his father's analysis of
the above problem, the Rav posits two aspects to *miẓvat Amalek,* the
command to destroy Amalek's descendants (Deuteronomy 25:19),
one that devolves on each individual, and the other, a communal
command to war against Amalek. While the command to eradicate

195

all of Amalek's offspring is literally limited to lineal descendants, the commandment to war against Amalek takes on a broader interpretation, encompassing any nation which sets out to destroy the Jewish people. Because any nation can thus become Amalek, the commandment is operative in each generation, until God's battle is won.[3]

Ẓafenat Pane'aḥ in his commentary to Exodus offers a slightly different approach. Amalek and Israel differ from all other nationalities. They are metaphysical entities wherein the entire nation is constituted from its individual components. Sennacherib, by dissolving the nation-states of the ancient Near East, eradicated all nationalities but Israel and Amalek. As long as one Jew or one Agagite survives, his respective nation lives.[4]

Our tradition tells us that those Amalekites who survive rank in the forefront of our enemies in each generation. Without identifying specific individuals as Amalekites, we may identify certain actions with those of Amalek and his cohorts.

Amalek, is then, the metaphysical antithesis of the Jewish people. Any nation which determines to eradicate the Jewish people as a whole has the halakhic status of Amalek. This re-creation of Amalek generations after Sennacherib has one clear historical example—the battle against Haman.[5] We turn now to a consideration of Megillat Esther and the Purim experience.

The holiday of Purim has a double aspect, an aspect reflected by the two lots (*purim*) of it name. Our childhood memories of Purim abound with merriment and joy. Yet behind the mask of the clown lurks a darker side, a specter of doom deferred, of destiny defied. If the wicked Haman is hung, the drunken tyrant still reigns, with golden scepter firmly in his hands. If Mordecai rides on high dressed in the royal robes, it is only after sleepless nights and days of fasting and screaming.

It is not only our modern sensibilities, shocked by the atrocities of the Holocaust, which are disturbed by the too-familiar decree of Haman "to destroy, to slay, and to cause to perish" (Esther 3:13). The sense of menace intrinsic to the Megillah itself is noted in both

Talmuds.[6] Indeed Maimonides and the Ra'abad stress the source of the Fast of Esther as intrinsic in the Megillah itself.[7] We can only reexperience deliverance if we reexperience the peril as well; the Fast of Esther and the subsequent reading of the Megillah defeat Haman's decree of old.

No Hallel is recited on Purim. Our praise is cloaked in the terms of the Megillah itself, sans the name of God. In the works of Rabbah, "We are still servants of Ahasuerus,"[8] our salvation is not complete enough for a full Hallel. The drunken king, still befuddled and unable to distinguish between Haman and Mordecai, has granted the Jews a reprieve. Still, his love for Esther knows its limits—"to half of the kingdom" (Esther 7:2).

To the religious Jew, then, the phenomenon of the Holocaust is not a new, anomalous occurrence, as has been argued by some historians, most recently by Lucy Davidowicz in *The War Against the Jews*. The phenomenon is subsumed under the class of Amalek, a presence confronting the Jewish people in the Torah, Nevi'im, and Ketuvim. The Holocaust is unique in the scale of destruction brought about by Amalek.

The rabid irrational anti-Semite is typified by Amalek, who first warred on the Jewish people in the desert and has continued his enmity against them throughout the ages. Haman the Agagite is the clearest archetype of Amalek presented in the Scripture.

The motivation of Haman for his genocidal plan has always seemed obscure. The Megillah's explanation, "But it seemed contemptible in his eyes to lay hands on Mordecai alone" (Esther 3:6), posits Haman's determination to eliminate an entire nation in terms of his hatred for one particular Jew. Hitler's description of his own conversion to anti-Semitism, as described in a famous passage of *Mein Kampf,* is hauntingly similar: "Once, as I was strolling through the Inner City, I suddenly encountered an apparition in a black caftan and black hair locks. Is this a Jew? was my first thought." After studying the man, Hitler next asked himself: "Is this a German?" Seeking an answer, he "bought the first anti-Semitic pamphlets of my life."[9]

Hitler, if he is to be believed, was drawn to anti-Semitism as a result of his instinctive reaction to the very presence of the Jews. Only afterwards does he learn of the Jews—"for they told him of the people of Mordecai" (Esther 3:6). From that moment on, Hitler and Haman determine that the Jewish presence must be totallly extirpated. Neither victory nor defeat can swerve Amalek from his need to be freed from the Jewish presence—best expressed in the infamous words of Haman, "all this is worthless in the presence of the Jews" (Esther 5:13). The demonic drive to purge oneself of the Jewish presence takes precedence over all other drives for power and happiness. Indeed, Hitler's "war against the Jews," according to Ms. Davidowicz's thesis, was the very constant of his being, with the drive for world power and dominion a mere end to satisfy this need.

In his commentary on Deuteronomy 25:17, the Malbim points out that the usual objectives of military action were specifically precluded by the Torah in the case of Amalek: no territory was in dispute, no future military threat was deterred or military might demonstrated, and religion was not the motive. Amalek's hatred for the Jew is total, not predicated upon external, rational reasoning. Unlike Pharaoh, whose purpose was to enslave and subdue, Amalek attacks the weak and unarmed, the women and children, the old and the lame.

While Hitler's espousal of a total racist hatred of the Jew is well-known, that of Haman's is not as readily apparent. His order to destroy every man, woman, and child of the Jewish nation bespeaks the Amalekite racist philosophy; however his words to Ahasuerus, "There is a certain people scattered around . . . and their laws are diverse from those of every people" (Esther 3:8), are phrased in the same form as anti-Semitic propaganda throughout the centuries— the Jews are a disloyal alien element in our midsts, whose laws and culture are totally inimical to the interests of the state.

This propaganda is meant only for Ahasuerus; Haman's hatred is inborn and instinctive. The racist nature of Haman's thinking is best reflected in the seemingly innocent remarks of Zeresh: "If

Mordecai, before whom thou hast begun to fall, be of the seed of the Jews, thou shalt not prevail against him" (Esther 6:13).

The reference to Jews as "the seed of the Jews," the only use of this phrase by a non-Jew in the entire Bible, is distinctly reminiscent of Hitler's racist terminology. The entire incident, however, reflects upon the mental image of the Jew in Haman's inner circle. Zeresh has not turned into a philo-Semite; her words echo the fear of the Jew which is part and parcel of racist anti-Semitic dogma.

Our sages have interpreted Zeresh's words as follows: "This nation is compared to the dust and compared to the stars: When they descend, they descend to the dust; when they rise, they rise to the stars."[10] In the distorted world of Amalek, an idea of this kind has deadly implications. To quote Dr. Lucy Davidowicz:

> German hysteria was rooted in fear. . . . What the Germans hated and feared most in themselves they projected onto the Jews, endowing the Jews with those terrible and terrifying attributes they tried to repress in themselves. . . .
>
> There were, fundamentally, two totally disparate and mutually contradictory images of the Jew that collided with each other in the paranoid propaganda of national Socialist anti-Semitism, both inherited from the recent and medieval treasury of anti-Semitism. One was the image of the Jew as vermin, to be rubbed out by the heel of the boot, to be exterminated. The other was the image of the Jew as the mythic omnipotent superadversary, against whom war on the greatest scale had to be conducted.[11]

A careful analysis of Ahasuerus' actions leads one to conclude that it is not Mordecai but Ahasuerus who has diminished Haman at this point. Nonetheless, Haman and his coterie interpret his setback only in terms of the Jew Mordecai, and not Ahasuerus himself. So, too, Hitler, in his last message to the German people, after having murdered six million Jews, but with defeat before his eyes, inveighed against his enemies the Jews. "For the last time our mortal enemies the Jewish Bolsheviks have launched their massive forces to the attack. Their aim is to reduce Germany to ruins and to exterminate our people."[12]

THE KING AND HIS RING

The actions of Ahasuerus in the Megillah narrative are contradictory and enigmatic. Our sages are in dispute as to his intelligence: do his seemingly irrational actions mask the craftiness of a master politician or a fool manipulated by those about him? His brutish nature and moral insensitivity, however, are beyond dispute. Concerned chiefly with satisfying primal needs, Ahasuerus' court becomes a nest of conspiracies and petty jealousies, of underlings pandering to the king's lusts and fears, and struggling for power.

In this atmosphere of a large empire beset by social tensions, Haman gains ascendancy over his fellow officers. According to our sages, Haman had previously played a role in the removal of Vashti, citing her act as a threat to the empire. In a time of unrest, Haman rises as the king's executioner, who will restore order and stability to the empire while the king attends to his partying and feasting.

Haman's approach to Ahasuerus, "there is a certain people," is a litany of charges against Jews. It is noteworhty, however, that this crucial diatribe fails to identify the peculiarly disloyal nation being accused—the word "Jew" is never mentioned! There are times when omissions are more significant than words. Again we quote from Ms. Davidowicz:

> The very idea of the destruction of the Jews as a political goal ended, when Hitler first began to advocate it, camouflage and concealment.
> . . .
>   How does one advocate publicly an idea or a program whose novelty lies in its utter radicalism? No matter how anti-Semitic the Munich of 1919 and 1920 was, the explicit transformation of a slogan like *'Juda verrecke'* into a practical political program would have brought on the censorship of the local authorities and discredited the

incipient National Socialist movement even among conventional anti-Semites. In this situation Hitler availed himself of a time-honored device—the use of esoteric language. ... Exoterically understood, the text is unexceptionable, but to the insiders who know how to interpret the words, the message is revolutionary and dangerous to the status quo.

   ... according to the earliest reports of Hitler's speeches, the code words he used for Jews outnumbered the plain references: usury (usurers), profiteering (profiteers), exploiters, big capitalism ... , international money power, Communists, ... aliens, foreigners.[13]

Haman uses similarly esoteric language in addressing Ahasuerus. The word "Jew" never appears in his denunciation. Moreover, the phrase describing the fate of these traitors, "let it be written that they be eliminated" (Esther 3:9) is rather ambiguous in comparison to the language of Haman's ultimate decree: "to destroy, to slay, and to cause to perish" (Esther 3:3). Nazi propaganda, too, spoke of the removal of the Jewish people by unspecified means. The details of the methodical murder of the Jews were carefully kept from the general public.

This is not to argue that Ahasuerus did not know that the Jews were the ultimate target of Haman's plot. The monstrosity of consigning an anonymous nation to doom cannot be ruled out in the case of the a moral eunuch like Ahasuerus; however, the king's lack of curiosity about an entire nation accused of disloyalty does strain one's credulity. Ahasuerus' terror of assassination, carried to the extreme of barring even the queen from his court, would hardly have allowed him to be indifferent to the identity of an entire nation of conspirators.

The Megillah itself makes this very point when it relates the response of Ahasuerus to Haman's proposal: "And the king took his ring from his hand and gave it unto Haman the son of Hammedatha the Agagite, the Jews' enemy" (Esther 3:10). Though the Jews have not been mentioned, the king knows Haman full well and therefore knows about his hatred of the Jews. Haman, whose maniacal preoccupation with the Jews has driven him to genocide, is hardly one to hide his true feelings. As he hands over the royal ring, the king could hardly fail to be aware of Haman's fanatical racism.

Similarly, after Haman's decree is promulgated, the Megillah tells of the public reaction: "and the king and Haman sat down to drink; but the city of Shushan was perplexed" (Esther 3:15).

The entire city is in an uproar because of Haman's decree—but the king and Haman resume their carousing. Are we to believe, then, that the king is still in the dark as to the parties alluded to anonymously by Haman? Can the entire city of Susa, the palace guard and officers, be involved in a monstrous genocidal plot, and the king somehow remain oblivious to it all? Certainly, the intention of the verse quoted above is subtly to link the king with Haman in this nefarious deed.

The role of Ahasuerus in Haman's plot is a key to the proper understanding of the Megillah. Written under Persian rule, the Megillah could not be completely candid as to the depth of his involvement, and left the matter somewhat ambiguous—"we too are subjects of Ahasuerus," as the Talmud puts it. Ahasuerus however, was equally circumspect. He obviously assented to Haman's plans, as shown by his presentation of the royal ring, but his oral response deserves careful study. The phrase "the money is given to you" (Esther 3:11) has long troubled commentators, Ahasuerus is not noted for his generous nature, and would harldy have given Haman such a large sum of money. Indeed Mordecai is concerned about "the sum of money that Haman had promised to pay" (Esther 4:7). Clearly the money is destined for the king himself.

The king's second phrase, "the people also, to do with them as it seems good to you" (Esther 3:11), parallels Haman's request, "if it is good before the king" (Esther 3:9). The king, telling Haman to do what is good in his own eyes, distances himself from the act—it is Haman's judgment that will dictate, not Ahasuerus'. The king's surprising "the money is given to you" is a similar effort to avoid responsibility for the atrocity about to be committed. Haman offers payment for the Jews' destruction directly to the royal treasury;

Ahasuerus is more circumspect. Money of this nature would directly implicate the king in murder; rather the money should be given to Haman, who will know its final destination.

Our sages have commented on Ahasuerus' procedure in the case of the Jews as compared to the previous case of Vashti.[14] Whereas the seemingly trivial incident of Vashti is discussed openly and fully with a cabinet of seven advisers, the fate of the Jewish people is decided in private by the king and Haman. Without in any way diminishing the moral message of Ḥazal, the lack of full cabinet discussion points up the essentially extralegal nature of the proceedings. Ahasuerus has granted his ring and his blessing, but he has vested authority for the acts upon Haman himself—and not upon himself. Only in this way can we comprehend Haman's later execution for conspiring against the Jews (Esther 8:7).

Having discussed the moral culpability of Ahasuerus and Haman, it is of interest to consider the issue of Hitler and the Final Solution. Ironically, there is no written order signed by Hitler authorizing the Final Solution of the Jewish problem by means of mass extermination. The Nazis indeed considered the total elimination of the Jewish people as "a page of glory in our history which has never been written and is never to be written."[15]

This is not to argue, as Neo-Nazis and some Hitler apologists would have us believe, that the Holocaust was carried on unbeknownst to Hitler. It is the case, however, that the direct order for the implementation of the Final Solution came from Himmler, speaking in the name of the Fuhrer, rather than from Hitler himself. Such a chain of command was commonplace in Hitler's Germany. Hitler would make his desires known to a small coterie of close associates, generally Himmler and Bormann. They would then translate this "Order of the Fuhrer" into a practical plan of action.[16]

Haman, in his decree against the Jews, also speaks in the name of the king; as the bearer of the royal ring, Haman has such authority. Because the order is identified with Haman, however, the king can later claim ignorance of the details of Haman's letters[17] and hang him for conspiring against the Jews. Ahasuerus is equally careful in his dealings with Mordecai, who is charged, "Write concerning the Jews as is good in your eyes" (Esther 8:8), the very same language used previously. While Mordecai and Haman may use the king's name and signet, they bear responsibility for the propriety of their acts. The king himself does not intervene until after the battle on the thirteenth of Adar, when the Jews have emerged victorious. If Ahasuerus, as we have argued, is aware of the details of Haman's plot, how then are we to understand his actions, both his public humiliation of Haman and Haman's subsequent execution. While the salvation and survival of the Jews is providential and miraculous, it is a miracle that works in the realm of the natural. What then is the rational explanation for the actions of Ahasuerus?

We can only speculate on Ahasuerus' sleepless night. Perhaps it was the sound of Haman's carpenters building the high gallows for all to see that hammered into his consciousness; perhaps the hidden terror that had seized his still silent queen. In any event, Ahasuerus, no longer heady from Haman's promises of riches and security, grapples with the growing sense of menace that threatens to envelop him. Having given the ring and the right to make arbitrary life-and-death decisions to Haman, he has set up a rival who may eventually threaten his hold on the throne.

The king dares not consult his trusted seven ministers in this matter, for the plot against the Jews, by its very nature, is illegal and monstrous. Furthermore, the king can no longer be certain of his ministers' loyalty; by his own order they are subservient to Haman and report to him. In desperation the king turns to his "book of records of the chronicles" (Esther 6:1). There he finds the perfect ally against Haman—Mordecai the Jew.

The King had doubts about Haman's loyalty before Esther's party, and Esther has no difficulty in persuading him of Haman's villainy. Since he had framed his decree to include women and children, the queen herself is threatened, with the king helpless to intervene. Haman is more interested in arming his cohorts than in the king's welfare. "The adversary is not worthy that the king be endangered" (Esther 7:4).[18] Once Haman's forces are armed and organized, the king will himself be the victim, quickly following the queen in the campaign against the Jews. The king moves with dispatch; Haman turns from cohort to conspirator, from savior to Satan. He is hung for his heinous crime—the war against the Jews.

Hitler, too, was eventually defeated by powers that attempted to reach accommodations with him. They, too, came to understand that Hitler was not merely concerned with Jews, but sought absolute power for himself. No "danger to the king," no economic or military hardship could deter him from his megalomaniacal goals. Indeed, the Nazi pursuit of the Jews took precedence over all other state priorities. Even as Jews were in demand as slave labor for military projects, the annihilation of the Jews continued unabated, against the vehement protests of German military leaders.[19]

Ahasuerus' embrace of the Jews is far from complete. Having eliminated Haman's threat to his throne, he forgets entirely the threat to the Jews, and only reluctantly lifts his golden scepter in Esther's direction. The Jewish problem is an intrusion which should be solved by the Jews themselves. Regretfully, he hears of the fallen in Susa. The burden pursuing Amalek is shifted to his seemingly implacable queen, who persuades him to grant her one more day of combat.

If the Allies finally did come to recognize the true nature of Hitler's goals, and moved against him, they too were not essentially concerned with the fate of the Jews, doing little to negate the murderous Nazi designs. Thus they moved against the murderous Hitler only as they dimly perceived a threat to themselves. The Jews, meanwhile, were allowed to defend themselves in their walled cities and ghettos if possible. Without a Mordecai at the helm, the king's forces did not concentrate on saving the Jews, but on saving themselves and defeating Hitler.

It is true that after the war, the criminal murderers were hung for their acts against the Jews, much as the sons of Haman are finally hung after their defeat in Shushan. It is only now that the king becomes directly involved, and his reluctance is evident. The plot against the Jews is recognized as a plot against humanity. Amalek disappears from the scene, waiting to rise again.

Having discussed at length the actions and motivations of Haman and Ahasuerus, we now turn to a few considerations concerning the role played by Mordecai. Rashi (Esther 9:26) acknowledges that the Megillah is obscure about Mordecai's reason for refusing to bow down to Haman.

Our sages relate that Haman had made himself into an idol (or wore an idol on his chest).[20] Bowing to Haman, therefore, was no mere act of subservience but bespoke idolatry; Haman was not merely a politician but a cultist leader.

It is not farfetched to presume that Haman was an outspoken anti-Semite even before his confrontation with Mordecai. His confrontations with Mordecai escalated his animosity to a genocidal level. Mordecai would not bow to Haman because of his intuitive insight into his perverse nature. To blame Haman's later actions on Mordecai, as some have done, is typical of anti-Semitic thought. The Jews are responsible for all the world's evils, even those they bring upon themselves. In this world, even the Holocaust is the result of a Jewish conspiracy.

There is considerable controversy among historians as to the roots of modern anti-Semitism. Indeed, in an age of little faith in established religions, the anti-Semite can hardly be said to be motivated by religious reasons. Yet in a very real sense, anti-Semitism itself becomes the new religion, with Haman or Hitler as its prophet; in the total subservience to such cultist leaders there is a grotesque parody of the religious experience. The similarity between some contemporary cultist leaders and Hitler has been brought home to us by the Guyana suicide-massacre. There is no doubt, however, that Hitler, too, saw himself as involved in a holy mission: "Hence today I believe that I am acting in accordance with the will of the Almighty Creator: by defending myself against the Jew, I am fighting for the work of the Lord."[21]

We must remember, too, that Mordecai and Esther respond with religious faith. If Haman's cult is based on the need for Jewish annihilation, Mordecai's is replete with faith in Jewish survival— "relief and deliverance will arise to the Jews from another place" (Esther 4:14). Indeed, the crux of the Megillah lies in the religious reaction of the Jews of Shushan, "the matters of the fastings and their cry" (Esther 9:31).

We have discussed above the racist quality of Zeresh's superstitious fear of the Jew. We must recognize an essential element in the Jew's own self-image. Jewish survival in a largely hostile world has never been predicated on Jewish racial superiority but on the beneficence of the Almighty; the success or failure of the Jews in their struggles with their enemies depends on the moral stature of their cause. Whereas Amalek views the Jews as a people with perverse racial quality, which must ultimately be confronted, the Jew recognizes that survival depends on his deeds, not his genetic inheritance.

This lesson is expressed best in the initial confrontation with Amalek—with Moses standing on high, his hands uplifted and the staff of the Lord in his hands (Exodus 17:11). Israel's victory over or defeat by Amalek lay not with themselves but with the arms of Moses, held up by Aaron and Hur. As Israel raised their eyes to the hands of Moses, and to heaven, their cause prospered.[22] In this sense, Mordecai's resistance to Haman and refusal to bow to him were not the source of annihilation but rather the source of salvation for the Jewish people.

The distinction between the Jews' concept of themselves as a chosen community and the Amalekite racial view of the Jew is also evident in the Megillah's account of the holiday of Purim itself, which is accepted "upon them, and upon their seed, and upon all such as joined themselves unto them" (Esther 9:27—i.e., by born Jews and those who choose to join the covenantal community. Finally, let us note that Haman is dispatched by Harbonah, a Gentile, who is remembered positively along with Mordecai and Esther.[23] If Jews are the chosen enemies of Amalek, they are not alone in the battle against evil, which is ultimately the concern of all mankind.

If we have discussed certain ambiguous aspects of Mordecai's behavior; we must focus equally on Esther's enigmatic role in the battle against Amalek. Esther's invitation to Haman troubled Ḥazal.[24] Even more puzzling is her seeming pliability in the face of Haman's pleas after he has despaired in placating the King (Esther 7:7), which contrasts with the later decree utterly to destroy Haman's hordes, men, women, and children.

Esther's ambiguous reaction to Haman reflects the instinctive Jewish reaction of mercy and forgiveness, even toward enemies. Esther's royal forebear, King Saul, similarly pondered the unforgiving and harsh command entrusted to him by Samuel.[25] Ahasuerus, now alerted to the danger to his person from Haman, suffers no doubts about his future actions; Esther, confronted with Haman's pleas for mercy, seemingly wavers in her determination.

The tension experienced by Esther and King Saul expresses a basic moral problem—how to combat evil without becoming evil oneself. Indeed the traditional Jewish values of accommodation, peace, and forgiveness are challenged by the phenomenon of Amalek, the bestial and irrational hater of Jews and Judaism.

The campaign against Amalek has been led by the dual leadership of the Jewish people—represented by Aaron and Hur, with the priestly-prophetic role assumed by Aaron, Samuel, and Mordecai, and the political, by Hur, Saul, and Esther. Indeed Saul and Esther, concerned with tactics and pragmatic considerations, waver in their zealotry against Amalek. The prophet, who sees at a glance the entire destiny of his people, has no misgivings.

Gersonides, discussing Samuel's confrontation with Agag (1 Samuel 15:32), Agag, when he saw the prophet, immediately detected his saintliness and mercifulness, and assumed that his life would be spared. Samuel, however, stresses Agag's crimes and executes "before the Lord," measure for measure (1 Samuel 15:33).

Judaism recognizes the distinction between the absolute justice of God and the justice of man, which because of man's finitude is perforce imperfect. "An eye for an eye" is the measure of justice demanded by the written Torah; the Oral Torah, however, recognizes the general impossibility of achieving such justice. The hall-mark of God's punishment is its measure-for-measure quality.

The war against Amalek is not only man's but God's. The Almighty's throne is not complete until the evil of Amalek is eli-minated. Israel partakes in the Almighty's battle, just as the Almighty fights Israel's battles. As such, Israel is commanded to exact measure-for-measure retribution on Amalek, to return cruelty for cruelty, death for death.

This measure-for-measure quality is stressed not only by Samuel but in the Megillah itself. Indeed, Mordecai's decree is so literal a cop of Haman's that it is read again with an added *vov* to assure an absolute identity of texts. The phrase "and to take spoil" (Esther 8:11) may have been inserted for the sake of parallelism; no spoils are ever taken by the Jews (Esther 9:10). The miracle of Purim truly resides in the exact turnabout, the reversal of roles. The cam-paign against Haman is part of God's eternal battle against Amalek; as such only the most exacting punishment is possible.

The Torah, in commanding us to remember the acts of Amalek, recognizes that historical forces for peace and accommodation can be as strong as those sustaining hatred and rivalry. Israel is admon-ished not to despise the Egyptians and the Edomites, nations that perpetrated wrongs of greater historical significance against Israel; but Amalek's utter evil is singled out for eternal notoriety.

Instinctively, the Jewish people have reacted to the Holocaust in this traditional way. Firstly, we are commanded to remember and never to forget that which Amalek did unto us. The Holocaust must live with us—for it is not a part of the historical past but Israel's metahistorical essence. Secondly, we must pursue absolute justice for our slain brethren—not out of vengeance but out of a sense of a historic mission to restore the throne of the Almighty. Thirdly, we must recognize that Nazism and its offshoots are not merely another political phenomenon, with inherent rights in a democratic society, but evil itself, to be combated by their own antidemocratic methods if necessary.

Within the exact reversal enacted in the Megillah, there are two decrees identical in all but the reversal of the pursuer and the pursued. By implication, Haman's *pur* (lot) has been doubled into Purim—two identical lots or destinies interchanged. But what is the larger significance of the *pur?* Why does a *goral* (lot) typify the Megillah and the holiday?

An oft-quoted passage from the Gemara equates the name Esther (*ester*) with the word *hester* ("hiding"), indicating that the confrontation with Amalek is best described in terms of *hastarat panim,* i.e., God's presence being hidden from us. The destruction of the Temple is ever-present in Esther; the haunting *Eikhah* melody subtly intermingling with the Megillah tune. No prophet arises to speak in God's name. Esther herself is but a morning-star, illuminating a dark and lonely night.

Haman's decree, ordering the total annihilation of the Jewish people, is unspeakable in its depravity. In a theological sense, the decree in its totality and finality bespeaks the end of both the Jews and their God. Even Hitler, in all his brazenness, never openly spoke of the extermination of the Jews that was under way. How then did Haman dare to openly command what was obviously an atrocity of unprecedented scope and evil?

Throughout the Bible, the function of the *goral* (lot) was to speak the unspeakable, to decide what no man may decide. Whether the *goral* allotted the portion of every Israelite in the land of Canaan (Numbers 26:55) or the guilt of Achan in violating the *herem,*[27] it spoke that which no man may speak. Particularly in the Yom Kippur service (as we will see below), the lot was the vehicle to express the otherwise inexpressible.

So, too, in the context of *hastarat panim,* the Megillah speaks through lots, through *purim.* Haman, with his *pur,* choosing the day of destruction, divorces himself from the essence of the order. It is destiny that calls forth the destruction of the Jews; he is merely the mechanism through which the die is cast. So, too, Eichmann in Jerusalem explained that he had merely been the tool of destiny, a destiny which doomed six million Jews.

Yet another term for lots, *holesh,* and another purpose for the lots, is alluded to by Isaiah (14:12 *holesh al-goyim*). The lots is used in the context of war to select the victims for attack on any specific day, a usage applied by Ḥazal to Joshua's battle with Amalek (Exodus 17:13).[28] Unlike a battle waged over a short period, the battle throughout the generations between Israel and Amalek involves a war of attrition, a constant random attenuation of enemy forces. Rather than speaking of a cataclysmic battle, our sages have described Amalek's tactics as a series of sporadic attacks, stealing souls from the camp of Israel from under God's protective clouds.[29]

So, too, our brethren during the Holocaust, in other camps and under malevolent clouds, faced a random *selection* every day of their existence, a multitude of *purim* to decide their day.

The service of atonement calls forth, too, the casting of lots. Two identical goats are assigned by lot—one to holiness and ultimate sacrifice in the Holy Temple, the other to be banished to the desert and desolation. The two services are performed by two contrasting personages—the high priest, representing Aaron in each generation, who enters the Holy of Holies; and the *ish ha-itti,* the anonymous and transient functionary who carries the goat to Azazel and destruction. The assignment of the goat to Azazel is by lot alone; no man may pronounce any name but the Almighty's upon a sacrificial animal.

The Purim story similarly posits two near identical *ishim* (men), Mordecai, the *Ish Yehudi* the exile of Jerusalem, who, like the priest of old, changes his garb five times to reflect his proximity to God's presence; and Haman, the *ish itti,* who becomes Azazel himself, the angel of destruction. Just as the goat for Azazel is unspeakable, so, too, the rendering of the ring to Haman is unthinkable in theological terms. God speaks at last through the *pur,* the seemingly random interchange of identical objects.

It is ironic that atonement of sins is granted to Israel not through the ministrations of the high priest but the actions of the *ish itti.* The confrontation with evil inherent in the goat for Azazel results in Israel's absolution. In a time of *hastarat panim* and exile from the Temple, Haman's ascension to power, brings about a return to God, forgiveness, and redemption.

We too have experienced *hastarat panim* and the sacrifice at the abyss, at the hands of the *ish itti*. The atonement of the "deaths of the righteous" is equal to that of the atonement service,[30] bringing about forgiveness for Israel.

Rav Zakok ha-Kohen sees the battle with Amalek as an essential precursor in the establishment of lasting *kedushah,* just as the giving of the Torah followed Joshua's battle, and the construction of each Temple followed by a generation the battles of Saul and Mordecai, respectively, against Amalek.[31] Thus we are challenged, one generation after the Holocaust, to create in our own lives, in our Torah institutions and in the land of Israel, an eternal *kedushah* that will lead to the final redemption. Only then will Amalek be totally defeated, and God's name be restored to its full glory—"For on that day will God be One and His name be One" (Zechariah 14:9).

NOTES

1. Maimonides, Hilkhot Melakhim 5:5; *Sefer ha-Mitzvot,* positive commandment 187.

2. Berakhot 28a; Maimonides, Hilkhot Issurei Biah 12:25.

3. R. Joseph B. Soloveitchik, "Kol Dodi Dofek," in a final note (see pp. 118–19 in this volume).

In a subsequent interview, Rabbi Soloveitchik elaborated on his view that a nation could be transformed into Amalek in a metaphysical or halakhic sense. This status of Amalek would not, according to the Rav, create halakhic obligations concerning innocent offspring and spouses because Maimonides clearly limits actions against Amalek to unrepentant elements who have refused to make peace with Israel. However, the animals and possessions of such a nation might very well be included in the injuction, for it also applies to the animals of Amalek (according to Rashi, Deuteronomy 25:19). Such an injuction appears to be the reason for the refusal on the part of Mordecai and the Jewish combatants against Haman to partake of the spoils of battle. (See e.g., Rabbenu Behayya on Exodus 17:16.)

4. R. J. Rozin, *Zafenat Pane'ah al Shemot* (ed. R. M. M. Kasher) on Exodus 17:14.

A similar argument is advanced by R. Moshe Sternbach, *Mo'adim u-Zemanim,* vol. 2, chap. 164. For an alternative approach to the contradiction in Maimonides, see also the discussion in Rabbi M. M. Kasher, *Torah Shelemah,* Exodus, vol. 14, p. 340.

5. Midrashic and exegetical literature abounds with examples linking Purim to Amalek primarily because of Haman's descent from Agag, the Amalekite king. By designating the confrontation with Amalek as the Torah reading for Purim and the Sabbath before Purim as Parashat Zakhor, the halakhah too recognizes this connection.

6. Megillah 2a, according to the text of Maimonides and Alfasi: *ho'il u-mistaknin boh;* Yerushalmi Megillah 1:5.

7. Maimonides, Hilkhot Ta'anit, 5:5; Ra'abad, quoted by R. Nissim in his commentary on Alfasi, Ta'anit 7a.

8. Megillah 14a.

9. As quoted by Lucy S. Davidowicz, *The War Against the Jews, 1933–1945* (New York: Holt, Rinehart & Winston 1975,) p. 9.

10. Megillah 16a.

11. Davidowicz, op. cit., p. 165.

12. Hugh Trevor-Roper, ed., *Hitler's War Directives,* p. 212.

13. Davidowicz, p. cit., pp. 151–152.

14. Esther Rabbah 4:5 in the name of R. Isaac.

15. From an address by Himmler in Poznan, October 4, 1943, to the leaders of the SS (*Trials of Major War Criminals,* 29, Doc. 1919-PS, pp. 110–173).

16. See, for example, Serge Klarsfeld, ed., *The Holocaust and the Neo-Nazi Mythomania,* pp. 35–73, for a discussion of the authority for the Final Solution.

17. See Ibn Ezra's commentary to Esther 8:8.

18. The interpretation of Esther's argument offered here was presented by Rabbi J. B. Soloveitchik in a public lecture at Yeshiva University.

19. Davidowicz, op. cit., pp. 188–200.

20. See R. Baruch Epstein, *Torah Temimah* on Esther 3:2.

21. From *Mein Kampf,* quoted by Davidowicz, op. cit., p. 27.

22. See Mishnah Rosh Ha-Shanah 3:8.

23. Y. Jacobson, *Ḥazon ha-Mikra,* vol. 2, p. 200.

24. Megillah 15b; see also Rashi's commentary on Esther 9:26.

25. See Rashi on 1 Samuel 15:5, reflecting the rabbinical opinion in Yoma 22b.

26. Ḥullin 139b.

27. See Sanhedrin 43b.

28. See *Torah Shelemah,* vol. 14, pp. 265–266, n. 104.

29. Mekhilta to Exodus 17:8, in the name of R. Eleazar ha-Moda'i.

30. Yerushalmi Yoma 1:1.

31. R. Zadok ha-Kohen of Lublin, *Resisei Laylah* end of chap. 18: "it was before the introduction of any complete aspect of *kedushah*—before the giving of the

Torah, and before the construction of the First Temple—that immediately in the kingship of Saul there was an awakening of interest in the building of the Temple, but it was first necessary for Saul and David to eliminate Amalek. Similarly before the construction of the Second Temple [it was necessary] to eliminate Haman's Amalek; and so it will be in the future before the construction of the Third Temple, may it be built speedily in our days."

Some Lessons

A Time to Keep Silent and a Time to Speak

Dr. Norman Lamm

It is very difficult for me to speak on this topic. I will not tell you any personal experiences of the Holocaust, for I cannot: I have none. I was a youngster living in Brooklyn when the Shoah occurred. Neither will I speak this evening as an historian, teacher of philosophy, or amateur of literature. I appear before you without any such scholarly or artistic pretensions. Rather, I wish to engage in some deeply felt private reflections—meditations, if you will—between me and myself: an inner dialogue, with you as courteous outsiders listening to this strange man talking to himself.

I confess that I am beset by deep ambivalence in talking about the Holocaust, even at this late date, almost forty years after the event. I have done my share of talking and writing about the Holocaust, and yet, I am unnerved whenever I am called upon to do so.

My problem is that, having accepted to speak at this Holoaust Remembrance gathering, shall I speak at all? Can I? May I? Am I perhaps here under false pretenses?

My doubts apply only to me and others who, like me, were not *there*. Those who were need not share my hesitations. For there is a real, palpable curtain—or even a wall, a tangible obstruction—that separates those who were seared by the flames and survived, and those who merely wept; between me and those who had the Shoah inscribed into their flesh and psyches forever.

For those of us who did not experience the Holocaust firsthand: is it perhaps best that we keep quiet together? It was Ecclesiastes (3:7) who said that there is a time for everything—"a time to keep silent, and a time to speak." My dilemma is that when it comes to the Holocaust, I simultaneously feel an urge to speak and a summons to silence.

The Holocaust is in many ways the obverse of divinity. The Holocaust was a satanic revelation, an historic apocalyptic disclosure of the reality of evil, ugliness, darkness.

When Moses saw the burning bush, he was attracted to it by his innate curiosity. But when he understood that it was a divine revelation, "Moses hid his face, for he was afraid to look upon God" (Exodus 3:6). What holds true for the revelation of holiness holds equally true for the apocalyptic revelation of overarching evil, the kind that surpasses all human understanding. For, to gaze, to state, to conceptualize, to describe, to bewail, and to formulate—is, by its very nature, to limit and, therefore, to diminish.

An example: The Talmud (Berakhot 33) tells us that in the days before the prayerbook was fixed in permanent form and reduced to a literary text, a reader was reciting the prayers in public, and was lavish in extolling God's attributes. R. Hanina turned to him sarcastically and said, "Is that all that you have to say in praise of the Lord?" What Rabbi Hanina meant to say was that man must never say more than that which tradition ordains, because when we add we thereby diminish. Augmenting words of praise is limiting the praise to our few meager adjectives. The more speech, the more insult, and therefore silence is the greatest praise.

What is true for divine compassion is true for the terrible wrath of the Divine. Anything we articulate about the suffering of the martyrs insults them, because human language is inadequate to convey the dimensions of what occurred. We trivialize such ineffable evil and suffering by mere verbalization.

So silence is recommended, lest talk become drivel, writing prattle, and symbols sacrilege.

When Job was smitten with his unbearable torments, his three friends came to console him. "And when they lifted up their eyes afar off, and knew him not. . . . So they sat down with him upon the ground seven days and seven nights, and none spoke a word unto him, for they saw that his grief was very great" (Job 2:12–12). If silence is the only response to the suffering of one Job, what shall we say of six million Jobs?

There is a third and deeply sensitive personal reason why those of us who were not present in what Elie Wiesel has called "The Kingdom of the Night" ought to hold our peace. Again, let us resort to a biblical metaphor, because when we try to speak about what happened in the Holocaust, only biblical metaphors have that sweep of terror and of grandeur and of mystery—and at times even those do not suffice.

At the destruction of the cities of Sodom and Gomorrah, as the Lord was about to "overturn" the two evil cities, angels hurried Lot and his family out, and told him, "Look not behind thee" (Genesis 19:17). Why so? Rashi, the great exegete and commentator, explains that Lot was forbidden to observe the destruction of Sodom and Gomorrah because he deserved the same fate as his countrymen but was saved only "by the merit of Abraham," his righteous kinsman.

Lot and Sodom are, for me, metaphors for us American Jews and the Holocaust. We dare not look too intently upon the victims, even as Lot was not permitted to look back upon the perpetrators— because we might well have been in their place!

Call it survivor's guilt or whatever you will. It is indeed mind-boggling: why was I spared in New York, while dozens of my cousins, uncles, aunts, and my aged great-grandmother were butchered in Poland? Lot at least had "the merit of Abraham." What merit did I have that my martyred kinfolk did not? Why were they murdered, why was I spared?

"Look not behind thee." Contemplation, description, and analysis of this twentieth-century diabolical paroxysm and satanic convulsion threaten the very structures of our thought and values and the very foundations of our faith and feelings. It is a philosophical atom bomb, and if we tinker with it carelessly, it threatens to destroy our entire axiological universe. Think about it too long, and you lose your equanimity—indeed your very humanity—and, like Lot's wife, you turn into a pillar of salt.

And yet, although this is a "time to keep silent," it is by the same token a "time to speak." While silence has much to commend it, if we are indeed silent, then both we and the world will forget. And forgetfulness, as the Midrash taught—and as S. Y. Agnon was fond of repeating—is the root of all evil. With all that the talk and activity about the Holocaust have often been cheapening and trivial; with all the failure of books and monuments to offer even a glimmer of solace to match the unspeakable grief; with all that our preoccupation with the Holocaust has tended to distract us from our own complicity and responsibility—the failure to speak up is far worse.

In America—and from America the poison spreads abroad—we are treated to a "revisionist" view of the Holocaust that appears in "academic" guise, declaring that the Holocaust was a hoax. The whore dresses up like a princess: the hoax theory appears in an academic "journal" accompanied by all the scholastic paraphernalia designed to impress the uncritical and the naive. It is an instance of insufferable pedantry at the service of unspeakable hypocrisy.

Yet some benighted souls confuse the freedom of speech and academic freedom, as if the civil right of any citizen to deliver himself af any remark, no matter how stupid or false or inane, means that professors have the intellectual right to exploit their academic standing in order to propagate deliberate lies and vicious misstatements of fact.

So, let it be said here, in this hall of learning, from the podium of Adelphi University, that this is a dreadful and unpardonable error. A professor of astrophysics who denied the existence of galaxies and attributed their properties to the intervention of pixies and fairies would be booted out of the university. A professor of economics who ascribed market fluctuations to devious little gremlins would be laughed out of the classroom. A professor of psychiatry who recommended exorcism of the devil as normative therapy for neurosis would even lose his tenure.

Shall, then, professors, of electrical engineering or history or chemistry be allowed to deny verifiable facts about contemporary history—in the presence of survivors who bear the scars on their bodies and souls, and the numbers tattooed on their arms—with impunity as they claim the dignity of academic freedom? I grant their claim to the civic freedom of speech. But as academicians? Have we no longer any standards in the world of scholarship?

We must break our silence and speak up—loud and clear.

In West Germany, Chancellor Helmut Schmidt plans to arm the Saudis—and announces it on Holocaust Remembrance Day itself. Without mentioning any moral debt that Germany owes to the Jews, he speaks of Germany's "moral commitment to Palestinians." What colossal hypocrisy!

It is hard to believe that this is 1981 and not 1984—George Orwell's *1984*—when the leader of a country that brought unparalleled devastation to the world and decimated the Jewish people not only thinks about arming the enemies of Israel (the only country that afforded the last shred of dignity to the remnants of the Holocaust), but has the temerity to describe such actions as "moral." For shame!

For thirty-five years, since Adenauer, West Germany has been trying to atone for its sins, and somehow allow itself to reenter the community of civilized nations. Herr Schmidt has now undone it all, and for all time.

Neighboring Poland has now acted in a way that should elicit from us not silence, but also not formal speech—rather, peals of horrible laughter and wretched amusement. For Poland has proven that there need not be Jews in order for one to be anti-Semitic . . .

Russia, we have just learned, did not permit Russian Jews to gather in a forest clearing outside Moscow to commemorate Holocaust Day. The Russians did not allow the survivors even to gather and say Kaddish for the millions who were martyred. This is the country which first pulled the shroud of obscurity over Babi Yar, not permitting a memorial plaque to mention that it was *Jews* who were so barbarically killed there. Now it repeats its offense, and even the memory of these Jews is not permitted to be preserved.

It might be in place to recall that European anti-Semitism did not begin with Germany in 1939. Hitler owed much to Russia: It was exactly 100 years ago, in May of 1881, that the Russian Minister of Interior prevailed upon the Czar to pass the infamous May Laws; one-third of all the Jews were to be killed, one-third baptized, and one third exiled. Thus was the "Jewish problem" to be solved. So Russia, which was one of the teachers of modern anti-Semitism, today will not even allow the Holocaust to be commemorated by its survivors.

At such a time, and in the face of such provocations, we dare not keep silent.

Hence, I return to my inner dialogue. My dilemma is: to speak or to keep silent. If I speak, I risk trivialization and vulgarization; if I do not, I encourage amnesia, the possibility that neither my children nor my friends, Jews or Gentiles, will ever learn anything from the Holocaust, and that the world will yet allow it to be repeated.

Hence, we must choose to talk and study and read and analyze and remember and remind. But we must be doubly and trebly careful to choose our words with great care. We must resolve with all our hearts that:

The Holocaust must not be vulgarized into lurid entertainment for both adolescent and adult addicts of the violent and the prurient. *The Holocaust* must not be turned into an industry and into a form of show business. The *Holocaust* must not be used as a means to further private ends, even private ideological ends, so that it is invoked as an excuse, no matter how irrelevant, to propagate cherished ideas.

The Holocaust must not be diminished by abusing the terms "Holocaust" and "genocide" for every object of political, social, and economic oppression. I bristle when I hear the terms applied to Vietnam and El Salvador, or by the sundry American liberation movements. The term is used with such abandon that all meaning is squeezed out of it. It becomes profane, as if you were saying that the molester not only tortured his victims to death but also ran through a red light. It must not even be misused in this manner by Israeli officials when speaking of the Christian enclaves in Lebanon, who are threatened with defeat and cruel oppression, but hardly with genocide itself.

The Holocaust must be commemorated by paintings, statues, and monuments, but never, never be reduced to merely statues and paintings and books and poems, as if with these objets d'art we have fulfilled our moral obligations to the martyrs.

The Holocaust must become part of education, but must not be used to distort education, especially not Jewish education. Holocaust studies must become a permanent part of the curriculum of all decent human beings, and especially all Jews. It must! But I am apprehensive about the proliferation of Holocaust courses.

Many Jewish students who otherwise have no contact with their tradition and their people have, as their main or sole exposure to 3,500 years of Jewish history, only: "Holocaust studies." They learn how Jews died, but know not how they lived. They learn of the culture of the murderers, but have not the slightest notion of the culture of the victims. I am aghast because, victimized though we were for three and a half millennia, it is scandalous to teach my children and my students that our role in history was primarily that of the perpetual victims. An exclusively martyrologic interpretation of Jewish history is simply all wrong.

For they created one of the most vibrant cultures in the history of man—Polish Jewry.

Polish Jewry rivals Babylonian Jewry and Palestinian Jewry in the second century. Purely from a cultural point of view, it was one of the most creative communities on the face of the earth. It is therefore a well-intended but cruel joke that we play upon the East European Jewish victims when we conjure them up only in relation to the genocidal plans and acts of the Nazis, as if this exhausted their importance for human history.

Shall we ignore all that they created—in religion and in literature, in language and in politics, in social thought and in philosophy—and invoke their memory only by the recollection of the obscenities visited upon them by the Western world? My heart grieves for all those youngsters who flock to the "Holocaust courses" and can tell us only how many Jews of Lublin were killed in Auschwitz, and how many fell in the Warsaw Ghetto uprising, but know nothing of the Lublin Yeshiva and of Warsaw Jewry's religious and literary and social and political creativity, of Yiddish and Talmud and Musar and Hasidim and labor groups and education.

Therefore, we must never teach our young people, whose primary exposure to Judaism is through Holocaust studies, that East European Jewry was simply a group of victims who died at the hands of the Nazis. This is not what the study of the Holocaust should do; it should not rob the victims of the eternity of their heritage.

- *We must* remember their lives, and also what might have become of them had they survived.
- *We must* continue to support the State of Israel, which, had it existed then, millions of the martyrs might be alive today.
- *We must* struggle against evil and bigotry and racism wherever we find them and whatever victims they claim.
- *We must* carry on their culture and their faith and their vitality—to the very end of days.

And for this—silence will not do.

So, having spoken I conclude with an apology for having done so.

Better yet, I close with a prayer—the kind of prayer with which we conclude our daily prayers, on the style of "My God, keep my tongue from speaking evil, and my lips from uttering deceit":

Forgive me, O Lord, for having profaned the greatest and most horrible mystery of the history of our people with empty words from unclean lips.

Forgive me for daring to disturb the eternal and infinite and endless cry of anguish, silent and thunderous as the grave, with twitting and wayward words that barely rise above the banal and blasphemous.

Forgive me for the arrogance of attempting to find meaning in that convulsion of divine wrath which not only consumed six million lives—ten times the biblical number of Israelites who left Egypt, old and young, mothers and babies, scholars and ordinary people—but annihilated meaning itself. For the Holocaust was the "black hole" of history, which, like the black hole that astronomers claim to have discovered in the galaxies, buries all within it and allows no light to escape.

Forgive me, O Lord, for Thou knowest that silence would have been worse than speech. For while speech may not shed light, at least it can protest the darkness.

This selection was originally given as the keynote address at The Holocaust Through Contemporary Eyes, the Second Long Island Academic Tribute to the Martyrs of the Holocaust, held at Adelphi University in Garden City, N.Y. in 1981.

Yom ha-Shoah

Rabbi David Stavsky

Why are we here tonight? What is our purpose here this evening? It goes without saying that we are here to remember the *kedoshim,* the martyrs: mothers, fathers, sisters, brothers, aunts and uncles, our dearest ones, whose lives were brutally snuffed out in the worst mass murder in Jewish and world history.

For them, we say Yizkor; for them, we light candles, and for them we humbly bow our heads to say Kaddish. For them, we pledge never to forget their love or the songs they sang or the words which they spoke.

However, no words which I utter this evening will adequately describe the pain, the hurt which you and I, the *she'arit ha-pelitah,* the remnant of the flock, feel and know. Of the sixty or seventy surviving families in our community, each could write its own book of hundreds and hundreds of pages. You, my friends, could write, not only with ink, but with tears that would remain indelible. You could write chapter and verse with deep signs, a *krechtz* to punctuate your paragraphs. You know the stories best, and only you can tell them best.

Then why am I here tonight?

In July 1952, I made my first trip to Israel. Jerusalem was a divided city then. The Kotel was not in our hands. It was Tishah be-Av, and I went to the only holy shrine in Israeli hands to daven *Minḥah.* It was Har Ziyyon. And there I saw it: the *Martef ha-Shoah*—the Holocaust Cave. This was in pre-Yad Vashem days. I looked around the cave on Mount Zion and saw the flickering candles burning near a lampshade. I picked up the lampshade, touched it, and realized it was made of human skin. I saw a small keg full of bars of soap—R.J.F.—*Reines Jüdisches Fett.* I stumbled out of the *Martef ha-Shoah,* sat down on the steep steps that led to

King David's Tomb on Mount Zion, and started to cry. I was twenty-
one years old, and this was my personal confrontation with the
Holocaust. It hit me. I could not believe what I had held in my
hand. I wondered how many bodies it had taken to make that soap
and whose skin they had cut to make that lampshade and which Nazi
beast had used that soap.

So why am I here tonight? Not to tell that story. Not to open
more wounds and cause more pain.

In 1978, I was sent on a mission to visit the concentration camps.
Ruth and I were in Dachau, and we saw that the Germans, trying to
hide and deny the past, had turned Dachau into a rose garden. A few
days later, I went to Mauthausen. Yossi, an Austrian Jew who lived
in Vienna, was the U.J.A. escort assigned to me for the day. After an
hour's drive, we arrived in Mauthausen. We walked into the tremendous courtyard. At the entrance, there was a steel chain hanging
from a wall. The chain was used by the S.S. guards to break the neck
of any inmate they wanted to punish and kill. There is a photograph
in our lobby of that horrible chain.

Silently, I followed Yossi through the camp. We went to the
stone quarry, with the 186 steps. There the Jewish slaves were forced
to carry the boulders on their backs, and if they fell, they were
thrown down those 186 steps to their deaths.

When the Dutch Jews were shipped to Mauthausen, they were
thrown over the steep cliff of the quarry. The S.S. guards laughingly
called it the "Parachute Jump."

Silently, we continued our walk until Yossi took me into the
crematorium. I saw the ovens. Unlike the crematorium in Dachau,
which the Germans cleaned up, in Mauthausen you can still see the
ashes of human beings—ashes over forty-five years old.

Unthinkingly, I opened the door to the room next to the crematorium. It looked like a room in a bathhouse, all tiled, a few
chipped tiles here and there. Not much different from any community shower room. It measured about twenty feet by twenty feet. I
went inside, and Yossi closed the door behind me. Suddenly, I

looked up and realized that no water had ever run from those spigots. I was in a gas chamber. I started to shout, "Yossi, Yossi!" I felt faint. Finally, Yossi opened the door, and I thought of all of the souls which had perished, had choked to death in this gas chamber. One hundred ten thousand of our brothers and sisters were cold-bloodedly murdered in Mauthausen.

Why am I here tonight? Not to add to your pain or mine. Why am I telling you this story? And who am I to tell you this story?

I am telling you this story because I believe we have a mission. For me to tell you about that mission, I must review two Hebrew words. They sound exactly the same but mean the very opposite. The Hebrew word *lo* has two letters: *lamed* and *alef, and it means* "no." *Lo* with an *alef* means "no." The other Hebrew word also is *lo,* again with two letters, but this time *lamed* and *vav,* and it means "to have."

Let me explain. *Lo tignov,* which means "thou shalt not steal" when spelled with *lamed* and *alef,* could be read "for him you could steal" if spelled with *lamed* and *vav.*

Only three times in the entire Five Books of Moses do we find that the word *lo* is spelled one way but means the opposite. And these three times, I submit, tell us what our mission is, what it means to be a post-Holocaust Jew, why never again will there be lampshades made of Jewish skin, bars of soap made of Jewish fat—and shower stalls which spew forth Zyklon-B gas.

In the opening parashah of the Book of Leviticus, the Torah tells us that if a person sins and another witnesses it and does not testify, the sin belongs to him as well (Leviticus 5:1).

The word *lo* in this verse is spelled with an *alef* and means "he does not"—he does not speak up. But it also can be read as "to him," meaning "he now owns that sin."

In simple language, "to be or not to be." Do you keep quiet about heinous crimes? Do you remain silent when crimes are perpetrated by brutal murderers? Do you look away when, in 1987, the media continues to hack away at Israel, at the Jews. In the media's eyes, we were wrong in Lebanon, we were wrong in bombing the nuclear reactor in Iraq, and we are simply always wrong, wrong, wrong. We are never right.

American Jews were silent and are still silent.

Gerhart Riegner was the representative of the World Jewish Congress in Geneva, Switzerland. On August 1, 1942, he learned from a most reliable German source, a leading German industrialist, that there was actual documentation of Hitler's orders to murder all the Jews in Europe. The secret was out. It was official. On August 8, Riegner went to the U.S. consulate in Geneva. Howard Elting, Jr., the vice consul in charge that day, said the report seemed "fantastic," meaning preposterous. Therefore, one delay followed another, cablegrams to the State Department went unanswered, and American Jewry and world Jewry were being lied to and deceived.

Riegner then sent a cable to Dr. Stephen Wise, head of the American Jewish Congress, c/o the State Department. The text read as follows:

> Received alarming report that in Fuhrer's headquarter plan discussed and under consideration according to which all Jews in countries occupied or controlled numbering three and one-half to four million should after deportation and concentration in east be exterminated at one blow to resolve once and for all the Jewish question in Europe.

The State Department at first decided to keep the information from Rabbi Wise. Finally, a month later, they called Wise to Washington, handed him the cablegram, and made him promise that he would not disclose the contents to the press or public.

Wise agonized. He wrote to his friend John Haynes Holmes, "I am almost demented over my people's grief." But he kept his promise. For months, he did not state what he knew. Privately, he started to enlist the help of Washington officials, but his pleas fell on deaf ears.

How could he have made such a promise? As a Jew he had pledged at Mount Sinai not to make such promises.

Let me quote from the *New York Times* of March 21, 1984, from a report by former Supreme Court Justice Arthur J. Goldberg, who headed a commission to find out what the established Jewish leadership did to rescue the Jews who were being shipped to Auschwitz and gassed at the rate of ten thousand a day.

> A fundamental reason for the overall failure of the Jewish organizations, in the commission's view, was that they were disunited, financially limited and lacking in political influence. Moreover, according to the report, many of their leaders were afraid of stirring up anti-Semitism in the United States and impeding the Allied war effort.
>
> In an appraisal of that it calls "discreet 'backstairs' diplomacy" by the "upper class" American Jewish Committee, the report noted, with each worsening event, the Committee reacted by contacting yet another official or revisiting the same ones to call their attention to the new situation.
>
> "They were still trying to persuade the same officials (about rescuing the Jews) when the war ended," said the report.
>
> "Although the American Jewish Congress was more inclined to call for highly visible, militant actions—boycotts, street demonstrations, rallies," the report notes that in 1940, its leader, Rabbi Stephen S. Wise, "refused to sanction any tactics that would embarrass the pro-British administration of Franklin D. Roosevelt and check its Lend Lease scheme."

What did the Jew in Auschwitz think? The Jew in Auschwitz, Treblinka, Mathausen said to himself, "If only President Roosevelt knew, if only Churchill knew, if only the Pope knew, they would bring this hell to an end." The irony is that they all knew but chose to remain silent.

As the *lo* with the *vav*, which means that repressed articulation, that deathly silence, makes *him* part of the crime, *he now owns the sin,* the sin of silence.

Yes, American Jews were silent for too long. We were lulled into silence. We were lulled into the *sha-shtill,* be quiet, don't rock the boat syndrome. The anti-Semites could become upset; you might cause waves; you would not be considered, *sha-shtill; lo yagid;* don't speak! The Jews were burning, ten thousand every day in Auschwitz, but the Jews were told not to protest.

But the Torah tells us that he who does not speak up, he who remains silent, also carries the sin of the crime.

Oh, how we were lulled, how we were fooled. How we were told to be patriotic Americans, that we must first win the war and forget about rescuing Jews, that we should not criticize the government.

The Jew on the Lower East Side of New York City worshipped President Roosevelt. Mi She-berakhs for his good health were made in every shul every single Shabbat, including my father's Hasidic shtibl on the East Side. Playing on the word *velt,* the Jew on the street said, *"Es zeinen foran drei velten: di velt, yenne velt, un Roosevelt"* (There are three worlds: this world, the world-to-come, and Roosevelt).

Yes, Washington knew, Jewish leadership knew, but we were tranquilized and silenced.

My mission, my pledge, is never to remain silent when Jewish life hangs in the balance.

The second time the word *lo,* "not," is changed to be read *lo,* "to him," is in Parashat Shemini. In introducing the various kosher and non-kosher foods, the species and their kinds, the Torah tells us "that if an insect, a creeping thing has four legs and "spring legs above their feet with which to leap" (*asher lo khera'im mi-ma'al*), you may eat from that species (Leviticus 11:21).

Listen to the words. Those that have spring feet! The word *lo* is spelled with an *alef,* which means "not." They do not have spring feet. Yet this is read as *lo,* the possessive, "to have." They do have little feet. What does this mean? Simply stated, for the species to be kosher, they have to have spring feet. I daresay you must be a people who are capable of leaping forward, not just crawling, not begging, not being one who crawls on his hands or crawls on all fours. That, the Torah tells us, is a species of *tamei,* unfit.

We must be a people who move forward, achieve and create, leap at opportunities for Torah and Judaism. The survival of the Jewish people comes from the spirit and energies of a Rabbi Akiva, and a Bar Kokhba, not passivists but gallant, heroic activists. Crawling is despicable. Indeed, that is what the enemies of Judaism want and demand. They demanded it from the court Jews in Spain and in Russia. And that "court Jew" Caspar Weinberger demands it today. But we will not have it anymore. Our mannerisms may not be proper or predictable, but we are not going to crawl when it comes to intervening on behalf of our dignity. We are not going to crawl or hide when it comes to defending Jewish honor or values.

Kol ha-kavod Operation Thunderbolt-Entebbe.

Kol ha-kavod General Ariel Sharon for standing up to *Time* magazine and making it apologize. You were defending Jewish honor and dignity.

Kol ha-kavod Operation Moses, the rescue of Ethiopian Jewry.

Kol ha-kavod, my friend, Prime Minister Menachem Begin for not meeting with smiling former President Jimmy Carter when he came to Jerusalem this past March. You were defending Jewish truth and honor.

And I submit we have not as yet heard the end of the Jonathan Pollard case and the excessive punishment he received, thanks to the work of Secretary of Defense Caspar Weinberger.

Now all eyes are focused on Jerusalem. All eyes are focused on the trial of John Demjanjuk, known as Ivan the Terrible. There are many reasons why the trial is taking place in Jerusalem today. The most obvious is that an accused killer should be brought to justice. However, I think there is something which transcends the trial. What we are witnessing in Jerusalem is Jewish sovereignty and Jewish pride in that sovereignty. We are not crawling. We are standing on our own two feet. The trial is being conducted in Hebrew, in the free, open court of a free Jewish people in their own homeland and sovereign state. The Israeli flag stands in that courtroom with dignity.

What we are witnessing and what the world is witnessing is *lo* with an *alef*, no nonsense. We have, thank God, removed the sackcloth of the Shoah and are wearing, as Mordecai did, *bigdei malkhut,* garments of royalty. Mordecai was the first to teach us not to crawl, not to bend the knee, and that is what is so important about what is taking place in Jerusalem these days.

I pledge a mission for the next generation, for children of the survivors to pledge that crawling is over for the Jewish people.

Finally, the third time the word *lo,* "no," is substituted for the word *lo,* meaning "to have," is in the last portion of the Book of Leviticus. The Torah discusses the laws of real estate and says: "And the house which a person owns in a city in Israel which has a wall around it, that house remains with the original owner and returns to the original owner and can never be sold to someone else forever."

Thirty-nine years ago this week, the Children of Israel came back and said, "That house, that house and the other house, which were empty and deserted for two thousand years, are ours. There is a wall, a solid wall—both physical and spiritual—which protects our rights to the land, and no one can take it, no one will take it from us again. We will never be divested of our sacred real estate. On the walls of Jerusalem, I have appointed watchmen. The martyrs, the *kedoshim* of the Holocaust are our *shomrim,* our guardians and watchmen. Every night their souls leave the smokestacks of the fiery ovens of the Holocaust, and they travel. They come from Poland, Hungary, Czechoslovakia, Germany, Russia, Rumania, Slovakia. These *neshamot,* these souls, come from Terezin, Buchenwald, Bergen-Belsen, Treblinka, Mathausen, Auschwitz, and they enter the watchtowers."

About a month ago, the Yiddish newspaper *Der Allgemeiner Journal* carried a story about a wedding which took place in Israel, in a community called Kiryat Tsanz. Thirty thousand people gathered to celebrate the wedding of a Hasidic rebbe's young daughter, the Klausenberger Rebbe's daughter, to her young man, Eliezer Shapiro. People from all over the world, Hasidim of Klausenberg, came to celebrate this great simḥah.

Well, weddings are, of course, nice and important, and I suppose thirty thousand people is an impressive number of guests, but why am I telling you this? Because during the Holocaust that same rebbe, as a young man, lost a wife and eleven children. Yes, eleven children. He came to the United States wearing sackcloth and ashes. And then he went on to Israel to rebuild his life, to find his physical and spiritual house. He vowed to rebuild his life and start all over again. Indeed, Kiryat Tsanz and the Laniado Hospital in Netanyah, Israel, stand as testimony, "I have returned to reclaim my house." *Lo homo*—"to him belongs the wall."

Who was the first Jew to recover after a tragic death? It was Abraham. He had just returned from Mount Moriah, where he had taken his son, Isaac, to what would have been the first Holocaust, the first act of *Kiddush ha-Shem,* a test of faith. Abraham returned from the mountain and heard that his beloved Sarah had passed away. He was overtaken by grief. His loyal companion and partner in God's special mission, to bring the people closer to God, was gone. He was bereft, crushed, downcast.

He went to the people of Heth to purchase a burial plot. The Canaanite tribe saw in Abraham a broken-hearted man who would now surely give up his newly founded religion and his faith in a God whom he could not see, feel, or touch, and become one of them. They, in fact, told him to assimilate, to give up his Judaism, to become one of them. "You are a prince amongst us," they said.

At this point, the Torah tells us, *va-yakam Avraham.* "Abraham arises," he gets up, he recovers from the face of his beloved, deceased Sarah.

"Oh, no," he said to the people of Heth. The word *va-yakam* means more than "get up," it means "established"—to be uplifted, to grow spiritually. He drew strength from inner resources, from the depths of anguish and depression. "I must continue Sarah's dream and mission. I must do it for Sarah's sake." (Oh, what about the Sarahs! As the Rivkilays, the Rocheles, in Poland, Hungary!) "I must find a burial place for her and then find a wife suited for our Isaac, so that Sarah's Sabbath candles will once again cast a glow of faith for our people."

The torch would be passed. Abraham purchased a *kever,* a grave in the land of Israel, because at that very moment he realized that the same three letters, *kaf-vet-resh,* spelled out two other important words. They spelled out *boker,* "morning"—a new dawn, a new beginning. And *kaf-vet-resh* also spelled out *karaiv.*

Yes, Abraham teaches us recovery from *Kiddush ha-Shem,* to go from *gevurah* to *gevurah,* from strength to strength. Six milion Jews did not, *ḥas ve-ḥalilah,* die in vain. They created a new world for Judaism. They gave us *aḥuzat erez,* a piece of the land, the Holy Land. They gave us *boker.* They created a "new dawn" for us. They, yes, they gave us *karaiv.* They brought us closer to God.

They created a new agenda for Jews all over the world. A recovery of self-esteem and pride. And we will educate others as to who we are. Yes, there was the horrible, horrible Holocaust, and why it happened we will never, never know, but it was followed by a mandate to recover, to return, and, indeed, that is what is taking place throughout the world today.

Judaism teaches that there is but one road to recovery, and that is to assert your pride in your Judaism, to strengthen your commitment to the practice of your faith, to sing Ani Ma'amin, "I Believe," I believe in the coming of the Messiah. To sing it in Auschwitz and in Treblinka. To sing it on the displaced-persons ships going to Israel in 1947. To sing it while building kibbutzim in the arid desert of the Israeli Negev. To sing it while building the beautiful high-rises in Jerusalem. To sing it on Passover night with your children at your Seder table in Columbus, Ohio.

A song of recovery. A song of the Renaissance of Judaism.

Why are we here tonight? Because God in His infinite wisdom gave us a mandate to change the word *lo* with an *alef,* which means "no," to *lo* with a *vav,* which means to "have."

Yes, for every one of us in Columbus, Ohio, to know that we owe the *kedoshim,* the sainted victims of the Holocaust, three sacred pledges.

One, we must speak out when Jewish life and pride hang in the balance or we will become a partner to the crime.

Two, we must have spring feet, lift ourselves up, and stand on our own two feet. We must not crawl, but we must create, achieve, build a better Jewish world for all mankind. We must create more Torah institutions, to improve the quality of Jewish life by allowing us to become more knowledgeable Jews, to be learning Jews, not yearning Jews.

And finally; we must understand that Jerusalem and all of Israel is not for sale. It is not negotiable. It cannot be bartered. It is a walled city for eternity. There are souls, *neshamot,* guarding that city and that country. Those souls come from the battlefields of six Israeli wars. They form the wall, and the State of Israel and Jerusalem are ours, forever and ever.

May the world listen. May its people know that there will never again be lampshades made from human skin, nor soap made from human fat.

We are a people who pledge here, tonight, to reaffirm our love of God and our love of each other, because we are one people, and just as we say Shema Yisrael—we believe that our God is one—our hearts are also one. We are one.

Thank you for the privilege of sharing this evening with you.

This Week and Last Week:
Reflections on the Fortieth Yom ha-Aẓma'ut

Rabbi Haskel Lookstein

I

One can understand Yom ha-Aẓma'ut best only from the perspective of Yom ha-Shoah. The greatness of the establishment of Israel becomes even more apparent and more miraculous when one compares it with the greatest modern tragedy of our people.

It is not simply a contemporary coincidence on the Jewish calendar which schedules Yom ha-Aẓma'ut and Yom ha-Shoah one week apart. It is not exclusively an historical phenomenon which we commemorate when we observe the anniversary of the rebirth of Jewish nationhood, which came three years after the conclusion of the annihilation of six million Jews. The linkage of Yom ha-Aẓma'ut and Yom ha-Shoah is, in reality, a basic principle of Jewish thought and halakhah.

Purim, for example, is made more meaningful by virtue of the fact that it follows Ta'anit Esther. The celebration is enhanced by reliving the anxiety and struggle that are commemorated by the fast on the day before.

When we celebrate the liberation from Egyptian slavery, Jewish tradition requires us to begin the story of the Exodus with a description of the horrors of slavery. *Mathil bi-genut u-mesayeim be-shevah.* Because we describe the pain and suffering, the bitterness and the tears of slavery, "therefore we are obligated to thank and praise God, who has liberated us from slavery to freedom, from sadness to joy, from bondage to redemption, and from mourning to festivity."

When a Jew brings his first fruits to the Temple in Jerusalem, he is required to verbalize the humble beginnings of our people and the process from a time when we were wandering Arameans to the moment when we celebrate the harvest in a land flowing with milk and honey.

II

Let us, therefore, pause for a moment on Israel Independence Day and consider some of the changes and transformations that have taken place in our lives from the 1940s to the 1980s.

First, it is clear that we have gone from a situation of abject powerlessness to a status where one of our greatest problems is how to use power effectively. Forty-five years ago Jews were marched out of a town into the fields, ordered to dig a large trench and to remove all of their clothes. Then, standing at the edge of the trench, they were shot and they fell into the graves which they had dug for themselves. There is no greater powerlessness than that.

Today, our major problem is how to harness our power in order to achieve national goals. We have to decide when to use rubber bullets and when to fire live ammunition. The decisions about when to shoot at women and children who are throwing rocks and Molotov cocktails are not easy to make, anymore than it was easy to decide in 1982 whether to invade Beirut or to remain on the outskirts of the city. These are agonizing decisions, but thank God we have to make *them* rather than the ones we faced during the Holocaust.

We also have new political power that we did not have in the 1940s. On October 6, 1943, a group of five hundred rabbis came to Washington to petition President Roosevelt personally to establish a government agency to rescue Jews from the horror of the Holocaust. Those rabbis never got to see the President. But now we know that the decision of the President not to meet the group was supported by a Jew who should have known better. Listen to an excerpt from the diary of a White House aide who happened to be present on that fateful day.

> October 6, Wednesday, 1943. . . . A delegation of several hundred Jewish rabbis sought to present [Roosevelt] a petition to deliver the Jews from persecution in Europe, and to open Palestine and all the United Nations to them. The President told us in his bedroom this morning he would not see their delegation; told McIntyre to receive it. McIntyre said he would see four only—out of five hundred. Judge Rosenman, who with Pa Watson also was in the bedroom, said the group behind this petition was not representative of the most thoughtful elements in Jewry. Judge Rosenman said he tried— admittedly without success—to keep the horde from storming Washington. Said the leading Jews of his acquaintance opposed this march on the Capital.[1]

Today, thank God, we have another kind of posture when we face a President of the United States. We all remember how Elie Wiesel spoke to President Reagan during the Bitburg crisis. Both on national television and during a private meeting, he and Peggy Tishman and Malcolm Hoenlein told the President exactly what the President had to hear even if he didn't want to hear it: "Your place, Mr. President, is not over there with the killers, but here with the victims."

III

If we have gone from a state of powerlessness to one of power, we have also moved from cowardice to courage. Fifty years ago, on November 13, 1938, three days after Kristallnacht, as the headlines of newspapers all over the country screamed the news of Jewish suffering and tragedy in Germany, the General Jewish Council— that day's equivalent of the Presidents' Conference—met to decide how American Jews should respond to this terrible crisis. After some hours of debate, the Council reached the following conclusion: "Resolved that it is the present sense of the General Jewish Council that there should be no parades, public demonstrations or protests by Jews."[2]

Contrast that position of fear and trembling with the parade that was held on Fifth Avenue last Sunday. Schoolchildren by the tens of thousands marched up the Avenue, cheered by hundreds of thousands who lined the parade route, all of us proclaiming the glory of being Jewish and loving Israel. What a transformation!

It was not always this way. In the 1930s and 1940s we did not wear a *kippah serugah* outdoors. The slogan of the day was, "A yarmulka is an indoor garment." When we carried Jewish books outside, we carried them in such a way that the title which proclaimed their Jewishness was held inward, toward our bodies, rather than outward where people might see. We were frightened in those days and very reticent about our Jewishness. We walked around like question marks, bowed and cowed. Today, after the great achievements of Israel in gathering the remnants of the persecuted, absorbing all of the Jews from Arab lands, attracting Soviet Jews, and building a modern Jewish state, we walk around like exclamation points, proud of who we are and what we are.

Nineteen forty-eight, 1956, 1967, and other important dates have made a difference. The renaissance of Soviet Jewry has had an impact on *us*. If they can publicly proclaim their Jewishness in the streets of Moscow, Leningrad, and Kiev, surely we can do no less in the free and open society of America. I recall in the early seventies leading a group of Ramaz students down Fifth Avenue on Solidarity Sunday and passing a church which was letting out its worshippers at noon. Suddenly I heard fourth-, fifth-, and sixth-graders from our school begin to shout: "We are Jews; we couldn't be prouder; and if you don't like it we'll yell a little louder! We are Jews . . ." They kept repeating the statement. All I could think of was how different it was during the days when I grew up in an anti-Semitic Yorkville where we would never have dared to think such words, let alone proclaim them publicly.

Today we have moved from an understandable cowardice to an exhilarating courage. We are no longer question marks; we are exclamation points!

IV

Finally, we have also moved from hopelessness to faith. After the Holocaust we were all depressed, desolate, destroyed spiritually. There seemed to be no hope in the world, no future to Judaism, no way out of our misery.

My revered teacher, Rabbi Joseph B. Soloveitchik, once asked why we were privileged to be the generation that moved from servitude to freedom and from exile to redemption. Weren't there many more worthy generations than ours which would have merited the glorious gift of Jewish independence in our Holy Land? He answered: "We didn't get Israel because we deserved it; we got Israel because we needed it!" Had Israel not been reborn out of the ashes of the Holocaust, Judaism and the Jewish people, as we know them, might not have survived. It was finally God who helped us to transform hopelessness into faith.

V

We look back, therefore, and we are able to say with the psalmist: "I thank You because You have answered me; You have been my salvation." The stone which the builders disdained became the cornerstone of a new Jewish existence. The DP's, the Jews from Arab lands, and the Soviet Jewish assimilationists all became the foundation of a glorious people reborn in its land. Surely this is the work of God; it is miraculous in our eyes, and therefore: "This is the day the Lord hath made, let us be joyous and happy in it."

Do we have problems? Certainly we do. Do we have enemies? Of course we have. But today, as opposed to yesterday, we stand together, we stand with courage, we stand with faith, and we pray together: "Please God, save us."

And now we know that salvation will come. It will come from our brothers and sisters in Israel. It will come from you and me and from all American Jewry. And, from the perspective of the last forty years, we know it will come because God wants it to come.

NOTES

1. Haskel Lookstein, *Were We Our Brothers' Keepers: The Public Response of American Jews to the Holocaust, 1938–1944* (New York: Vintage Books), pp. 165–166.

2. Ibid., p. 59.

Holocaust: From the Perspective of a Native American

RABBI MARK KUNIS

When I was asked to contribute my thoughts on the Holocaust, I at first declined and only later accepted the task, but with some reluctance. After all, I am not a survivor or even a child of a survivor of the Holocaust. In fact, I was born after this dreadful experience had ended. What light could I shine upon an event from which I was so totally removed?

But at the time I was also busy with my preparations for the Passover holiday, and a striking phrase from the Haggadah kept ringing in my ears: "In every generation each individual is bound to regard himself as if he had personally gone forth from Egypt." And the thought suddenly struck me that since the rise of Hitler in 1933, in every generation each individual Jew *must* regard himself as if he had personally experienced the terror of Auschwitz and the horrors of Treblinka. The fate of every Jew is inextricably bound up with the fate of every other Jew. So although I did not physically experience this most awesome devastation of a people on the face of the earth, it nevertheless still holds for me deep and profound meaning. And perhaps, and I emphasize "perhaps," because my eyes did not witness the ovens of Dachau, there is something significant I can contribute to the perspective of the Holocaust.

Since 1976, everyone seems to have caught Bicentennial fever. We celebrated the Bicentennial of our Independence in 1976 and the Bicentennial of the Constitution in 1987. In 1989 we will have the Bicentennial of the Presidency and Congress; and in 1991 the Bill of Rights.

It was two hundred years ago that our country recognized that it could no longer bear the domination of its mother country, England. With most of its citizens recent immigrants or products of immigrants, the United States was founded as a haven for the oppressed under the principles of freedom and justice.

In the 1970s, with the collapse of South Vietnam, our country once more reaffirmed its commitment of those principles. Although we were in the midst of the worst recession in half a century, with severe inflation and almost ten percent of our population unemployed, we warmly opened our arms to over 127,000 Vietnamese refugees. Congress promptly appropriated $405 million to transport, feed, house, and resettle them. Among the refugees were a few thousand illiterate peasants and fishermen who were in no physical danger, but seized the opportunity to come to this legendary land of opportunity they had heard so much about. Also included were a number of prostitutes, black marketers, corrupt officials, and army officers. But they all worked hard and have flourished, becoming, on the whole, good citizens.

As an officer on one of the rescue ships stated: "You just have to understand what the skipper of one of our ships out there does when he looks down from the bridge and sees all the outstretched hands reaching up to him. He doesn't ask whether the people were heroes or cowards, whether they were rich or poor, even whether they were for or against us. He's only got one choice, actually."

And actually, this is our American tradition. George Washington admonished his countrymen "humbly and fervently to beseech the kind Author of these blessings . . . to render this country more and more a safe and propitious asylum for the unfortunate of other countries."

And Thomas Jefferson in 1801 asked: "Shall we refuse the unhappy fugitives from distress that hospitality which the savages of the wilderness extended to our forefathers in this land? Shall oppressed humanity find no asylum on this globe?"

In the annals of time, two hundred years is a very brief span, yet in these two centuries we have become the greatest and most prosperous nation on earth. And this greatness was in no small way achieved by the blending of diverse nationalities in our melting pot. Even after the introduction of restrictive immigration laws, we still relaxed those restrictions in time of crisis. When the Russians stormed into Hungary in 1956, thousands fled west. Of these refugees, forty thousand were welcomed into the United States. Following the Bay of Pigs fiasco during President Kennedy's administration, and in more recent years, Cubans came over in large numbers.

There was only one ugly chapter in American history where this great land of ours failed to extend its hand to those seeking asylum and refuge. The leading character in this chapter was the Jew caught up in the tragic decade between 1933 and 1943.

Many of us are under the mistaken impression that with the rise of Hitler to power in Germany, none of the German Jews took him seriously enough to flee before they were taken to the ovens. In fact, thousands upon thousands of Jews in all countries threatened by Hitler did make application through our American consuls for visas to come to the United States. And often, obtaining a visa was not only time-consuming, but extremely dangerous. Frequently, the long lines of people outside the consulates would be attacked by storm-troopers and beaten, or herded into trucks for shipment to concentration camps. Once inside the consulate there still was no guarantee, for unlike the penniless Vietnamese, Cubans, and Hungarians, the vast majority were denied visas because, in the official words of the U.S. State Department, they were "likely to become a public charge." Doctors, lawyers, professors, businessmen, some with wealthy relatives in the United States willing to pledge their support, were denied because they were likely to become public charges. In addition, any record of arrest by the German police was enough evidence to reject one's application for a visa. The following statement by C. Paul Fletcher of the Visa Division in Washington, where he complained about the difficulty in obtaining German police records, is indicative of the attitude of our State Department: "The statement relative to the unavailabil-

ity in Germany of complete police records, strengthens the conten-
tion that the United States is being made the dumping ground for
criminals."

Criminals? These weren't criminals. They were merely human
beings trying to escape the horrors they saw before them. But they
were Jews, and so, for some, it was easy to see them as criminals.

Those specific opportunities for rescue were ignored by our
government are now a matter of record, and are rapidly becoming
public knowledge due to documented works like Arthur Morse's
While Six Million Died. But the fact remains that between the years
1933 and 1943, over one million places on the United States immigrant quotas went unfilled. One million places that might have
saved one million lives without any real effort.

Let me just bring to your attention one brief incident that will
forever remain a stain on the image of mankind.

On May 13, 1939, the Hamburg-American Line's luxurious *St.
Louis* sailed from Germany with 936 passengers. They were bound
for Havana, Cuba—930 of them Jewish refugees, among the last to
escape from the Nazis' narrowing vise. Inscribed on each passport
was a red *J* and in each mind the memory of six years of ever-
increasing terror.

Each refugee had managed to scrape together $262 for passage,
plus $81 as a guarantee for return fare in the event Cuba would not
accept them. But this, they were assured, was but a mere formality,
since they had purchased in good faith what they considered to be
legitimate visas.

The documents, however, turned out to be merely landing permits.
Colonel Manuel Benites, director of Cuban Immigration, sold over
four thousand of these permits on Cuban government stationery,
with appropriate seals, at $150 each, thereby amassing a personal
fortune.

For 734 of the refugees, Cuba was to be but a temporary sanctuary, a way station en route to their future home—the United
States. They had fulfilled the U.S. immigration requirements,
completed all the forms, and now held quota numbers which would
permit them to enter the United States from three months to three

years after their arrival in Cuba. Since the refugees could not get into the United States immediately, the Cuban landing certificates were literal life-savers.

Or so it seemed. Colonel Benites, who had sold the landing certificates, had failed to share his profits with Cuban President Bru or the Army chief of staff, Batista, and suddenly the landing certificates were no longer valid. The Joint Distribution Committee, the major Jewish relief organization, negotiated with the Cuban government—but to no avail. It seemed that the only hope for these 930 Jews was the United States, the land of freedom and opportunity.

When the negotiations were completed, the captain of the St. Louis sailed past Miami to give the passengers a brief look at their future home. The U.S. Coast Guard quickly dispatched a cutter to follow the ship and prevent any refugees from jumping overboard and swimming ashore.

Unfortunately, President Roosevelt was so concerned with the oncoming election for an unprecedented third term that he sought to pacify those southern senators and "patriotic" groups stirred up by the Nazi propaganda. He calmed concerned Jews with vague promises and appointed committees with incompetent chairmen or with individuals not overly sympathetic to the Jews. The word out of Washington to the Joint Distribution Committee was that there would be no compromise with the immigration laws—even for those who already possesed U.S. immigration numbers. The St. Louis changed course back toward Europe. The fate of its passengers, despite all efforts, would remain intertwined with that of the rest of European Jewry.

Hitler lost no time in making sport of America's response to the St. Louis. It was only one of the many indications that his treatment of the Jews would not expose Germany to the wrath of the United States. The August 1939 issue of Der Weltkampf commented as follows: "We are saying openly that we do not want the Jews, while the democracies keep on claiming that they are willing to receive them—and then leave the guests out in the cold! Aren't we savages better men after all?"

Emma Lazarus would have rolled over in her grave had she

known that her fellow Jews would be turned away while her poem, enshrined forever in bronze at the base of the Statue of Liberty read:

> ... Give me your tired, your poor,
> Your huddled masses yearning to breathe free,
> The wretched refuse of your teeming shore.

Many of us are still perplexed at the implications of the Holocaust. Some of us question God's Judgment in allowing the destruction of six million Jews along with many more millions of non-Jews. Others just can never understand why rabbis and lay leaders keep bringing up something that happened over forty years ago. Look to the future and to the State of Israel, they say. Just speak to any Hebrew school principal and ask him how many times parents complain that the Holocaust, with its horrors and atrocities, is not the sort of material they want for their children.

What is the answer to the questions raised by the Holocaust? Why bother rehashing what is now past history? Simply because the fundamental question of the Holocaust is not "Where was God?" Many ask how God, who is all-merciful, compassionate, and omnipotent, could allow six million of His chosen people to perish in such a cruel and violent manner. The problem, posed in absolute terms, becomes unanswerable when we read God's governance of the world in absolute terms, as though He alone directed the panorama of events. But Jewish tradition has always reminded us that when God created the world He willed to "shrink" His own domain, and admit man as His partner and coworker in the drama of life. To make this partnership real, man had to be given a zone of sovereignty where he could act freely in accordance with his own vision of the good. This was a perilous gift God gave man, for he so often uses his freedom arbitrarily, selfishly, unwisely, bringing untold suffering on himself no less than on others.

Why did God endow man with this dangerous gift? He did so in accordance with the design of creation, to bring into being a creature who would grow in wisdom and in goodness, and choose the right course, in acts of voluntary decision. God, in this respect, acted like a parent who permits his child to cross the street on his own, or to make other grave decisions on his own. The child may injure himself by being left on his own, but this is a necessary price a parent pays to permit his child to grow toward maturity.

So the fundamental question posed by the Holocaust is not "Where was God?" but "Where was man?" Where was our government when the passengers of the *St. Louis* cried out for help, as did the Vietnamese, the Cubans, and the Hungarians? Why did we permit our government to maintain its overtly anti-Semitic State Department under Secretary of State Cordell Hull and Assistant Secretary Breckinridge Long in the face of political expediency? Why did we allow, along with England, France, and the rest of the world, countless opportunities for rescue to slip through our hands and thereby encourage Hitler to proceed further? Why was the Red Cross, the international agency for relief, silent in the face of atrocity? Why was the Vatican silent?

No, my friends, the question is not "Where was God?" But "Where was man?"

Why remember the Holocaust? We remember the Holocaust so that we can take a good look at ourselves, and remember how low the level of human dignity can sink. We remember the Holocaust because, for the majority of the victims, there is no one to recite Kaddish. We remember the Holocaust because we see how misused this term and the term "genocide" have become in our everyday speech; how President Reagan could belittle human sensitivity and honor the S.S. with his visit to Bitburg; how Pope John Paul II could herald the process of denying that the Jews were special victims of the Holocaust with the beautification of Edith Stein, his audience with Kurt Waldheim, and the construction of a monastery on Jewish graves at Sorbibor and a convent at Auschwitz. We remember the Holocaust because it is important for all Jews to share in memory. And finally we remember the Holocaust because the power of remembrance is a power for good.

When two members of Milwaukee's Nazi Party were brought to trial for ambushing a local Jewish leader, the lawyers involved had little trouble in selecting an impartial jury. Of the twenty-three people asked if they were aware of the bitter enmity between Nazis and Jews, none referred to World War II or any of its horrors. One woman stated: "I've heard of Nazis, but I don't listen to the news that much." Another said that she knew Nazism as a dictatorship, but she "really couldn't say more about it."

The *Jewish Post and Opinion* once reported a survey of New Orleans teenagers—much the same as our children. The majority of the teenagers polled indicated that they would not be concerned at all if Israel were destroyed by the Arabs.

Do we take the chance that forty years hence our children might say to their children, as many of our parents did to us, that "We didn't know?"

If we have learned anything from the Holocaust, we have learned to take our enemies at their word. That when Hitler threatened to exterminate the Jews, he meant it. And now when Arafat and his ilk threaten to exterminate Israel, they mean it.

Yes, we are all children of Auschwitz. But to be a child of Auschwitz does not mean to be cast into perpetual grief. Not, at least, for those of us who were not there. Nelly Sachs, a survivor and Nobel laureate, wrote a poem whose first line tears its readers apart: "We are gardeners who have no flowers." She wrote that in her anguish, in her solitude.

But the overwhelming testimony of our behavior since those days in the Kingdom of Darkness refutes Nelly Sachs. Are the people of Israel not our flowers? Are the Jews of Russia who defy the KGB by applying for emigration and learning Hebrew and Torah not our flowers? Are our own children, alive, not our flowers? Are we not even, some of the time, gardeners to our own souls?

To understand the past, you have to know the future. The future of the Jewish people after the Holocaust was not to become paralyzed with perpetual grief. The future of the Jewish people was to build the State of Israel and to procreate, to found schools, and to write books, and yes, to laugh, to plant and to worship God. We are not victims because the Jewish soul refuses to become a victim. We are survivors!

Jews are gardeners, and we have flowers in abundance, Nelly Sachs notwithstanding. Gardening is, in fact, one of the things we know how to do with uncommon skill. We have made contributions to mankind far beyond our numbers with our scholars, our scientists, our doctors, our businessmen, our authors, our artists, our composers, and on and on. But the thing we know best, and do best, is planting, gardening. We plant with heavy hearts, even broken hearts. Our hearts are broken not only by memory, but also by the knowledge that comes with our collective memory that the world will almost surely try to trample that which we have planted before it can be harvested. But we plant on, because as surely as we know of cruelty and evil, we know also of redemption. We, who are not more than the remnant of a remnant, we know that we will outlast them, for as the psalmist teaches: "They who plant in sorrow shall surely reap in joy." And in the meantime, we go about our business, which for the Jew is life and its sanctification. And that, for me, a native American, is the lesson of the Holocaust.

Faith and Doubt

RABBI BERTRAM LEFF

Rosh ha-Shanah is designated in our prayers as the birthday of the world. Rabbi Levi Yitzchak of Berdichev, in his magnum opus, *Kedushat Levi,* presents a very significant analysis of this concept. There is a controversy in the tractate Rosh ha-Shanah 10b as to when the world was created. "Rabbi Eliezer says: In Tishrei the world was created; Rabbi Joshua says: In Nisan the world was created."

Rabbi Levi Yitzchak indicates that there is no conflict between Rabbi Eliezer and Rabbi Joshua; rather, each opinion delineates a different relationship with God.

Nisan symbolizes the straight path to God, for the month of Nisan is also known as Aviv. The letters of Aviv are *alef* and *bet,* the first two letters of the Hebrew alphabet, followed by a *yud,* symbolizing God. Thus, Aviv—that is to say, Nisan—represents the "straight" commitment to God and His teachings.

Tishrei, on the other hand, symbolizes our return to God—our repentance and teshuvah. The name Tishrei is formed by writing the last three letters of the Hebrew alphabet in reverse order, symbolizing our stepping backwards toward God, the *yud* in Tishrei, marking our return after repenting for our sins. Thus it is understandable that Rosh ha-Shanah should occur on the first of Tishrei, marking our return and coming back to God.

However, we are left with one problematic letter, the last letter of Aviv—the *bet.* What does this letter tell us about the human condition?

I maintain that the last letter of Aviv conveys the message that our Aviv relationship with God is not always straight. There are

255

times of religious crisis, when there are more questions than faith in the justice of God in His encounter with His creations. There are times when doubt overwhelms faith.

The Holocaust will always be that event in Jewish history which overwhelms the faith of the most pious Jew, creating legitimate doubt in the soul of Man. However, doubt is not heresy but an inevitable result of the human condition.

When does genuine doubt and the crisis of faith become heresy? Only when we allow our doubts to destroy our everyday religious life and practice, our commitment to the Torah of Sinai.

Elie Wiesel's writings on the Holocaust illustrate the tension between faith and doubt.

In Wiesel's first book, *Night* we encounter the Hasid of Vishnitz, Akiba Drumer. The presence of this devout Jew gave the inmates of Auschwitz a spiritual uplift. His deep and solemn voice "would break our hearts" as he sang Hasidic melodies in the "night" of Auschwitz. Akiba Drumer was a man of faith. He said, "God is testing us. He wants to find out whether we can dominate our base instincts and kill the Satan within us. We have no right to despair. And if He punishes us relentlessly, it's a sign that He loves us all the more." In Auschwitz, it was good to know that one person among them still had faith in God and hope for the future.

But the hell of Auschwitz was too much even for the pious Hasid of Vishnitz, Akiba Drumer. Doubts began to intrude and cracks began to form in his faith. "He had lost his reason for struggling." When the selection came all he asked of us was . . . "In three days, I shall no longer be here. . . Say the Kaddish for me." Did Akiba Drumer lose his faith in the "night" of the Holocaust? Emphatically, NO!

Did Akiba Drumer's aleph—beth—Aviv—relationship with God encounter the beth of doubt and crisis? Yes. Not heresy, but the legitimate struggle for understanding God's ways. Questions, doubts, religious crisis, all are a legitimate result of the Holocaust. The last words of Akiba Drumer were, "Say the Kaddish for me," reflecting his faith in the midst of doubt, voicing his commitment to Judaism even in the night of Auschwitz.

Elie Wiesel replicates Akiba Drumer's experience of faith and doubt in "The Death of My Father," an essay included in his *Legends of our Time,* published ten years after *Night.* Wiesel describes his thoughts on the day before the Yahrzeit of his father, who perished in the fire of the Holocaust. The death of his father in Buchenwald reminds Elie Wiesel of a deeply religious man "who on the Day of Atonement, in despair took Heaven to task, crying out like a wounded beast. 'What do you want from me, God? What have I done to you? I want to serve you and crown you ruler of the universe, but you prevent me. I want to sing of your mercy, and you ridicule me. I want to place my faith in you, dedicate my thoughts to you, and you do not let me. Why? Why?'"

Wiesel declares his crisis of faith, his accusations, and his doubts. "Perhaps someday someone will explain how, on the level of man, Auschwitz was possible; but on the level of God, it will forever remain the most disturbing of mysteries."

Wiesel's commitment to Judaism is maintained. "All things considered, I think that tomorrow I shall go to the synagogue after all. I will light the candles, I will say Kaddish, and it will be for me a further proof of my impotence."

Faith and doubt—a legitimate response to the Holocaust.

Our teacher, Rav Joseph B. Soloveitchik, taught us about the tension between faith and doubt when he wrote in his magnum opus, *Halachic Man.* "Out of the straits have I called, O Lord" (Psalm 118). "Out of the depths I have called unto Thee, O Lord" (Psalm 130). Out of the straits of inner oppositions and incongruities, spiritual doubts and uncertainties, out of the depth of a psyche rent with antinomies and contradictions, out of the bottomless pit of a soul that struggles with its own torments I have called, I have called unto Thee, O Lord.

Rav Soloveitchik, Elie Wiesel, and the Vishnitzer Ḥasid, Akiba Drumer, understood R. Levi Yitzchak's Aviv relationship with God;

the straight path of faith—of the *alef,* the *bet,* and the *yud* that encounters the *bet* of doubt and crisis.

Is not this Aviv relationship the essence of Rabbi Levi Yitzchak of Berdichev's song "A Din Toyrah mit Got"? Rabbi Levi Yitzchak of Berdichev, son of Sarah, wishes to bring God to judgment; to stand before the Almighty and ask: "What do You have against Thy people, Israel?"

He refuses to stir from his place "until an end is made to the sufferings of Israel." With a sense of crisis and doubt, Levi Yitzchak questions the justice of God. But then the song concludes with a declaration of faith in God, with the words of the Kaddish: "Magnified and sanctified be the Name of God."

Akiba Drumer did not lose his faith in Auschwitz. Elie Wiesel did not stray from the teachings of his martyred father. Levi Yitzchak of Berdichev brought God to judgment, but in the end sanctified the Name of God. Rabbi Soloveitchik taught us the legitimacy of spiritual doubt and uncertainty. All encountered the mystery of suffering—the Holocaust, but all emerged out of doubt with the faith of the Kaddish.

Holocaust Commemoration

Rabbi Stanley M. Wagner

In 1943, when there could no longer remain any illusions about the devastating tragedy which was enveloping Europe, a courageous Labor Zionist leader by the name of Chayim Greenberg wrote, in the *Yiddisher Kemfer,* a condemnation of American Jewry which is not only worthy of repetition, but which, I believe, is of signal import even today. He said:

> The time has come, perhaps, when the few Jewish communities remaining in the world which are still free to make their voices heard and to pray in public should proclaim a day of fasting and prayer for *American Jews.* No—this is not a misprint. I mean specifically that a day of prayer and fasting should be proclaimed for the five million Jews now living in the United States. They live under the protection of a mighty republic governed by democratic laws. They move about freely through the length and breadth of the land. The vast majority of them have enough food to eat, clothes to wear, and roofs over their heads. And if any wrong is committed against them, they are free to protest and to demand their rights. *Nevertheless, they deserve to be prayed for.* They are not even aware what a misfortune has befallen them, and if they were to look at themselves with seeing eyes, they would realize with shock how intolerable this misfortune is. This misfortune consists of the vacuity, the hardness, and the dullness that has overcome them; it consists in a kind of epidemic inability to suffer or to feel compassion. In pathological fear of pain, in terrifying lack of imagination, a horny shell seems to have formed over the soul of American Jewry to protect and defend it against pain and pity. At a time when the American Jewish community is the largest and most influential in the world, at at time when the eyes of millions of Jews in Europe who are daily threatened with the most terrible and degrading forms of physical extermination are primarily turned to

American Jewry, this American Jewish community has fallen lower than perhaps any other in recent times, and displays an unbelievable amount of highly suspect clinical health and evenness of temper. If moral bankruptcy deserves pity, and if this pity is seven-fold for one who is not even aware how shocking his bankruptcy is, then no Jewish community in the world today (not even the Jews who are now in the claws of the Nazi devourer) deserves more compassion from Heaven than does American Jewry.

My dear friends, this is a harsh and severe excoriation of the American Jewish community of the Holocaust period who, in the eyes of the author, were shamefully and painfully guilty of transgressing the commandment "Thou shalt not stand idly by the blood of thy brother." But if this commemoration is to play a meaningful role in the life of this community, then it dare not be *only* an expression of *yivada ba-goyim le-eineinu nikmat dam avadekha ha-shafukh* that the shedding of Jewish blood "be made known *only among the nations in our sight.*" We Jews have some remembering to do—what others have done to us, yes, but also what we have done to ourselves.

Reb Naḥman of Bratslav tells the story of a town that had a particular dilemma. It was suffering from a severe famine. And the only grain which was available turned those who ate it into madmen, crazy people. Were people to starve, or to eat the grain and go insane? The rabbi of the town, facing these cruel alternatives, ordained that the people should eat—that is, all but a few persons, who were charged with the perpetual responsibility of reminding the remainder of the community of their madness.

Somehow I feel that our Holocaust commemoration must include more than just a pious remembrance of the *kedoshim u-tahorim she-nehargu al kiddush ha-Shem,* of those holy and pure— our fathers and mothers, our sisters and brothers—the noblest and most glorious of our people—who died martyrs' deaths; it must include more than just a recounting of the enormity of the evil, of the abominations, of the malevolence of the Nazi beasts; it must include more than just a retracing of every nation's complicity in those extraordinary events—*their* shameful silence, their devastating paralysis, as apathetic bystanders to the most obscene undertaking in the history of mankind, genocide, the extermination of a people.

If this or any Holocaust commemoration is to have any significance, then I submit it must *also* provide *us,* especially American Jews, with an opportunity to do teshuvah, to repent. This is the moment that *we* are being called upon; herein *we* who are gathered here today are charged with the responsibility to remind the Jewish community of its madness *then*—of its spiritual poverty—of its criminal indifference, of its unbelievable supineness, of its nauseating nonchalance, in the hope that it will evoke the repentant response among all of us today. *Harei nikhlamnu u-boshnu be-ma'aseinu,* we are remorseful and embarrassed by our deeds, and *we will never ever recommit them.*

And it is the hereafter that should occupy our attention. George Santayana once said that "a people which does not profit from the lessons of history is doomed to repeat them." God forbid that there should ever be a recurrence of the Holocaust. Yet had we not been taught *before* the truism that in every generation there are oppressors, tormentors, persecutors who rise up against the Jewish people? Had we not been told that "the Lord will have war with Amalek, the *enemies* of our people, from *generation* to *generation*"; that the Lord will do *His* share to campaign against those nations who are bent on our destruction—God will "utterly blot out their remembrance"; but that accompanying the mitzvah of *zekhirah,* of being on guard, of being aware of the danger to our existence as a people by virtue of the designs of the anti-Semites of every age, is the command *Timheh,* the clear-cut and unequivocal responsibility of *self*-protection, of *self*-defense, of *our* duty to take whatever steps are necessary to preserve the integrity of Jews everywhere.

And most certainly we should have understood that when one segment of our people is being humbled, when one portion of our nation is being attacked, when our brethren in any part of the globe find their lives endangered and they become helpless victims of an inhuman, horrendous assault of maniacal proportions, we dare not countenance the stifling of the voice *Lo tishkaḥ,* "Thou shalt not forget," and action is mandatory—inaction is *criminal.*

We learned, we knew—but we forgot.

Boshnu ve-nikhlamnu—we are ashamed, we are filled with remorse. In the late 1930s and early 1940s, we forgot the lessons of Jewish history. We forgot that Hitler was Haman and Antiochus and Torquemada and Chmielnicki all rolled into one. We forgot that the Jewish people are one body, and that if one part of the body is diseased, if one part of the body is wracked with pain, then the *whole* body suffers. We forgot th fundamental principle of Jewish existence—*kol yisrael arevim zeh ba-zeh,* the people of Israel are responsible each for the other. When one Jew bleeds—it is *my* blood that flows. When one Jew is imprisoned—it is I who am behind the bars. When one Jew is attacked—then it is I who must rise to his defense.

Timḥeh—there are forms of anti-Semitism which God assumes that *we,* the Jewish people, will deal with. *Lo tishkaḥ*—we dare not forget ever again this lesson which, in an excruciating fashion, has been engraved on our consciences.

But there are those who regard our commitment to commemorate the Holocaust and perpetuate the memory of those *korbanot,* those *Olot u-zevaḥim,* those blessed souls who we sacrificed on the altar of indifference, as an obsession. There are those who cry out: "Enough—*ḥatanu*—we have sinned—*pashanu,* we have transgressed. How long shall we have to carry the burden of our guilt?"

To them I say that we must carry this burden until every Jew in Russia is permitted to live in peace and security or leave in dignity; until every Jew in Arab lands is removed from his enslavement and is no longer at the mercy of his tormentors; until the State of Israel is strong, physically and spiritually, and invulnerable to the onslaught of enemies whose highest aim in life is the slaughter of our people; until every bigot, every anti-Semite, every enemy, is crushed and no longer threatens Jewish existence.

Until that day shall Yom ha-Shoah, this Holocaust commemoration, *strengthen* our memories and sensitize us to the need for our eternal vigilance.

But I pray that we shall soon be witness to the *U-va le-ẓivyon go'el*—that moment in history when the Redeemer shall come to Zion—and a millennium of peace, harmony, and brotherhood shall be ushered in—for us and for all mankind. Amen.

Reprinted from Stanley M. Wagner, *A Piece of My Mind,* (New York, 1979), pp. 128–131.

The Parasites Among Us

Rabbi Bernhard H. Rosenberg

If someone murdered a loved one of yours, would you benevolently erase the atrocity from your mind? If the murderer still lived, would you seek to convict him or merely discover other avenues of interest to preoccupy your time?

Six million Jews were brutally murdered, yet some wish to conveniently forget. Why live in the past? The dead cannot be revived! Let us speak for the living; let us turn toward other outlets of concern.

The Nazi mentality still exists; we dare not naively believe that anti-Semitism has vanished. Hatred and bigotry are a cancer which eventually returns to haunt its innocent victims. Unless intense treatment and annual diagnostic tests occur, tragedy is inevitable.

Some naively believe that public denunciation and continued documentaries will awaken latent Nazi tendencies. Allow me to suggest the opposite. Those who truly wish to destroy the Jewish nation certainly do not need additional incentives. Like parasites, they survive at the expense of others. These cannibals of society eagerly wait to devour their prey; they feed upon fear and desperately search for defenseless scapegoats. An apathetic approach combined with the fear of retaliation merely furnishes fuel for those seeking scapegoats. Too often we dismiss the obvious in order to achieve peace of mind.

As we travel backward into the time machine of history, this truism becomes evident. The National Socialist Party declared a boycott, to begin on April 1, 1933, of all Jewish businesses in Germany. Naively, the following sentiment was expressed in the April 3rd edition of the *London Times:* "There is no spontaneous hostility to the hard-working small Jewish shop-keepers or trader." The *New York Times* reported: "There has been nothing spontaneous about this boycott any more than there is any active anti-Semitism in the German masses if they are left alone."

Eventually the press awakened to the reality of an impending nightmare. In response to Kristallnacht the *New York Times* observed: "It is assumed that the Jews, who have now lost most of their possessions and livelihood will either be thrown into the streets or put into ghettos and concentration camps or impressed into labor brigades and put to work for the Third Reich as the children of Israel were once before, for the Pharaohs." Following the atrocities of Kristallnacht, the *London Times* exclaimed: "It is not to be believed that the Nations . . . cannot find the means of assisting unwanted citizens to leave Germany and of providing the territory in which those Jews can form a liberated community and recover the right to live and prosper. There is no difficulty which a common will and common action cannot overcome."

Now we can openly admit: too little, too late! Fear and appeasement provided the Nazi Party with the subterfuge they eagerly sought. Isolationism blinded the eyes of our so-called leaders. Various pleas remained unheard and unanswered. A cable sent to Breckinridge Long, on March 26, 1943, stated: "Gravest possible news reaching London past week shows massacres now reaching catastrophic climax, particularly Poland. Also deportations of Bulgarian and Rumanian Jews already begun. European Jewry disappearing while no single organization rescue measure yet taken . . . extermination reaching peak. Urge Allied relief."

Ironically, between 1933 and 1943 there existed more than four hundred thousand vacant places in the United States based upon the United States immigration quotas of countries under Nazi domination. Yet Cordell Hull insisted: "I cannot recommend that we open the question of relaxing the provisions of our immigration laws and run the risk of a prolonged and bitter controversy in Congress on the immigration question—considering the generous quantity of refugees we have already received."

Today we cry out for our six million brethren. We lament, we shed tears of anguish. We remember those of our Christian brethren who perished at the hands of the crazed Nazi machine. We offer a prayer to God to remember the souls of those Christians who took their lives in their own hands in order to save the remnants of our flock.

Yes, today we all offer a prayer to God. Let us pray that we will always speak as a united front.

If they had only opened their eyes. If they had only seen:

• How they forced our brethren to wash the dirty boots of S.S. officers; and how they beat them after they finished.

• How savagely they raped our sisters, wives, and mothers.

• How they used our limbs for their medical experiments. After all, they were curious. What does happen when you tear a man's arm from his body?

• How Nazis loved animals, especially wild, savage animals that they kept. Our children were used to feed them. The beasts were hungry.

• How S.S. officers drowned rabbis in the urinals of the concentration camps.

• How they forced parents to stand at attention and look into the eyes of children whom they hung.

• How they carefully took aim and smashed the heads of infants against the cement, or how they tossed babies in the air in order to practice target marksmanship or in order to catch their flesh with their pointed bayonets.

• How they played catch with our Torah. How they loved to enwrap bearded Jews in the holy parchment and set it aflame.

The free world's eyes were blinded, their ears deafened.

In the *New York Times* of December 4, 1942, the headline on page 11 read: "Two Thirds of Jews in Poland held slain—only 1,250,000 said to survive of 3,500,000 once there."

Perhaps if we as a nation had spoken as one unit, our leaders would not have turned a deaf ear. The Holocaust can happen again. Ruthlessness and hatred still permeate the atmosphere. Awareness and action are our most potent and valued weapons. We dare not accept silence and inaction as our way of life.

I Am the Reminder

RABBI JACOB RUBENSTEIN

My colleague gazed at me with a mixture of anger and sadness. "It's so beautiful, and it's just not fair!" he exclaimed. Indeed, one of the most difficult things to accept was that the sun was bright and warm, the rows of birch and poplars lovely to look at, and the atmosphere serene.

It seemed frighteningly wrong that the sun should ever shine at Auschwitz or that there should be light and fauna at Treblinka. It would be fitting that the sun never shone and the grass never grew, because they are places of unutterable terror. Yet every day, from all over the world, people gravitate to the world's most grisly tourist center. Some come to see if it could really be true, or to remind themselves not to forget, or, like me, to pay homage to the dead by simply visiting their place of suffering and death.

I had already walked the streets of cities which had street signs with Jewish names, where Jewish symbols still abounded on houses and buildings, where outlines of mezuzot remained on the door-posts of homes once inhabited by Jews. People gazed from behind window curtains and partially opened doors, wondering who had returned. Stares and whispers followed our group as we walked through neighborhoods that once were replete with Jewish life.

The guides avoided difficult questions, and we avoided debates. They were not expressive on issues of Jewish life in Poland, they didn't translate everything that could be read, nor show us all that could be learned. In private, however, an aknowledgment was heard that the spirit of Poland has not been the same without the Jews. Five thousand Jews remain from the 3,250,000 of prewar Poland. Their average age is seventy-eight. Even with the conciliatory posture in Poland today, many still live incognito. They are too old to leave, too poor to care. They too are haunted by the sights of the past and the phantoms that invade their sanity.

On a memorial plaque in the Temple Synagogue of Cracow the survivors recall those who were killed by the Nazis and their collaborators (*she-nehergu al yedei ha-nazim ve-ozerehem*). We ask the head of the community to elaborate on this unique inscription, and the halting reply is, "We live well with our neighbors." We forget that after we leave she will still remain. While the guide speaks, she quietly admits seeing thirty-seven people shot in the square, then turns quickly to follow the group. She listens stoically, without emotion, as we enter the Rama's Shul and the Alte Shul where the *hakafot* on Sukkot are abbreviated in memory of a bloody pogrom, and where all jewelry is removed on the first night of Hanukkah in recollection of a massacre and plundering. It was one thing to hear of atrocities of the past, but a sobering shudder chilled us when we witnessed the defaced street monument of the Warsaw Ghetto.

We went to *kever avot*. We visited the minutely organized factory of torture and death—Auschwitz. We walked in a funeral procession and made our seven stops. Our souls felt the rip of keriah. We grieved. We noticed the absence of the word "Jew" on the signs explaining the camp to its visitors. We noticed the sculpture in the shape of a *zelem* at the entrance to the camp, and we were not too surprised when the explanatory film (Made by a Ukrainian unit of the Russian Army) mentioned the word "Jew" only once. We entered the prison chambers in the death block and noticed the whitewashing of all graffiti on the cell walls except that of a priest.

Auschwitz is sanitized and sterile, and the memory of the Jewish dead is whitewashed from its visitors. We walked the long corridors where rows of faces stare from the walls. Thousands of pictures—the photographs of prisoners. Thousands of them—Polish criminals and disagreeables—not one Jewish name. Thousands of pictures of people who knew they were going to die. Their date of entry into the camp and date of death recorded. Thousands staring at you in single framed photographs. Thousands of Polish names welcoming the compulsory school visits of Polish schoolchildren.

We observe the dungeons, the flogging post, the firing-squad wall, the sterilization block of Dr. Mengele, the mounds of human hair, the piles of brushes, pans, clothing, and shoes—remnants of our people. We stand in horror in front of the suitcases and observe that they had forgotten to remove the Jewish names—all had Jewish names.

And then we walked where they were herded naked, with whips and blows, into the chambers. I walk into the gas chamber; standing in the dark, breathing the air with nausea. I turn the corner into the crematoria, unable to encompass them—shivering not only from the cold, but from the highly efficient terror machine. I felt the need to cry—but I can only stare; I can only mourn the *hurban!* What a *korban!*

The guide avoids translating the Polish signs explaining the exhibits. We insist, but who knows what they really said? To him and to others it was Germany's war against Poland. And when all the Jews have disappeared from Poland, who will be there to remind them? My visit to Poland was an orchestrated reminder—but I had my own personal mission: I had my own Kaddish to recite. I had to visit *my* own *kever avot.*

I had seen the Warsaw Ghetto where my parents were herded. I had seen the site where my family had been forced to enter the train to the camps. But I, unlike others in my group, had to go home—to visit their shtetl, their birthplace, their house and my sister's playground.

The shtetl is small. No more than a hundred dwellings, dwarfed by a large red church. Many of the homes have not changed in over a hundred years. It is an inspiration for a painting—a fable. But what I was to experience was no fiction.

When the taxi pulled up to the front yard of what had once been my parent's home, the town's policeman took immediate notice. Within moments he charged me and, without eye contact, shouted and barked commands. My roommate, who accompanied me, thank God, quietly asked me to acquiesce. I stood in shock but I smiled, not accepting his intimidating scowl. More shouting followed—a shove. I smiled at the treacherous homecoming. My eyes beheld a look of real hatred. It wasn't supposed to happen, not in 1987. I signaled my driver. After asking for our passports and the driver's identity card, the officer carefully filed his report while we stood in the freezing cold. "Why had we come? They're all gone. What do we want? There's no one left. What were their names? I don't recall them. Why are you taking pictures?" The driver translated the curt questions with embarrassment.

Children were being called to quickly come home. People stood at a distance observing us with curiosity. Much animated conversation took place between the policeman and my driver. Condescending gazes, sarcastic tones, and hostile looks at us peppered the exchange that seemed endless. The driver explained that we were with a large group of rabbis from America—he had to have us back in Warsaw within a few hours, otherwise we'd be missed. The policeman's tone changed. He became civil, returned our passports, and asked what had happened to my family. Fabricating my words, I explained that everyone had made it, that all were doing well and living a life of paradise. He seemed comfortable that I would have no claims to property. He had demonstrated his official standing to all observers—he had proven himself! No one noticed that my dance in the cold had written the words *zakhor al tishkah*. I told my roommate that in my personal view, *zakhor* meant that we should remember and *al tishkah* indicated that we should remind others. The shtetl's Jews are gone—no one is left to remind them. We were the reminders, the embodiment of *al tishkah,* remember—don't forget. Yes, Yakov Bergman and Shmuel Rubenstein are in Paradise, but they returned with me to remind the village of Stoczek. The tears came later and then I sang. The song came to me from wartorn Lublin. In Nazi-occupied Lublin, the local fascists and Nazi sympathizers rounded up the Jews in an *aktion.* In a cruel, dehumanizing manner they compelled them to sing before their deaths. With whips, rifle butts, and sticks they were forced to sing before their execution. Ironically, they sang *"Lomir zich iberbeten"* ("Let's make up" or "Let's forgive each other"). When the Jews faltered in their singing they were viciously beaten. Then one religious man loudly changed the words to *"Mir velen zey iberleben*—we shall outlive them!" They sang loudly, with excitement and energetic animation, "We shall outlive them!" Globocnik, the Nazi commander, understood their words and ordered the Nazis and Poles to beat them to stop their singing. But the Jews danced and sang even louder. "We shall outlive them." They fell beneath the blows of death, but we remain to sing.

Our generation must sing a new song to the Lord because we are the generation which merits from their *kiddush ha-Shem.*

In memory of the immediate families: Shmuel and Rifka Rubenstein; Yeta Rosa, Yisrael Shimon, and Mayer Leib Rubenstein and families; Yakov and Razel Devorah Bergman; Yoel and Sarah Yelta (Bergman) Krystal and son Hershel; Aryeh and Rachel Leah Rubenstein and daughters Chaya Yetka, and Sarah Rifka; Shaya and Esther Pearl Bergman and daughter Razzie; Zisha and Rifka Rubenstein and their three children Shmuel, Basha, and Yelid; Michlah Bergman, Yisrael Bergman—herded from Stoczek to Wnegrow to Warsaw to Treblinka.

Some Historical Reflections

Rabbi Louis Bernstein

I

Observances of Yom ha-Shoah and studies of the Holocaust are valuable particularly if post-Holocaust generations are able to learn from that terrible era and apply the lessons to their own period. As the years pass and the number of Holocaust survivors decline, as those years and occurrences fade in memory, the memoirs of the survivors remain eternal monuments for researchers. Official archives and records, until now sealed from the public view, have become increasingly available to researchers and the public in the last decade.

Yet even with the staggering amount of source material, historians can still not digest the total magnitude of the event. We can but come to grips with some of its aspects. One sad conclusion is inevitable—more Jews might have survived had Jewish leadership been more sensitive to the inevitable.

Researchers have not even begun to investigate the role of Orthodox Jews during the Holocaust years. When they do, *Refugee and Remnant: Rescue Efforts During the Holocaust* by Dr. Zerach Warhaftig will be an invaluable source. Dr. Warhaftig, who served for many years as Israel's minister of religions, was a leader in the attempt to save yeshivot and rescue religious Zionists during the Holocaust years.

In 1940, Warhaftig attempted to convince the heads of the Lithuanian yeshivot to organize themselves to attempt to reach Palestine via Russia. The crowned leader of Lithuanian and Polish Orthodoxy was Rabbi Chayim Ozer Grodzinski. He was unable to comprehend the clear handwriting on the wall, and Warhaftig's warnings and pleas fell on deaf ears.

On 10 Nissan 5740, Warhaftig reported in a memorandum to the Berit Olamit of Torah ve-Avodah in Tel Aviv:

> Va'ad ha-Yeshivot [i.e., Rabbi Chayim Ozer] still equivocates over the aliyah of yeshiva students. I have held long discussions with Rabbi Chayim Ozer Grodzinski and he still hesitates whether bringing the yeshivot or their students to Israel will enhance the study of Torah. He fears the environment of Eretz Yisrael, he still believes in the Diaspora, he still deceives himself that the Polish yeshivot will find a secure haven in Lithuania and then will return to Poland. It is because of these doubts that he believes that each yeshiva should decide the issue of the aliyah of its students, and each yeshiva has its own approach. A few (Kaminetz, Mir, and others) are totally committed to aliyah to Eretz Yisrael, while others still are skeptical. (p. 147)

Earlier, Rabbi Chayim Ozer told Warhaftig the reasons voiced by *roshei yeshivot* opposed to aliyah at meetings to which he, Warhaftig, had not been invited.

> (1) There is no need to be alarmed. All places are endangered in this war. It is conceivable that Lithuania might be spared. (2) It is questionable whether all the yeshivot should be removed far from Poland. One must plan for what may happen when the war, with God's help, comes to a speedy conclusion and it is necessary to rebuild Poland—shall we leave it without the voice of Torah? (3) There is no possibility of obtaining large quantities of certificates. If only a few were obtained, it would mean splitting the student bodies, and this would undermine the yeshivot's existence. (4) It is doubtful whether the sparse Jewish population of the land of Israel can sustain the many added ones from Europe in addition to those already existing there. There is concern that yeshiva students seeking sustenance will leave the yeshivot and empty them. (5) Therefore, if a decision to leave is arrived at, the departure of yeshivot to the United States is to be preferred. (6) The offices of the Polish yeshivot in the United States would not use their incomes for guarantees (for loans to obtain certi-

ficates to Palestine), for this would result in limiting or eliminating their maintenance funds. (p. 146)

Warhaftig cites the names of leading rabbis who refused to use certificates provided for them. When youth aliyah certificates for religious youngsters were made available on condition that they attended a seminar, Chanoch Achiman organized evening classes twice a week for that purpose and included students from the yeshiva of Baranowitz for young people. Rabbi Elchanon Wasserman protested to Rabbi Chayim Ozer. He charged that the yeshiva was being ruined and that the youngsters might leave the life of yeshiva students in Eretz Yisrael. Warhaftig suggested that they be sent to the agricultural yeshiva being started in Kefar ha-Ro'eh, where they could continue their talmudic studies and Seder Zera'im. "The offer was not accepted, and Rabbi Chayim Ozer demanded that the youngsters from the Baranowitz Yeshiva be excluded. I complied with his request, of course, and I regretted that very much" (p. 148).

The inevitable and somber conclusion is that even the greatest Torah scholars do not necessarily qualify as historical and political experts. Some (if not many or most) of the Polish and Lithuanian luminaries misread the inevitable, because they lacked the knowledge and expertise to comprehend what was transpiring. And yet a new generation of Orthodox Jews is repeating the same disastrous pattern.

II

Could American Jews have done more to save their European brethren? The answer is certainly yes, but no competent historian will speculate whether their efforts might have been successful, certainly not to what degree. What is painfully clear is that American Jewry, by its own divisiveness, limited serious rescue efforts.

Two of the finest books written about America and the Holocaust are *The Politics of Rescue* by Henry L. Feingold (1969) and *The*

Abandonment of the Jews by David S. Wyman (1984). A common deno-
minator prevalent in both books is that competition for exclusive
headlines gave the enemies of rescue efforts great comfort. Feingold,
in his final chapter, "Rescue in Retrospect," concludes:

> Much of their formidable organizational resources were dissipated in
> internal bickering until it seemed as if Jews were more anxious to tear
> each other apart than to rescue other coreligionists. One has only to
> read Long's description of the numerous Jewish delegations, each
> representing a different group, to realize how tragic the situation of
> American Jewry was. That a community which desperately needed to
> speak to Roosevelt with one voice remained in an organizational
> deadlock is no small tragedy, and when one realizes how appallingly
> irrelevant the issues and personalities dividing them were, one can
> only shake one's head in disbelief.

The Long referred to in the preceding paragraph was Breckinridge
Long, the assistant secretary of state, who consistently blocked all
efforts at rescue and even impeded refugees with legal papers from
coming to the United States. He describes how Jews quarreled outside his office.

David Wyman devotes two chapters to the conflict between the
Rescue Committee and the Zionists. They carried their fight into
congressional offices. The quarreling between the Bergsonites and
the Zionists did little to save Jews but enhanced the press's coffers
because of the large ads.

Jews, in 1988, still cannot channel their differences into civilized
discussion and resolution. Leaders of Reform Judaism and even
Foreign Minister Peres have carried Jewish differences to the Congress of the United States. The letter of thirty senators critical of
Prime Minister Shamir was the result of encouragement, silent or
active, by the foreign minister. There is no winner when Jews carry
their internal quarrels to Gentiles. The young generation must learn
the lesson from the Holocaust that "the righteousness of the Gentiles is sinful." There are only losers. Santayana's pithy aphorism
that he who fails to learn from history is apt to repeat it, is a lesson
still not learned by Orthodox American Jews.

We Continue to Continue

Rabbi Dr. Emanuel Feldman

The Talmud tells us the story of the death of R. Hananiah ben Teradyon at the hands of the Roman oppressors (Avodah Zarah 18a). Because he defied their ban on the study and the teaching of Torah, they wrapped him in a Sefer Torah scroll, placed bundles of branches about him, and set them on fire. Then they placed tufts of damp wool over his heart so that he would not expire quickly. His daughter said: "Oh, that I should see you in such a state." He replied: "If I alone were being burned, it would be hard enough. But now that I am burning together with the Sefer Torah, whoever will seek to save the honor of the Torah, it will be as if he is saving my honor." His disciples said to him: "Our Master, what do you see?" He replied: "The parchment is burned, but the letters are soaring on high."

When the attempt was made to exterminate totally Am Yisrael in the *Hurban* of Europe, it was not just the people which was being attacked, not simply another form of genocide. For Hitler knew one truth: he was attempting to destroy the ideas, the principles, and the teachings which this people Israel has brought into the world: that there is a God who created us; a morality and discipline which guides all of life; that man is not a beast but was created in the Divine Image; that to become human, man must learn to dominate his physical impulses; that the physical can be elevated and transcended by the spiritual impulses; that if we allow the physical to dominate, we will soon turn into beasts.

For Hitler, Judaism was an evil, and Torah was a poison designed to destroy the world, because it prevented man from living as an animal. And so the God of Israel, and the Torah of Israel, and the bearers of these tidings, the people Israel—the conscience of mankind—would have to be utterly destroyed. And once the conscience is destroyed, there are no restraints, and you have arrived at the *final solution:* you can become a full, unfettered, conscienceless beast.

And so the Jewish people, wrapped in its Torah, was put to a slow, torturous, agonizing death. And with it, the executioner was certain that there died all that he hated: Thou shalt not kill, thou shalt not steal, thou shalt not commit adultery. All the thou-shalt-nots which stood in his way would also be killed—particularly the one commandment which stood out above others: *annokhi,* I am the Lord thy God who took thee out of the land of Egypt; no human, no idol may command your ultimate allegiance, only I the Lord am your God.

But the executioner was wrong: he could not destroy God or God's Torah, for the letters, the teachings, the *neshamah* of the Jew went up, soaring on high, eternal and indestructible.

Far from being destroyed, Am Yisrael stands, forty years after the Shoah, a vital, dynamic people, which has not only rebuilt itself physically, but somehow, through the divine miracle, is in the process of rebuilding itself spiritually. Jewish life and Jewish practice and Jewish commitment have not been forgotten by the Jews. Instead, slowly, gradually, step by painful step, schools are founded, yeshivot are begun, synagogues are built, young and old begin the return. "Whoever saves the Torah's honor," said R. Hananiah, "it is as if he is saving my honor, as if he is saving the Jewish people."

Zakhor and *hemshekh* are two key words today: "remember" and "continuity" go together naturally. But *zakhor* must be with a purpose. Not simply to say mindlessly "never again," as if somehow it was within the power of the victims to have halted the onslaught of the Nazi war machine. *Zakhor,* remember, rather, the sources of Jewish spiritual power, the many instances of Jewish spiritual heroism during the Holocaust, the spiritual beauty of prewar Europe. What other people would have been able to find the resources and inner strength, after such a destruction, to build and defend a state, to continue to teach its traditions? We remember the sources of Jewish spiritual power with a purpose, and that purpose is to create a *hemshekh,* a continuation, and to provide a home for those letters which soar in the heavens.

Holocaust Memorial Day is necessary: we must remember. But we must not allow it to become a once-a-year event, a kind of sad Mother's Day, in which one day of attention soothes the conscience of 364 days of neglect—and even that one day becomes nothing more than empty, secular expressions of mere indignation, of human and civil rights, or of defiance—as important as these are.

Joseph Friedenson, a survivor of several death camps and currently a writer in New York, tells the following story: It was a Sunday in one of the factories of the death camps. Suddenly, one of the Jewish prisoners realized that it was Simḥat Torah. On his own, he began singing a classic Simḥat Torah song: *"Mi-pi-E-l . . ."* At the top of his voice he sang it, and a number of the prisoners joined in with him: *"Ein adir kelokenu . . .* None is mighty like our God, none is great like Moses the son of Amram, none is faithful as the children of Israel . . ." Suddenly the chief guard appeared at the door and yelled out, "What is going on here!" The prisoners stood in stunned silence. The guard turned to Friedenson, who was fluent in German, and demanded that he translate the words of the song. Friedenson explained that it was not a song at all, but a prayer to God. He proceeded to translate. The German demanded: "You people believe all this? You really believe in those words?" Before Friedenson had a chance to reply, a young Jewish prisoner stepped forward and said, "Yes, I believe, we all believe!" The guard said: "This is unbelievable! Hitler will never succeed with you people!"

And he was right. As long as we remember the right things and for the right reasons; as long as we create a continuation for Torah in our Jewish living, our Jewish schooling, our Jewish learning; as long as we look for holy letters which still soar in the heavens above us, and strive to pull them down to our hearts, then he was right, and it is unbelievable: our enemies will never succeed with us.

Because we continue to believe. Because we continue to remember. Because we continue to continue.

Survivors Recall

Where It All Began:
A "German" Jew's Reflections on Kristallnacht

Rabbi Shlomo Kahn

Years ago, a popular nonpartisan religious weekly was published in Israel, *Panim el-Panim*. Its editor was the late writer and scholar Pinchas Peli (a professor at Ben-Gurion University). In one of his penetrating editorials, he made a striking observation.

Two segments largely make up the Jewish people today, Ashkenazim and Sephardim. Their names are Hebrew for two countries, Spain and Germany, an irony of the greatest magnitude. Precisely the two countries in which Jewish life had at one time flourished for generations became the prototypes of the most vicious persecution and the brutal destruction of Jews and Jewish life!

For a long time after the horrors of the Spanish Inquisition, Jews had an aversion to everything Spanish. Probably false (but not surprisingly persistent) is the rumor that a *ḥerem* was pronounced which prohibits Jews from residing on Spanish soil. I speak exclusively for myself when I express a personal similar aversion to the country of my birth, the country where I spent my childhood, the first twelve years of my life.

I lost no immediate family members in the Holocaust. Needless to say, I was never an inmate in a concentration camp. My late father was spared, by the *ḥesed* of God, the incarceration at Dachau following the infamous Kristallnacht. Yet *(be-li neder)* I shall never set foot again on German soil (and there are no German stamps in my modest stamp collection).

Have I no feelings of nostalgia for the environment of my childhood years? Of course I do. I remember the joy of taking walks in the beautiful parks in Stuttgart, the unforgettable scenic grandeur of the Black Forest, the majesty of the Danube and Rhine rivers. In my ears the songs, music, and nursery rhymes learned as a child still reverberate, as well as literature and poetry. No doubt, I would derive real pleasure from seeing once again the house where I was born and raised, the park where I played, the streets, the forests. But all this, and much more, I deliberately pluck from heart and soul, and try to erase from memory. The events of 1933 to 1945 are so searingly overwhelming that all the good and pleasant has become diluted, to the point of extinction (*bittul* is the talmudic term) in a bottomless sea of horror. I may not have many soul brothers among "German" Jews in these sentiments. I fully realize that many think differently even among those who suffered more than I did. I wish not to offend or accuse, but feelings of the heart cry out to be aired before I address myself to the main part of these reflections.

Since Kristallnacht unmistakably signaled the impending doom of German Jews, it is appropriate to sketch ever so briefly Jewish life in Germany, prior to relating my own experiences of the Kristallnacht nightmare. To provide a glimpse of German Jewry in the framework of a short article is a most formidable undertaking. Paraphrasing the Great Viddui of Rabbenu Nissim ("Were I to rise to mention my errors and explain them, the time would end but they would not end")—if I were to describe fully the history of German Jewry, I would have to speak and discuss, lecture and record, catalogue and list, and time would pass without exhausting the topic. What should I say?

How Jewish life and Jewish communities originated in Germany? That they existed since the time of the Second Temple? That Charlemagne, emperor of the Holy Roman Empire, was so concerned about the Jewish education of "his" Jews that he imported to Germany a Torah scholar from Italy of the famous Kalonymus family, to raise the spiritual level of German Jews?

There were eminent *kehillot* in Germany where Torah study flourished. There, in Germany, the study of Kabbalah developed with great intensity. There were the *Ḥasidei Ashkenaz* long before Hasidism, as it is known today, even originated.

Jews rose to prominence in Germany in all fields and areas. There were the Rothschilds in finance, of course, but also politicians, poets, literary giants, scientists: Paul Ehrlich, Heinrich Heine, Walter Rathenau, Albert Einstein—names chosen at random out of dozens if not hundreds, each of them and each one's particular field deserving of tribute.

Developments occurred on German soil, leading to concepts, ideas, and movements which had and still have incisive impact on Jewish life: Moses Mendelssohn and his ideology of raising the German Jew to a level culturally and linguistically equal to his environment; Geiger, Frankel, the originators of the Reform movement, in whose footsteps many followed, first in Germany, then in Hungary, and finally finding fertile ground in America; earlier, much earlier, the concept of *shtadlanut,* pacifying an oppressive, anti-Semitic government with a policy of humble petitioning and payment of money, whose illustrious champion, eminently successful, was the learned Rabbi Joselmann of Rosheim; last but not least the great renaissance of Torah-true *kehillah* life championed by Rabbi Samson Raphael Hirsch and his *Torah im derekh eretz* approach, which led to a split in German Orthodox Jewry between the Wuerzburger Rav, Rabbi Seligmann Baer Bamberger, and Rabbi Hirsch. (I tactfully refrain from taking sides—the Wuerzburger Rav was my mother's grandfather, while I grew up in the congregation of Rabbi Hirsch's grandson, the late Rabbi Dr. Joseph Breuer.)

Were I to do justice to all of the above where I merely gave headlines of extensive topics without even scratching the surface, this article would grow into a thick volume. I shall therefore confine myself to two areas: (1) a short description of Jewish life in Germany in the period immediately prior to the rise of Nazism, and (2) the German Jew's feeling toward "his" country.

On Kristallnacht, hundreds of synagogues were burned down and others were demolished. In other words, there were hundreds of *kehillot* in Germany at that time. Obviously some were large congregations boasting hundreds of members while some were small, numbering only dozens of families. Basically, Jewish life in Germany can be divided into life in the large cities and life in the country, in the hundreds of little towns and villages.

There was a world of difference between the two. Cities held the educated, highly cultured citizens of Germany. Cities contained centers of education, museums, libraries, concert halls, as well as the opportunities for careers. There abounded the professionals, the politicians, people engaged in commerce and industry. The towns and villages, on the other hand, although containing a small share of similar opportunities, had largely citizens who occupied themselves with small-town means of livelihood: farming, trading, small ships, traveling salesmen. The Jews of Germany were well integrated in the fabric of German society, hence this picture of roughly dividing city life and life in the country was reflected, to a large degree, among the Jewish population as well.

As a result, in the cities the Jew as an individual became much more easily integrated and assimilated. He could lose himself easily in the busy, pulsating city life, was not conspicuously Jewish but rather more anonymous and therefore accepted readily as an equal. Not so in the small towns and villages. There everyone knew everyone else personally. The Jew remained recognizably Jewish in the eyes of his fellow residents.

While a basic gut feeling of anti-Semitism is somehow part and parcel of the very nature of the German, this did not disturb a pleasant interaction between Jew and Gentile. Let me illustrate from personal experience. I was born in a large city. I shall explain a little later how my parents raised me with emphasis on Jewish identity over and above German patriotism. But first this illustrative anecdote.

In the house where I lived, indeed on the entire street where I spent the first seven years of my life, we were the only Jewish family. I had many friends with whom I played—all non-Jews. I was accepted, but I stress the word "accepted." They all knew that somehow I was different. It didn't interfere with our games. My late parents bent over backwards to forestall any possible animosity. For example, each year on Sukkot, all the boys and girls on our street were invited to a party in our *sukkah.* They came in their Sunday best, drank the hot chocolate, and ate the cake and candy. This was done deliberately to show them that despite our differences, we are not strangers, and it helped.

Yet these efforts notwithstanding, I remember vividly a conversation on a sunny Sunday afternoon in front of our house. We boys were sitting around during a break in a ball game, and the talk of us five- or six-year-olds turned to the question of why I was Jewish and all of them were non-Jews. They scratched their little heads and racked their little brains, and then the oldest came up with this answer: It wasn't my fault nor the fault of my father, he said. (Knowing me and my father and liking us prevented blame.) It was the fault of my grandfather!

Out of the mouths of babes and children comes uninhibited frankness. The Jew is different. Somewhere something went wrong. There has to be blame. We'll accept him, in spite of the fault, out of the goodness of our heart.

In the small towns this was more pronounced. Although life was peaceful and Jews were on good terms with the Gentiles in trading, business, social functions, town politics, entertainment, nevertheless the Jew was known as a Jew.

Again, a personal note. In the summer I would often stay with my aunt and uncle in a small town. It had a good Jewish population, an excellent *kehillah,* but although the relationship between Jew and Gentile was good, the Jew stood out. As children, we played chiefly with fellow Jews. When Nazi policy began to encourage anti-Semitic acts, it was simply impossible to submerge among the masses as in large cities. Quickly, and much earlier than elsewhere, life for Jews in towns and villages became an ordeal.

I mentioned earlier that there is latent, natural anti-Semitism in the German personality. This needs some clarification. Needless to say, the hackneyed phrase "some of my best friends are (or were) Germans" does apply to me. I remember them and will come back to it later, but there is this factual observation: The German mental-

ity is such that whatever is different and foreign is under suspicion
and automatically disliked. In Germany (in my time—perhaps this
has changed) you do not read a foreign-language paper or book in
public without arousing snickers, comments, or at least raised eye-
brows. You do not walk anywhere in public with a yarmulka. You
take off your hat in public or in the presence of Gentiles. So far did
this penetrate even the Jewish life of the religiously observant that
when drinking a lemonade in a restaruant, he would quickly recite
the berakhah and then take off his hat and drink bareheaded. Such
practices, totally out of touch with the freedom enjoyed in America,
must be kept in mind to understand some diehard German-Jewish
behavior still today.

On the subject of religious observance, another matter must be
explained. There were in Germany many more congregations than
available rabbis. Especially the great number of rural communities
could not possibly obtain the service of a local rabbi. A novel solution was found, superficially sound. Germany was divided into
geographical districts. In each of these sections, the rabbi of a large
city became the "district rabbi" with jurisdiction over his own
congregation as well as dozens of smaller communities clustered
around the city. Obviously he could not be in close touch with all of
those. He would arrange to spend at least one weekend a year in
each town, deliver a sermon, inspect the mikveh and the shehitah,
and observe the Sunday Hebrew school, but largely he left the
community in the hands of a spiritual leader more or less his
deputy, a teacher (*lehrer*), a position approximating that of assistant
rabbi but usually (not always) filled by a rather poorly trained individual. The man could lead services, read the Torah, sometimes act
as shohet and mohel and give lessons to the children in Hebrew
reading, writing, translating Humash and Siddur. If better educated
he could also teach Mishnah and in rare instances Gemara. As a
result of this system of community leadership, the level of Torah
knowledge in Germany, especially in towns and villages, fell to a
dismal low.

Another point of interest. German Jews (like Jews throughout galut) adopted the behavior and personality traits of the surrounding population. German thoroughness and refusal to compromise led to a unique religio-sociological development. German Jews insisted that a rabbi must have full training in all areas of halakhah, even those which did not often touch on day-by-day living. Semikhah had to be *yadin-yadin,* with expertise in talmudic civil law as well as ritual law. But as a rule, German yeshivot (rabbinical seminaries) could not match the intensive study of the yeshivot of Eastern Europe. In Germany, secular education was demanded, while in the East, all study concentrated on Torah and Talmud. Hence the average Germany-trained rabbi had to spread his knowledge in Talmud rather thin. He had to study all parts of the *Shulḥan Arukh* at the expense of the entirety of the Talmud.

All of the above had a deplorable consequence. It led to the paradox of well-meaning, pious, faithful Jews who conscientiously observed what they knew, often not understanding what it was all about. In the cities, the inroads made by Reform Judaism led to the assimilation of the cultured and intellectuals. In the country, the failure of proper Torah teachers led to lamentable ignorance.

A word about German-Jewish patriotism, so often discussed, condemned, defended, but primarily grossly misunderstood. Jews are classically patriotic toward their host country, loyal and grateful. The Torah commands us never to forget the hospitality we enjoyed in (of all places) Egypt, in spite of subsequent mistreatment. To this day, outside Israel the prayer for rain, *tal u-matar,* is added when rain is needed in Babylonia (Iraq!), because it was the host country of the great Talmud academies.

Naturally, Jews in Germany were good Germans. Many overdid it. I lack statistics but I have personal recollections. My family goes back, longer than I can trace, to Jews living in Germany, yet it was always stressed that we were Jews first, and only to a much smaller degree Germans. My grandfather was a well-integrated German Jew who was keenly interested in German politics, German culture, etc., but he raised my father with the oft-repeated caution: remember that we are strangers in this land. His mother (my great-grandmother) spoke fluent German but never learned to write it. She wrote German in Hebrew letters, then called *Juedisch-Deutsch*.

Love for Germany, in normally sensible Jewish circles, was very similar to the patriotism of American Jews, who are keenly aware that they are a minority, warmly support the State of Israel, but express gratitude and loyalty to the host country.

No doubt there are exceptions, but aside from the elderly, who had difficulties adjusting after emigration, the German Jew is no different from his brother in other countries. Naturally, Jews of Poland, Russia, etc., who constantly lived under humiliating anti-Semitism, have little loyalty to their host countries.

To integrate the culture, customs, and language of the country into aspects of Jewish life is rather normal and not confined to German Jews. The fact that many German-Jewish families sing some of the Seder songs in German is balanced by an experience some years ago when I attended the *berit milah* of several teenaged Russian immigrants. During the meal, the men broke into a Russian folk song, with obvious nostalgia.

Undeniably, German Jews have German characteristics, not only that the pronunciation of German has made inroads into their pronunciation of some Hebrew (and a variation in the chanting of Torah and Haftarah readings), but also personality traits. There is a strong emphasis on puctuality, orderliness, decorum (some of these found their way into the synagogue services), often objects of good-natured jokes but just as often admired and even accepted by others into their own way of life.

As mentioned at the outset, I had to be selective in presenting a picture of German Jewry. Regarding my own Kristallnacht experiences, I shall mention them briefly.

I was twelve years old at the time. Unaccountably, during that fateful night I slept fitfully, which was unusual. I woke up several times, and I'll never forget the time of 4:00 a.m. showing on the green luminous dial of my alarm clock. Later I learned that at that very time, the Nazi hoodlums had drenched the synagogue with gasoline and ignited it.

I rose shortly after six went to shul, a walk of about twenty-five minutes from home. Wherever I passed a Jewish-owned shop, I saw shattered glass—that is what gave the night its name, Kristallnacht, Night of the Broken Glass. I reached the synagogue and saw the fire engines standing by idle, for the men had orders to protect the neighboring houses, but not to extinguish the fire. In my confusion, I ran home without actually seeing the flames.

What followed was a nightmare. We heard that Jewish men were being rounded up for incarceration in concentration camps. My late father had already given up our apartment, for we were about to emigrate, and we stayed at a friend's house. That night my father took me and my nine-year-old sister (my mother had died a year earlier) to go into hiding. We begged Gentile friends to take us in—a friend who had served with my father in World War I, our family barber, the family of a former maid. Each politely but firmly refused. "What will the neighbors say?" they said. It was eerie, walking through once friendly, familiar streets, now dark and frightening, a fugitive and a wanderer in our own native city.

We finally stayed in the home of a Jewish family. We did not know it then, but my father was not on the "wanted" list, since he had registered for emigration. For two weeks we lived in constant fear. My sister stayed at the window, looking out, fearing the arrival of the Gestapo. Regularly she would call out: "Don't be alarmed when the door bell rings—I see the mailman coming!" Even during the night we were alert to street sounds while asleep. There was little traffic in our street. Whenever a car passed, I woke up—it might be the Gestapo.

Once, terror knifed through me. A car passed and stopped. Moments later the downstairs bell rang. I still feel the constriction of my heart at that moment. But it had a happy ending. A fellow tenant, a Jew, had been released from Dachau and was allowed to come home.

I want to conclude on a positive note. Last Simḥat Torah, when a Sefer Torah was handed to me for *hakkafot,* this thought rose in my mind.

Remember the scene from *Fiddler on the Roof?* They are leaving Anatevka. They have assembled in their little synagogue for the last time. They take the Torah scrolls from the Ark and carry them, cradling them lovingly. A camera shot focuses lingeringly on the memorial plates on the synagogue walls, as if to say: "We're leaving, leaving behind even the memories of our loved ones. But we leave with the Torah." On their way out, already beyond the town, they stop to daven Minḥah—business as usual. And then they go on, with their pitiful belongings, but proudly with their Sifrei Torah.

Let no one tell you that German Jews attach inordinate importance to material goods, to memories, to reminiscences, to peculiar customs. All this is there, of course, but above all is the Torah. It has sustained us through centuries and millennia. It is the only thing that matters.

God's Handboat

Rabbi I. Nathan Bamberger

There are certain moments in every person's life that can never be
forgotten. No matter what happens in our lifetime, certain events
will become fixed in our conscience and we will never be able to
overlook them.

Nineteen forty-three. What a terrible year for the Jewish people.
Nazi Germany is the cruel taskmaster of Europe. The trains with
their precious human cargo are rolling to the death camps. Sorrow,
famine, humiliation, hopelessness, despair, distress, and gloom
prevail in all the occupied countries under the vicious German boot.
No hope for the Jewish people.

One country, Denmark, is different. Let me tell you about the
night when I literally saw the hand of the Almighty. Let me share
with you the moment of my rescue from the clutches of the angel of
death.

A short history lesson will set the stage for the drama which has
been recorded as *the* unique event during the terrible war years.
Denmark, the northern neighbor of Germany, was occupied on
April 9, 1940.[1] The occupation was swift and thorough. Special
status was accorded Denmark and consequently also the Jewish citizens. For three years the Jews of Denmark lived a "normal" life,
although the public display of Jewish activities was toned down
considerably. By September 1943, the situation changed totally.
Martial law was declared. The king was made a prisoner in his castle.
Parliament was dissolved. The cabinet was discharged. The Danish
police were imprisoned, the navy destroyed, and a general strike
declared. While all these events took place within a two-week period, the German occupation forces, primarily the Gestapo, leaped at
the chance to "solve" the Jewish problem in Denmark.

Rumors had circulated that an *aktion* against the Jews was

imminent. On Erev Rosh ha-Shanah, when it was announced that the Jews should not stay at home the following night, most Jews complied. We went to a good Christian friend, a merchant in Copenhagen, who provided shelter and food for us. Rosh ha-Shanah and Shabbat Shuvah we remained in his house, praying for a good new year!

One question was on everybody's mind: How to get out of occupied Denmark and whom to contact to make a rescue possible. On Monday a contact was established with the Danish underground, who promised to send a car with a driver in the afternoon. When the car arrived, we had only to get into the car and the driver would take us to a safe place north of Copenhagen. Obviously there was no choice. The car did arrive, my family went into a strange car with a strange driver. No words were exchanged. Quickly we drove out of the city, and after one hour's drive we arrived at a farm. We were told to go upstairs in a barn . . . and lo and behold, there were no less than two hundred other Jews who also had been transported to this place. We were assured that rescue operations were in progress, and we had to wait our turn to be ferried to neutral Sweden. On Tuesday and Wednesday we stayed on the farm, waiting for the fishing boat that would take us across the sound. For two nights the operation was cancelled because the moon was shining too brightly. But Thursday night we were taken in trucks to the beach. In small groups, covered with straw mats so that German patrols would not become suspicious, we were driven to the edge of the water. Behind every tree, behind every wall and house, a member of the Danish underground was standing, ready to protect the human cargo which was being shipped across the sound to Sweden (Oeresund).

Now to the miracle. Approximately two hundred people, men, women, children, most still dressed in their Yom Tov garb, with nothing to carry, were taken by small rowboats for a few hundred yards out into the water. There they were taken aboard a fishing boat with one and only one command: Do not speak, and keep the children quiet. It was a long and tedious operation, but by midnight everybody was on board.

And then the engine would not start. Imagine, being caught on a fishing boat that could not start. The captain and his helpers worked feverishly to get the engine going. After one hour's time, the miracle happened. The engine activated, and ever so slowly the boat started its dangerous journey across the black waters. Not a sound was heard, but the prayers on everybody's lips must have reached the highest places. It felt as if the hand of the Almighty actually carried the boat to safety. After two hours journey, bright lights suddenly fell upon the boat. It was a Swedish torpedo boat with instructions to pick up any Jew who could make it out from the grip of death. The night before Yom Kippur became the night of our rescue.[2]

God's protective hand did not rescue us only from certain death in the concentration camps; His aid extended also to our possessions. In May 1945, after the Allies liberated Denmark and its capital city, Copenhagen, we were permitted to return from Sweden. Great indeed was our surprise when we entered our home. My mother, of blessed memory, had set the table before Rosh ha-Shanah. The candlesticks, the plates, the flatware, the silver cups had all been prepared to usher in the New Year. After twenty-two months the table was still set in exactly the same way as when we left. There had been no vandalism, break-in, or robbery. Our Danish neighbors made certain that our property was also protected from the hands of the savages.[3]

Thanks have been expressed to the Danes for their heroic actions in the hour of need. Similarly, thanks have been expressed to the Swedes for their willingness to accept Danish Jewry.

I do not know why the Jews from Denmark were saved. Many reasons have been advanced. This much, however, is sure. I felt the hand of God on that memorable night when we were taken from slavery to freedom, from darkness to light, and from death to life.

NOTES

1. A detailed history of the occupation of Denmark and the experiences of Danish Jewry during those five fateful years can be found in my book *The Viking Jews: A History of the Jews of Denmark* (New York: Shengold Publishers, 1983).

2. A total of approximately six thousand Jews were rescued from Denmark during October 1943. Some six hundred were caught by the Germans and sent to the Theresienstadt concentration camp. It should be stated that even in the concentration camp, the Jews from Denmark were treated "better" than the rest of the prisoners. In April 1945 nearly all returned to Denmark. Two children were born in the concentration camp. They are still alive today.

3. In this connection it should be recorded that the synagogues of Denmark as well as the cemeteries of Denmark were not destroyed or vandalized during the absence of the Jews. The Danes made certain that religious institutions, Jewish property and ownership were protected during the twenty-two months while Danish Jewry were in Sweden.

The Warsaw Ghetto Uprising

Rabbi Mordecai L. Glatstein

We enter the Holy of Holies and read Lamentations, written on the parchment of our hearts: "I am the man that hath seen the affliction of my people" (3:1). I am the victim and the witness.

The forty thousand men, women, and children knew what was going to happen. They trained and armed themselves as best they could with the few weapons available. Finally they had decided that this war was their Massada.

They knew the plans of the Germans. They knew they would be facing the terrible fire of Nazi tanks and mortars: even warplanes would ultimately be used against this starved and disease-ridden fragment of what had once been the culmination and pride of Jewish intellectual history. Polish Jews: the crown of world Jewry, with vibrant centers of Torah scholarship, academies of learning, writers, philosophers, rabbis, Torah luminaries, and zaddikim.

Against this enemy, the remnant of the Warsaw Ghetto, the Germans threw in their best military leadership, their best arms, their best strategies.

The Warsaw Jews carried out their uprising with intense disillusionment in their hearts; swallowing the world's betrayal and indifference, they fought for six weeks in a holdout without parallel in history. "I called them my friends but they deceived me. All her friends have dealt treacherously with her—they have become her enemies" (Lamentations 1:2).

Never in the sad and holy annals of the Jew's will to survive for his faith has a more desperately glorious stand been made than by those heroes who acted not only to save their own lives, but to save the dignity of the entire Jewish people. They fought like mythological lions, without arms, without help, without hope.

Do not put your trust in the cultures of the nations—they are a veneer of phrases and words. "In the beginning was the word"; but also in the end they gave us words.

Hitler alone could not have committed his ghastly crimes without the aid of thousands of his fellow Nazis and the complicity of the nations in their utter indifference and conspiracy of silence.

What was proclaimed in *Mein Kampf?* Hitler gave notice to the world of his intentions to destroy the Jews. Instead of sternly opposing his plan, the civilized nations gave him the green light. They recognized his government and granted him billions in trade, enabling him to accomplish his diabolical purpose of murdering the Jews.

When the Evian Conference of 1938 was convened by President Roosevelt to discuss the European refugee problem, all the participating nations refused to absorb Jewish refugees. Himmler, chief of the SS and the Gestapo, declared that the Nazis had recognized the indifference of other nations and felt it was safe to proceed with the extermination of European Jewry.

They hermetically closed their countries, their eyes, their hearts, and their conscience. Phrases of "love" preached for two thousand years meant nothing to their believers. Like the idols, "mouth they have but speak not; eyes they have but see not; ears they have but hear not" (Psalms 115).

The so-called civilized nations, their statesmen and leaders, stood mutely by and let the Jews perish when they could have saved hundreds of thousands by lowering the bars of immigration.

The British historian Hugh Trevor-Roper told an audience at Duquesne University that the Catholic church shared responsibility for the rise to power of Hitler and Mussolini. The Vatican achieved concordats with both dictators granting the church a privileged position in Germany and Italy. Trevor-Roper said later in an interview that Popes Pius XI and Pius XII were able to reach agreements with Hitler and Mussolini that they would not have been able to achieve with democratic regimes. He indicated that since the church influenced the voting of Catholic political parties in Europe, both Hitler and Mussolini were materially assisted in setting up their dictatorships by the activities of the Catholic (political) church. The historian said bluntly: "The popes were responsible for Hitler and Mussolini coming to power."

Trevor-Roper further observed that Hitler's rise to power in Germany was in fact a revolution with an unusual characteristic—it was peaceful. Yes, some opponents were murdered by the Nazi Party in 1934 and others were terrorized, but, he added, "Every other comparable revolution in history has had opposition that had to be crushed with great volume. Hitler's revolution was carried out in perfect peace." The Germans accepted him.

Arthur Morse has documented in his *While Six Million Died* how the indifference of the U.S. State Department furthered the Nazi murder plot. The perfidy and apathy of the Roosevelt administration, the Churchill government in Great Britain, the Communist Stalin regime, and the pope in Rome established a climate of silence and conspiracy. When the Allied forces first had news of the extermination camps, they did not publish it. ". . . for we are sold, I and my people, to be destroyed, to be slain, and to perish. But if we had been sold for slaves, I would have been quiet." How can mankind breathe freely and enjoy all that nature has created? Such a world has no right to laugh and live!

I saw the Warsaw Ghetto with thousands of skeletons extending their bony arms as if begging for mercy and life. I saw the Warsaw Ghetto littered with corpses—their faces distorted and swollen, their eyes wide open, skulls crushed. And blood everywhere, the blood of our children, our brothers and sisters, our fathers and mothers. No imagination, no matter how daring, could possibly conceive of anything we have seen and lived through. No language has been created to describe the enormity of the Holocaust and the slaughter of European Jewry.

The aftermath of the uprising: the Gehenna of Gehennas. On that day when we first saw men, women, and children being led into the house of death, I shed bitter tears of despair. We suffered most when we looked at the children, accompanied by their mothers or walking alone, and within a few minutes their lives were snuffed out under horrible tortures.

After the liberation, General Eisenhower visited the Feldefing D.P. camp. He asked me if I was going back to Poland. I answered him: "Poland is soaked with Jewish blood, how can you live in a cemetery?"

Deeper than the oceans and higher than the heavens was the tragedy of the Jewish people!

We were lonely and forsaken in a world of brutality and bestiality.

We cried out in anguish to save our naked lives: "We and our children will labor and toil, we give you all our possessions, our gold and silver, all our accumulated wealth of one thousand years."

—but in vain. Nobody came to comfort us, nobody came to break the wall of loneliness that surrounded us.

"They have heard that I sigh."

The yells of the women, the weeping of the children, the cries of despair and misery, begging for mercy, for God's vengeance, ring in my ears to this day! "God of Retribution, Lord God of retribution appear! Arise, thou Judge of the earth" (Psalms 94:1-2).

I will avenge their blood, which I have not avenged (Joel 4:21).

A Survivor's Reflection
on Marrying Off Children

Rabbi Dr. Isaac C. Avigdor

Considering the fact that a rabbi often participates in wedding ceremonies, various thoughts frequently come to my mind regarding the Jewish marriage rite.

Recently, at the wedding of our third son, old questions floated up in my memory—old questions intermingled with the problems of our generation of Holocaust survivors. The questions are many, but let's consider just a few of them.

First: There is an important statement in the Talmud which says that one is obligated to cheer the bride and groom with five sounds: ". . . the sound of joy and the sound of gladness, the sound of grooms and the sound of brides, the sound of people saying 'Thank the God of Hosts'" (Berakhot 6b). (Rabbi Naḥman bar Isaac adds that doing so is equivalent to rebuilding one of the ruins of Jerusalem.) The question arises: Why should the bride and groom have to be regaled, why should they be sad on their wedding day, as they stand under the bridal canopy, which is supposed to be the happiest moment of their lives?

Second: If solemn thoughts, or even sad feelings, are present at a wedding, they are present in the hearts of the two sets of parents. It might be more fitting, perhaps even the fulfillment of a religious duty, to regale the parents rather than the bride and groom.

Third: Under the bridal canopy the bridegroom recites the ancient formula as he places the ring on the bride's finger: "You are hereby consecrated to me . . . according to the law of Moses and of Israel." When performing other religious rites of passage, such as the *berit milah* (circumcision), *pidyon ha-ben* (redemption of the first-born), or bar mitzvah, we do not recite an equivalent formula. Why is this done only in the marriage rite?

Fourth: When a child is born, the parents recite the blessing, "Who is good and beneficent." They thank God for having granted them the gift of a child who will be a source of joy to them. A time comes when that very same father announces publicly, in the synagogue at his son's bar mitzvah: "Blessed be He [God] for freeing me from liability for this one's [the bar mitzvah boy's] wrongdoings." The father says, as it were: "This gift you have given us, God, is a great burden, and we thank You for relieving us of this burden, and of the liability for the boy's sins, which he henceforth bears." The time distance is not great between "Who is good and beneficent" and "Blessed be He for freeing me," but the contrast between them is like the contrast between black and white.

Fifth: Why is the figure of the mother-in-law universally such a negative one? She is the symbol of dissatisfaction; she is stereotypically a person whom it is impossible to please. How does the sweetest mother in the world turn into the sourest mother-in-law?

Sixth: How is it that when children grow up, they start rebelling against their parents: Many even go as far as to develop hatred and run away from home. And instead of respect and love, they bring their parents disgrace and aggravation. The conflict between the generations is an eternal one, and not only among Jews. It is a painful problem, one that afflicted Adam, the first human being, and our Patriarchs Abraham, Isaac, and Jacob. The Torah clearly relates the episodes concerning grief caused by children.

Seventh: It is difficult to understand the talmudic assertion that "matching up men and women for marriages is as difficult as the parting of the Red Sea was in the time of the Exodus" (Sotah 2a), in spite of the efforts of hundreds of commentators over the ages to explain it. What is the analogy between the miracle of splitting the sea and a couple's getting married? There is certainly no obvious similarity between the two.

It is worthwhile to analyze carefully what takes place when a man and a woman get married.

As early as in the Book of Genesis, in the account of the creation of Adam and Eve, mankind is told, "Therefore it is a man's duty to leave his parents and establish a permanent bond with his wife." The implementation of this command, however, is not so simple. There are children who are so attached to their parents that the obligation to separate themselves from them involves a great sacrifice on their part. I know many men and women who have never married on account of their fathers or mothers.

Our Patriarch Abraham's fulfillment of God's command to leave his father's house was the first of the ten tests to which God put him. The Torah's decree to leave one's parents conflicts in a way with the Fifth Commandment, which orders us to honor them.

That is why, under the bridal canopy, the groom says to his betrothed, "You are hereby . . ." He is saying, in effect: "I know that you feel as badly about having to leave your parents' home as I do about leaving mine. But it is all 'according to the law of Moses and of Israel.' That is what God wishes, and the Torah commands us to do two things: to leave our parents and to cleave to each other, body and soul, as a harmonious couple." Implementing the command to separate ourselves from our parents and leave them is a serious matter in the lives of two people. That is why the couple is serious, and perhaps even sad, on the wedding day. It is up to us to regale them and lift their spirits, as a special mitzvah.

It is an equally difficult moment for the parents, whose children are leaving them and giving all their love away to "strangers." A mother's emotions on the child's wedding day are expressed in the commandment to drive the mother bird from the nest before taking her chicks. The Torah understands a mother's heart, even the heart of a mother bird, and the pain she would suffer at seeing her chicks being taken away from her. So when we wish to take chicks from a nest, we must first send away the mother, so she shall not directly experience the loss.

According to that commandment, parents of children getting married should be sent away while the wedding takes place. Everybody understands, especialy the mother of a bride or groom, that a child has to marry in order to complete his or her happiness. Meanwhile, however, her soul is torn to pieces. The more devoted a mother is, the more jealous she is as a mother-in-law. The same applies to fathers, albeit in a slightly different fashion. At any rate, it is certainly true that the wedding day is a serious day for both the newlyweds and the parents.

Perhaps this is what the Talmud has in mind when it compares matching up a couple to the splitting of the Red Sea. At a wedding, too, there is a "splitting" of the laws of the natural, innate love that a child feels toward its parents, and parents toward their children. One of our sons once burst into tears and begged us to let him live with us forever. He said he did not want to get married. That happened when he was ten years old . . .

What does the Master of the Universe do? He comes to help us implement the division that takes place on the implementation of the "leave" decree. First God drips into our hearts that infusion called "love." The potential of human love between members of the two sexes is great. "Love is as powerful as death." Love helps the lad and the the lass overcome their longing for their parents. The "cleave" is the cure for the "leave."

God uses another means to help both the parents and the children, by planting jealousy and hatred, the very opposite of love, in their hearts. When children grow up a bit, they develop a tendency to individualism, oppositionism, and rebelliousness vis-à-vis their parents. They constantly find themselves being wronged and find shortcomings in their elders, and they are always finding cause to be piqued and to pout. These quarrels serve a special purpose in both directions: they wean the children of their dependence on their parents' home, and they prepare the parents for the day of separation. The atmosphere at home becomes so tense that the parents thank God from the bottom of their hearts at finally being rid of their son or daughter. This is where the "parting of the Red Sea" comes in, the parting of two generations. Things ease up a bit. The parents no longer have to be regaled, because their children's marriage is salvation from Heaven for them. Good riddance, thank God.

If all these problems are eternal and universal, the emotions upon escorting one's children to the bridal canopy are different for us Holocaust survivors. We who returned from that "other planet" react differently, both psychologically and physically, on such occasions.

I remember, when I was in the Mauthausen concentration camp, often wondering what I would do if I survived the war. Regarding getting married, I had many doubts whether I would ever be able to do so. For several reasons I excluded the possibility of starting a family. Even after the liberation, I thought about the time of Aaron, Miriam, and Moses' father, Amram, in Egypt, and as in the period of the destruction of the Temple and the horrendous persecutions, when Jewish men did not cohabit with their wives, in order not to bring children into the world to be murdered by the enemy. I have never been able to erase from my memory the image of children being murdered by the Nazis and flung aside like slaughtered chickens.

Another thought terrified me. Who knew what the Germans had done to our bodies? Who knew what kind of cripples would be born of a father who over the years had suffered illnesses such as typhus, cholera, and the like? Who knew what had been mixed into the concentration camp soup cauldrons?

Indeed, I married late. Various girls were suggested to me in Europe and, especially, in the United States. I was unable to make up my mind. Some nightmares and dark dreams continued to haunt me. I was afraid.

Once, after my father, of blessed memory, repeatedly asked when I would finally marry, I poured my heart out to him. He gave me the answer that Miriam gave her father, Amram, in convincing him to go back home to her mother and have more children.

"What gives you the right to play God?" my father argued. "We have to do our duty, and leave the rest to the Master of the Universe.

"Secondly, no Jew, especially not a survivor is allowed to continue carrying out Hitler's plan to exterminate the Jewish people, God forbid. Our not marrying means national suicide."

I got married, and when my wife became pregnant with our first child I promptly notified my father. Here is what he replied: "Have

no fear or worry. For having so devotedly fulfilled the commandment to honor your own parents, your progeny will be healthy and
you will derive much joy from them, please God, and they will be a
glory to our people and our family."

My father's blessing has materialized, thank God. Unfortunately,
however, he did not live to escort a single grandchild to the bridal
canopy. I have often thought what a joyous celebration it would
have been if he had lived to do so.

May his merits protect us and the entire Jewish people.

A Child of Survivors Speaks

Rabbi Bernhard H. Rosenberg

As a *ben yaḥid,* a child of parents who survived the horrors of the Holocaust, I am constantly asked to comment regarding my feelings and sensitivities. I applaud those individuals who have painstakingly embarked on new avenues to communicate with children of survivors. Indeed, many may be in need of specialized advice to aid them in confronting their innermost anxieties and tensions. Sharing emotions, communicating one's fears, is of utmost importance. Some may, as psychologists have often suggested, sense pains of guilt. Others may seek to rebel against an environment which projects images of nightmares. Still others may avoid any conversation or situation which might awaken latent emotions.

I, for one, wish to share my personal thoughts regarding the issue of "children of survivors." I do not pretend to be an authority on the subject, nor do I dare speak from psychological expertise. I merely wish to speak from the heart, as a child of survivors who cares and loves his brethren.

Many children of survivors have been categorized as possessing immense guilt. Others have attributed their zealousness for achievement to an intense need for survival. Yet others have been labeled as being overly concerned for their parents or quite the opposite, rejecting parental authority and fleeing from the stereotyped image of Holocaust survivors.

I personally feel no guilt for having the God-given privilege of being alive. I mourn for my grandparents, uncles, and aunts who perished at the hands of Nazi maniacs; often weeping for not having experienced their love. I cry in anguish when reminded that six million of my brethren, young and old, left this earth via gas chambers and crematoriums. I sense the pain of my family and friends who saw their elders shot before their very eyes and their babies hurled against brick walls and bayoneted. I experienced deep anger when I viewed the numbers branded on the arm of my father, of blessed memory. Yet I thanked God for sparing the lives of my beloved parents.

Yes, I blame humanity for remaining silent while my innocent brethren perished screaming in terror for someone to heed their outcries. Humanity; not God. We are not puppets to be controlled by our Creator. People caused the Holocaust; people remained silent. Leaders of countries refused to intercede on behalf of the defenseless.

Should I then hate humanity? Should I live with anger in my heart, rebelling against the environment, rejecting those of other faiths and cultures? Perhaps I should bend in fear like a blade of grass when the winds of anti-Semitism turn toward me. Perhaps I should walk along the rocky paths of society fearing what the future may bring.

I openly and candidly answer in the negative. No, I will not live in a shell of neurotic chaos, and I will not reject society. I refuse to live in a world which rejects hope, receiving nourishment from the seeds of hatred.

I admire and respect my beloved parents, Jacob and Rachel, and honor them for their strength and courage. Even Auschwitz could not diminish their faith. They could have rejected humanity; instead they aided others in their daily fight for existence. No, a world of anger and hostility was not their banner.

Refuse to discuss the Holocaust? Sweep these memories under the rug? No—this is not our mission to the world and ourselves. Let the truth be known! Let others realize what the world did to an ethical, moral, and religious populace. Let them hear the testimony of valiant survivors. Let them see our courage.

Feel guilt for surviving, for speaking on behalf of children who were silenced—*never!*

I became a rabbi to aid the living, to ensure our survival; to rekindle the Jewish flame. I am proud; proud of my heritage, proud of our strength, and proud of my beloved parents.

Contrary to what we are told, the passage of time does not ease the pain, nor does it diminish the scope of the horror that was the Holocaust.

Oh yes, there are those, few in number, who feel that it is psychologically healthier to avoid reminders that keep painful and unpleasant events alive. Why subject our young to the brutal story of Nazi bestiality toward the Jewish people? What purpose will it serve? It would be wiser not to talk about it so that it can disappear.

Never! We must never stop telling this story. Tell it we must, in every gory detail! We must tell it over and over again until it is etched in the minds of our young and until it has become part of their lives and heritage. We must do this because it is our sacred duty to alert them to the evils of men, so that they will never be lulled into a false sense of safety and security. We must alert them so that our children will be vigilant and will never be caught unaware as were the Jews who perished in the Holocaust.

Although we are cognizant that our children will be adversely affected, that they will feel great pain upon learning the true facts of the Holocaust, we know that this is something we must do.

One such story told to me concerned a Jew accused of possessing a firearm. He was placed on a gallows that had been built in front of his home. A noose was placed around his neck as a crowd gathered. His wife and young son stood by, sobbing. The Nazi officer in charge then gave the boy the horrendous choice of hanging his father or they would shoot his terrified mother. Each parent pleaded with the youth to save the other. When the distraught boy finally hanged his father, the butchers laughed and shot his mother. As the youngster, whose mind snapped, started to run away, the Nazi murderers shot him too.

Six million Jews were mutilated, shot, buried alive, and gassed. Among those innocent souls there were over one million children whose sin was being Jewish. Like our children, they attended school, played with toys and went to Hebrew school. Like our chilren, they too dreamed of becoming teachers, rabbis, mothers, and so forth. It was not to be! The night came when the dreams died with the children. This night was different from the other nights, for on this night they were sent to their graves. And the world slept while the children screamed in agony and fright. What we Jews want to know from the world is, What has been done and what is being done to prevent this from happening again?

The civilized world has learned of our tragedy. The media have shown newsreels of the camps, bodies, bones, graves, clothing, even the wedding rings and hair. Has the world erected a stop sign or a traffic light to end such destruction and to prevent another Holocaust?

In voting unanimously, prior to 1939, to refuse refuge to the desperate Jews of Europe who sought asylum, the governments of the world and their people became accomplices in the Holocaust. That same civilized world proceeded to do nothing to stop the genocide even though the *New York Times* openly confirmed the rumors that the Jews were being systematically annihilated.

In 1945, when the war was over and the smoke had cleared, wherever civilized men still lived, the horror that was the story of Auschwitz, Treblinka, Sobibor, and Buchenwald became common knowledge. People were outraged! Everyone, including the Germans, claimed that they had never known that this was happening. That did not stop the countries, those who were outraged as well, from placing quotas and restrictions on Jewish immigration

No longer are Jewish children being killed in gas chambers. Today they are slain on the highway between Tel Aviv and Netanyah. No longer are the Jews being hung. They are now being gunned down by Arabs in a room in Ma'alot. No longer are the Jews being used for experimental purposes. They are attacked at the Olympics in Munich, and they are dynamited in the synagogues in France. Unlike the Nazis, these murderers are quick to claim credit for the carnage. They scream with joy, "We did it, we did it!"

This annihilation is not the same as the Holocaust; the difference being that the murderers walk among civilized men and are respected. The Holocaust is the PLO attending the United Nations, being treated with respect, socializing with our senators and partying with the elite of the world. When the United Nations and the world behave in such a manner as to render the deaths of our children, our athletes, and our people meaningless, then we have a Holocaust.

It is not over for the PLO. They are not yet finished with the ugly work they started and must still do. There are kindergartens, super-markets, stadiums, and buses to be bombed, and the world is allow-ing it to happen, since it does not deal with the terrorists as it should. There was no ultimatum given to Idi Amin. Did the com-bined world threaten to destroy him if he did not return the victims to safety? No, they did not! That is what is utterly amazing and not the daring rescue executed by the Israelis.

We dare not be silent while atrocities are still being committed in the universe. Man has learned that to protect human life, human rights, and freedom, sacrifices must be made, and sometimes there must be armed resistance as well. From the Holocaust man has learned that he must remember and never forget.

There is a cloud, a stigma, if you will, that must be dissolved, erased, and dispelled once and for all times, so that our sad, proud, and heroic Jewish heritage can be passed down to future generations without shame.

For obvious reasons, one of which is lack of knowledge, all too many people still believe that the Jews of the Holocaust were cowards who went to their untimely and inhumane deaths without making any effort to fight and survive. After the passage of some forty-plus years, surely it is time to lift the veil of deception or mis-conception so as to enlighten those among us who have not yet learned the true story of what must certainly be the most shameful period in the history of mankind.

Controversial questions and issues rarely have simple solutions or answers. The question of why they didn't fight back is not only controversial but haunting. If one believes that the Jews of the Holocaust went to their graves like sheep to the slaughter, then one assumes that these Jews were cowards. Who but an anti-Semite would make so a vicious generalization as to infer that the Jewish people are different in that they are not imbued with the courage that results in acts of heroism? Who but an enemy of the Jewish people would point to the fact that the Jews waited placidly to be used as experiments or to be slain. These same anti-Semites propounded the theory that the Holocaust victims, guilt-ridden Jews, accepted their fate as just punishment for "crimes" they had committed.

Fabrications! Misconceptions! The Indians have an adage that refers to keeping one's counsel until one has been in a similar situation. Let us apply this to the Jews of the Holocaust and to ourselves.

Imagine a life of gainful employment, some peace and contentment, a life wherein you and your family are comparatively safe and secure. Then imagine that same life turned into an endless nightmare in which you and your loved ones, your friends, and your family are subjected to unspeakable horrors. Can you conceive of a world in which morality, kindness, humanity, and love are nonexistent? To this, add the fact that you did nothing to evoke this destruction of your world. Bear in mind that it is happening to you and your people only because you are Jewish.

Now that you are the victim, picture yourself brainwashed, intimidated by centuries of persecution at the hands of governments, inquisitors, and Hamans. Remember the centuries of Jews being victimized by prejudice and hatred, and then, maybe then, you will begin to understand the emotional upheaval of the Jew of the Holocaust.

You must under no condition, lose sight of the degradation and the dehumanization that you are subjected to with the Nuremberg Laws. Remember the beatings and painful acts of anti-Semitism that are being visited upon your beloved guiltless children and all the Jews of your town. Do not for one minute forget the economic boycott that has brought with it not only privation but fear of starvation.

You know that you are trapped and you must leave. You want to leave, but where can you go and how can you turn your back on the remainder of your family? The international conference at Evian,

France, has made it quite clear to you that the arms and the doors of people and of the world are closed to you as a Jew. Compare the "J" for *Jude* on your passport with the mark of Cain. You are not an acceptable emigre, hence you stay in hell, where on Kristallnacht your home, your business, and your shul are destroyed by those demons who must wipe everything Jewish off the face of the earth.

Then the arrests begin; people are sent to concentration camps, Jewish children are expelled from institutions of learning, and to be apprehended without that yellow badge is to invite death. How can you justify this nightmare to the innocent children? How can you allay their fears?

It does not stop there, for you must now be isolated like germs of contagion. Uprooted and resettled into crowded areas in ghettos, your numbers diminish because those among you who are aged or ill die from lack of nourishment and medical supplies. You hear infants, children crying with pain and hunger, and helplessly, you watch them expire. You cover your ears to deaden the wailing of the bereaved, and your howls of pain at the gross injustice fall on a world with deaf ears, blind eyes, and no heart. They hear not, see not and care not!

Now your travails really begin, for you and your family must report to a depot for a journey through hell to an unknown destination. Try, if you can, put yourself and your family into that boxcar where there are no sanitary facilities and where you are jammed together so that even those who die enroute remain upright. Can you go a step further and stretch your imagination so that you can smell the dead old Zayda who died hours and hours ago while pleading for a little air?

Conjure up the face of the beast posing as a man who points to the left or the right as you alight from the train more dead than alive. Of course, your destination was a concentration camp. You are separated from your wife and children, who are of no use to the Nazis and are therefore reduced to ashes in the crematoriums. You are overcome with new grief and you want to die; but you don't

You are overwhelmed by the amount of smoke that spews forth from those hateful chimneys and wonder why the entire world cannot see or smell it.

Now there are acts of insubordination which result in retaliations so horrendous that you learn that there is only one way to survive, by obedience. There is no escape, no place to go to, and no one who will help you.

How long has it been in time; how much longer can you withstand the hunger and the abuse? You will go on because you see those who are ill disappearing never to return. Like a branded animal, you live through freezing winters and torrid summers, and all you know and feel is pain.

Is that a dream you are having, one in which you feel that the day will come when this will end and you will live to build a new life as well as a better world? Are you now praying for that day as you try to blot out the beloved faces of your wife and children? Now you sob and beat your breast as they refuse to stay dead and parade pitifully before your eyes.

Fight back? How? Disarm the guards? With what?

Now that you've been there, can you recognize the courage it took to survive? Here we have real heroism! Beaten, starved, and barely alive, the will to survive, that small flickering flame, did not die. In this shell of a human being lived the dream to build anew. Here indeed was a lion of a man who managed to live by sheer courage.

Heroism and courage do not come packaged in any particular shape, style, or color; they take many forms. The world must not be permitted to lose sight of the courage and heroism shown by this small group of tortured survivors of Hitler's inferno in returning to the land of the living and the building of a nation. That nation will not be muted and has dedicated itself and its children to a new and decent life.

Inconceivable as it may be, the combined Nazi atrocities and the inhumanity of mankind were incapable of extinguishing that eternal Jewish flame, the spirit.

There are many who wish to forget about the Holocaust, obliterate the entire nightmare from the face of the earth. Let's ask the six million, one million children among them, what they think, what they would want us to do. Do they not have some rights left? Or shall we go along with those who wish to forget and deny that the six million once lived, loved, and were brutally murdered?

Once and forever, we must erase the stigma placed upon the Jews of the Holocaust. Upon the entire world and upon each of us rests the responsibility of relating the story of Hitler the infamous and his brutal Nazis. The onus lies heavily upon the Jewish people, for the burden of dispelling the *lie* that they went to their deaths like sheep to the slaughter is ours.

It is our sacred duty to tell our young that once upon a time there was a Hitler who could not destroy the courage and will it took to survive the inferno that he and his Nazis flamed, the Holocaust.

The gas chambers are gone, figments of the Jewish imagination some would have you believe; in their stead we have a new form of genocide: cults. Oh yes, they are not bloody nor are they brutal; but they are more deceptive, organized, and dangerous. Brainwashing has replaced gassing. With this method the so-called evangelists, Hare Krishna, Jews for Jesus, etc., are focusing in on our young everywhere.

Time passes, things change but remain the same. The anti-Semites still pander the lie that the Jews control industry, the mass media, our banks, and that they manipulate the economy and politics as well. They are out there still, and the masses have yet to learn a lesson from the tragic events called the Holocaust.

That flicker of hope in the victims of the Holocaust, which became a flame in the survivors, will never be extinguished. We have survived the crematoria, the inquisitions, the pogroms, because we do fight back; and it is because of this courage and heroism that the people of Israel will live, live, live!

The Sephardic Experience

Sephardim in the Holocaust:
A Lesson for All Jews

RABBI M. MITCHELL SERELS

This essay is not intended to make an ethno-centric presentation or to belittle the enormous evil perpetrated against the Jewish people in its entirety. The purpose is, however, twofold. First, to provide a record of the historical evidence on the Sephardic chapter of the Holocaust. Second, to provide the Sephardim who perished with a memorial.

The destruction of European Jewry has, of course, been studied extensively, but it requires further investigation simply because of its magnitude. Since the overwhelming majority of Holocaust scholars are of Eastern European background, it is only natural for them to turn their attention to the Ashkenazic communities. In addition, they are often unfamiliar with the Ladino, French, and Arabic documentation that would facilitate study of the Sephardic Holocaust experience.

To fill this desideratum, I will turn my attention to where my efforts can best bear fruit in reporting what happened to the Jews. By studying the situation of the Sephardim, with whom the Nazis had little contact during the formative period of Nazi planning before the war, we can understand the depth of the Nazi hatred for the Jews. While it is true that Hamburg had a Sephardic community (or Portugese as they preferred to call themselves) dating to the seventeenth century, and Vienna had a late-nineteenth-century transplanted community from the Balkans, both of these communities were annihilated. The Germans had had little contact with Spanish-and Arabic-speaking Jewry.

The chapter on the Holocaust amongst Sephardim must be told

321

and retold in order that the enmity and the depravity of all aspects of the Holocaust not be forgotten.

I shall therefore focus on three major areas relating to Sephardim during the Holocaust, namely, the Balkans, North Africa, and Iraq.

THE BALKANS

The Balkans, then under Ottoman rule, had welcomed Sephardic Jews at the end of the fifteenth century and at the beginning of the sixteenth century, when they left Spain following the Edict of 1492. After World War I, the countries of Greece, Yugoslavia, Bulgaria, and Albania, were formed with the largest group of Jews in Salonica, Greece. Indeed, the Jewish population was so prominent in the Greece in concert with the Axis powers. Some areas, particularly both spoken and literary, was Judeo-Spanish, popularly called Ladino. In addition the Alliance Israélite Universelle of Paris had provided many Jews with a French education. In general, the Jewish community had good relations with their Turkish neighbors but poor ones with the ethnic Greeks.

During the war, Greece, conquered by the Germans and the Italians, was divided into two zones of occupation. The Germans encouraged the formation of Greek anti-Semitic organizations which preyed on the general enmity between Greeks and Jews. In the end, the Germans deported the Jewish community of Salonica almost in its entirety. Ninety-five percent of these Jews were killed in Auschwitz.

The reasons for the Germans success were many. First, since Greek Jews did not speak the Greek language or have a great familiarity with the Greek culture or Orthodox Christianity, it was difficult for a Jew to disguise himself as an ethnic Greek. Second, since the Jewish population was large and concentrated, few Jews had friends in the Greek ethnic population who would hide them even for a price. Third, the Jews of these areas had generally lived quietly with their neighbors and were unaccustomed to virulent pogroms and anti-Semitic attacks. They did not have hidden gold or fluid assets, and were unprepared for the Nazi onslaught and were more readily broken in spirit. Fourth, the Jews of Greece knew little of the deaths in Auschwitz as the Germans, Italians, and pro-Nazi Greek groups controlled the media. The chief Rabbi of Salonica was a German Jew named Kronitz, who was arrested at one point, deported, and returned. The chief rabbi therefore portrayed himself as able to deal favorably with the German occupation authorities. In the end, he was a dupe of the Germans, and the few surviving Salonica Jews faulted him for not speaking out and for being an accomplice, willing or otherwise, in the annihilation of his community. When the Greek Jews were deported they readily believed they were being resettled in Poland with the rest of the Jews. Consequently, they exchanged their Greek drachmas for Polish zlotys, although Polish Jewry was already extinct.

The trains from Greece to Auschwitz took two and a half days, with their human cargo arriving tired, hungry, and thirsty. The Jews were generally in poor health when they left the warm Mediterranean for the cold of Central Europe. Very few were selected to be sent to the camps. Most were sent directly to their deaths in the gas chambers. These factors led to the nearly total extinction of the Salonica Jews.

Some, however, were able to obtain Spanish passports, or protection, or laissez-passer. The government of Generalissimo Franco extended some protection where possible and allowed these Jews to pass through Spain to Lisbon or to Spanish-occupied Tangiers. Once in Tangiers, the Jews were allowed to remain. Spanish passports were tendered to Jews in other areas of the Balkans as well as in France.

The Italians in the Balkans proved to be more humane than the Germans. But Italy was invaded by the Allies and the Mussolini government collapsed. Areas controlled by Italy were taken over by the German military. Those Jews then fell to the same fate as their Greek coreligionists.

In Yugoslavia, the Germans found ready accomplices in the Croatians. The Nazis had set up a pro-German Croatian puppet state headed by a Catholic priest. The Germans relied on the ethnic rivalry between the Croats and the Serbs. The Croats used three methods to lower the camp populations—starvation, typhus, and finally, gas vans. The gas vans were used first against the Yugoslavian Jews, the majority of whom were Sephardic, with additional Jews from various other areas. However, the Germans felt that the Croatians were unable to deal properly and effectively with the removal of the Jews. The Croatians would load Jews onto boats for transport to Poland; these boats were sunk in the middle of the river and the Jews drowned. But bodies were often washed up on shore, so the Germans ordered the rail transports to Poland to begin.

The fate of the Jews of Bulgaria was different. Bulgaria was a member of the Axis because of the monarchy's fears of its large Communist neighbor, the Soviet Union. The Jews of Bulgaria were for the most part Sephardim whose primary language was Ladino and they were tradesmen or skilled workmen. Jews had lived in Bulgaria even before the arrival of the Bulgars. There was no animosity between the two peoples.

As German allies, the Bulgarians attacked Yugoslavia and Greece in concert with the Axis powers. Some areas, particularly Thrace, were incorporated into Bulgaria's new territories. Since Bulgaria was ever desirous of territorial gain, the government felt justifiably rewarded for its pro-German stance. However, the Germans began to demand that the Jews under Bulgarian control be transferred to Poland. The royal government handed over the Jews from the new territories, but balked at sending the Jews from Bulgaria proper. Either because of royal protection, Communist demonstrations, a strongly militant Zionist organization, Spanish interest, a fear of a Russian offensive, or simply a lack of anti-Semitic feelings, Jews from Bulgaria proper remained protected. Most likely it was a combination of these various factors which uniquely protected the Bulgarian Jews. Despite the benevolent relationship with the Bulgar people, the overwhelming majority of Bulgarian Jews emigrated to Israel when the war ended.

Culturally, the Sephardim of the Balkans did not fit into the established pattern of Jewish behavior as projected by Nazi propaganda. The Sephardim were an ethnic group unto themselves who maintained separate cultural, linguistic, and ethnic entities. Nonetheless, despite the paradox presented by the Balkan Sephardim, since they were Jews, the German sent them to fiery graves. The Jewish people must be destroyed!

Further evidence is available from the extermination of the centuries-old Jewish community on the island of Rhodes. Rhodes was initially under Italian control. With the collapse of the Mussolini government, the island came under German administration. Although the military situation was already going poorly for the Wehrmacht, the Germans were prepared to sacrifice troops in order to destroy Jews. The Germans off-loaded armaments needed for their military forces in order to load the Jews of Rhodes aboard two transport vessels that would convey them to the Greek mainland. The Germans suffered weapons losses and thereby took fatalities so that Jews could be transported to their deaths. At all costs, even the cost of German lives and victory, Jews, simply because they were Jews, had to be destroyed.

With the death of this group of Sephardim also died their culture and, for the most part, the Ladino language. The Jewish dialect of the Balkan Jews, Ladino, died in the flames of the death camp. This element of Jewish culture was a victim of the Holocaust along with the people who spoke the language.

NORTH AFRICA

At the beginning of the War, the Arab countries were under the control of European powers. Morocco and Tunisia were French protectorates. Algeria was incorporated into metropolitan France.

Libya was ruled by Italy and therefore came under direct Axis control. The French North African administration came under the
Vichy French. In keeping with the anti-Jewish regulations enacted
by the Vichy government, the president-general of Morocco and his
counterpart in Tunisia enacted similar legislation under the protectorate agreements and had the indigenous native rulers sign the
documents.

Moroccan Jews, the largest Sephardic ethnic group, also suffered, but the Allied invasion and the collapse of the Vichy administration prevented wholesale slaughter. Work camps were established
but incarceration was limited to refugee Jews as well as Moslem
criminals. Five ships in the port of Casablanca were used as jails and
were eventually to be sent to Europe with their Jewish cargoes. Fortunately, the Allies invaded North Africa before the ships were
properly prepared for the voyage.

Less fortunate were Moroccan Jews who found themselves in
France either on business, for education, or because they had married Eastern European Jews who resided in France. Not considered
French because they were Moroccan, and not Moroccan because
there was no independent state, these 128 Jews, many of them children and teenagers, were sent to the Drancy camp and then shipped
to the death camps. The French handed over these Francophile Jews
to their German destroyers.

Tunisian Jewry did not fare as well on its own territory. The
Allies advanced in Tunisia after landing in French Morocco and
Algeria. They purposely avoided Spanish Morocco and Tangiers,
under Spanish control, where many Eastern European Jews had
found refuge. The Germans and Italians invaded Tunisia, over-
throwing the Vichy government and divided the country into two
zones of military command. The battlefront approximated the
Tunisian-Algerian border. In each zone, camps for Jews were set up
under the control of the Wehrmacht. These camps for Jews, in which
tens of thousands were incarcerated, and twenty-five hundred died,
were not run by the dreaded SS, but rather by the highly disciplined
German army.

The Italian-run camps were harsh because of their location in the southern area of Tunisia, but the members of the Italian military were in general more humane in an inhumane situation. Moreover, Tunisian Jews were well organized and were willing to take chances to protect their fellow Jews. The Jews were called upon to feed and clothe the Jews in the camps. In doing so, they assigned the task to keep a list of all inmates and published who died, how, and at whose hands. A system called the Terminities communicated the needs and news of inmates. Many Jews joined the Free French or acted as spies and saboteurs on behalf of the Allies. Some spied and had clandestine radios, others simply carried information by bicycle. The wearing of the yellow star badge was not consistently enforced. In Tunis, it was mandatory and enforced. In Italian areas it was only randomly enforced. Men like Paul Ghez and Community President Borgel, who gave his own fortune as a communal ransom, intervened constructively and actively. The Germans, when they began to withdraw, took Jews on their own boats under the impression that the Allies would not sink them if Jews were there. The Germans did this because they believed the Nazi propaganda that the Jews were the reason the Allies opposed the Axis. These hostage Jews died in Buchenwald and Dachau.

In Italian-occupied Libya, the Arab population was subjected to intense Fascist propaganda. Italian anti-Jewish legislation was more strenuously enforced in Libya than in Italy proper. Concentration camps were opened, round-ups made, stars worn, and children ejected from school. The full weight of anti-Semitic legislation was felt.

Camps were opened by the Italians to concentrate Jews into an organized slave-labor force. The Fascists were able to mobilize the local Italians and Maltese ethnics. The Jews had originally welcomed the Italians as the bearers of a culture that would save them from second-class status, but the German insistence on racial laws forced the Italians to adopt a racist policy. Although they were solicitous toward the Jews on the mainland, the Jews in their African colony were not so fortunate. The Italians had no enmity toward "their

Jews" but not so the colonists toward "their Jews." The Germans relied on local anti-Semitism in order to complete the final solution. When the Axis troops withdrew they left behind an indigenous Arab population steeped in Nazi propaganda. When the Khaddafi revolution seized power, the Jews realized they had to leave.

IRAQ

The exposure to Nazi propaganda was also felt in Iraq, which demonstrated pro-German sympathies. In April and May of 1941, Iraq tried to oust the British, but to no avail. The Arabs were already fiercely anti-British and therefore sympathized with the Germans. But they were also being bombarded by Nazi propaganda. The most effective propagandist for the Nazis was Haj Amin el-Husseini, the Mufti of Jerusalem. With Nazi subsidies, the mufti had incited the mob riots of Palestine in 1936–1939. The mufti fled to Rome, but realizing that Hitler was the moving force, he flew to Berlin in January 1941. The Nazis utilized the mufti in two ways—to broadcast propaganda to the Arab world and to form Moslem units, particularly in the Balkans, to fight on behalf of the Axis.

Iraq was vital to German interests because of its oil deposits and its strategic location. Oil would be needed for the war machine. Iraq, if it fell to the Nazis, would divide the British Empire and thereby leave the Asian areas of India and the Far East to the Japanese and the Middle Eastern areas to Germany and her Italian and Vichy allies. German trade missions and educational exchanges were pretexts for propaganda and for building on existing anti-British sentiment.

Four Iraqi military commanders, known as the Golden Square, organized a coup d'état on March 31, 1941, and appointed Rashid Ali el-Khailani prime minister. They began their revolt against the British shortly thereafter and as one of their first renewed de facto relations with Germany, promised oil from Mosul and railway and airport rights. The British, to protect their air bases at Habanniya and Shewaba, brought in troops from India and Palestine. Germany and Italy funneled aid through the Vichy forces in Syria and Lebanon.

During the April revolt there was a pogrom against the Jews. Hundreds were hurt or killed; many women were raped and children disappeared. During Shavuot, a more extensive pogrom, or *fard,* occurred. Nine hundred Jews were killed in Baghdad. Kurdish troops had to be brought in to quell the pogrom because the Iraqi troops had been exposed to Nazi propaganda and were infected with anti-Semitism. The mufti called for a holy war against the British but had to flee to Iran when the revolt was crushed.

In October 1941, the mufti was again in Europe, and on November 21, 1941, he had a two-hour conversation with Hitler. Hitler promised that German planes would bomb Tel-Aviv to bring about the elimination of the Jewish presence in Palestine. Anti-Semitic propaganda broadcasts increased even from Tokyo. Arab parachutists trained in German-occupied Athens dropped behind the British lines in the Middle East and North Africa. Fifteen thousand Moslems, mainly from Albania and Yugoslavia, were supervised by the mufti. He encouraged them to fight to exterminate world Jewry and end British imperialism.

El-Husseini promised to organize the Moslem population of Russia. In Hungary, he met with Eichmann and Hungarian anti-Semitic leaders, encouraging them to proceed with the liquidation of the Jews, for the fewer Jews left alive, the fewer would go to Palestine. After the war, the French and British authorities prevented him from being tried for collaboration lest this further incite the Arabs against the colonial powers. In 1946 El-Husseini was allowed to leave house arrest in France and go to Egypt, where he was welcomed by King Farouk.

Clearly, the evidence indicates that the Holocaust was not aimed only at European Jewry, nor was it only European Jewry that suffered. The aim was to kill all Jews regardless of geography, culture, or language. Nor were German Christians the only anti-Semites who played a role in the destruction.

The shock was more intense amongst Balkan and North African Jewry. Jewry's end came swiftly and intensely—especially that of the Yugoslav and Greek Jews. The destruction of Balkan Jewry belies the revisionist historians who view the Holocaust as a fight for *Lebensraum* (living space). The islands of the Aegean and Rhodes were not to be populated by others. The Germans viewed the Jew as a conspirator who had to die. When Jews themselves begin to blame the victims by attributing German anti-Semitism to assimilation or to Jewry's isolation, they do a disservice to the truth. The case of the Sephardim points to the singularity of anti-Semitism, the hatred of the Jew regardless of what he does or who he is. The Jew can therefore do nothing—except to be a Jew.

Resource Materials

Holocaust Bibliographies:
A Partial View

Rabbi Dr. Fred S. Heuman

The literature of the Holocaust has grown in the last three decades more than any other singular aspect of literature. It may well be that no topic in literature has ever had a similar mushrooming of literary creations in so many forms and in so short a period of time. The literary endeavors in nonfictional reminiscences, diaries, notes and documentations with commentaries, historical studies and descriptions stand alongside the plethora of fictional poetic and prose creations. This literary activity extends into various mediaforms: scripts for films, radio plays, television and video programs, the programs for memorial and commemorative occasions.

This growth has engendered bibliographical works which serve as surveys and guides. As more books are published, more bibliographical resource books are needed. These studies vary in their approaches and comprehensiveness. The aim of this investigation is to catalogue and critically examine the most signigicant bibliographical resource collections.

The creation of a descriptive survey of the bibliographical data would undoubtedly contribute to facilitate research in the field of Holocaust studies and to improve scholarly access to this resource material information. The scope should enhance its effectiveness. Besides the examination of strictly bibliographical works, bibliographical information in a variety of general works about the Holocaust will be examined. The data to be described will be deemed to be a highly effective means to disseminate bibliographical information.

At this time, no guide or evaluative study has been published regarding this extensive body of bibliographical literature. It would be of significance for scholarship to have bibliographical listings enhanced by a critical evaluation of their scope, comprehensiveness and relative usefulness. Thus this study is designed to supply these insights by an analysis of the bibliographical resource material. In addition, significant bibliographies are given, as already mentioned, in many literary works on the general topic of the Holocaust.

Yad Vashem, the Jerusalem Institute devoted to all aspects of the Holocaust, for example, has published a cumulative index of its volumes in Holocaust studies, *Yad Vashem Studies* (Jerusalem, 1983). It lists three cross-indices for volumes 1–15: contents, subject issues, and countries. Under subject issues, five bibliographical studies are listed (pp. 402–403). None are annotated.

Extensive bibliographies have been issued, in additon to the yearbooks, by the Yad Vashem Martyrs' and Heroes' Memorial Authority in Jerusalem and the the YIVO Institute in New York, which include works in English, Hebrew, and Yiddish. Both institutions are storehouses of Holocaust material and promote ongoing research. In addition, they publish single works and are equipped to answer inquiries.[1]

A compact and useful annotated bibliography, *The Holocaust and Genocide Curriculum Guide,* is published by the Anti–Defamation League of B'nai B'rith.[2] All 313 entries refer to works in English, and all are well described. The list includes books, journal articles, newspaper reports, and pamphlets. Some references are themselves compilations.[3] In addition, this guide lists 123 entries for audiovisual realia. A list of names and addresses for these materials is also appended. Some entries, such as the films on Hiroshima/Nagasaki and on the relocation of Japanese Americans, would, in the reviewer's opinion, tend to diffuse the uniqueness of the Holocaust.

Catalogues[4] and publishers' book lists[5] yield valuable information and can help in the acquisition of a bibliography by the owning of the books.

A massive work of bibliography by Edelheit and Eidelheit, *Bibliography on Holocaust Literature* (Westview Press, 1986), contains 9,014 items and an index of authors. It even catalogues a specialized bibliography such as K. Y. Ball-Kaduri's "Testimonies and Recollections About Activities Organized by German Jewry During the Years 1933–1935," an unpublished manuscript listed in the 1960 Catalogue of Manuscripts in the Yad Vashem archives. It also lists a bibliographical essay, E. G. Lowenthal's "Shadow of Doom—Post-War Publications on Jewish Communal History in German," from the *Leo Baeck Institute Yearbook* of 1966. Both entries remain, however, undescribed.

Now to a description. This most ambitious and massive *Bibliography on Holocaust Literature* by Edelheit and Eidelheit contains, besides the 9,014 items, an index of authors. It is divided into four sections, called parts, and twenty subsections as follows:

Part 1. Before the Storm
    Subsections: 1. Jewish Life in Prewar Europe
                  2. Modern Europe: Seedbed for Destruction
                  3. Anti-Semitism

Part 2. The Perpetrators
    Subsections: 4. Fascism
                  5. The SS State
                  6. The Nazis

Part 3. The Crucible
    Subsections: 7. World War II
                  8. Europe Under Nazism
                  9. The Concentration Camp System
                10. The Shoah
                11. Resistance
                12. The Bystanders
                13. The Free World Reaction

Part 4. Aftermath
    Subsections: 14. From Holocaust to Rebirth
                15. Reflections on the Holocaust
                16. Europe After World War II
                17. The Holocaust and the Literary
                     Inspiration

18. Yizkor Bicher—Memorial Volumes
19. Distorting the Holocaust
20. Historiography, Bibliographies, and
    Guides

It is quite comprehensive, but not complete. Subsection 17, for example, carries close to two hundred entries, yet lists no fictional work by Elie Wiesel.[6] Only two of his novels are listed elsewhere,[7] although there are thirty-two references to his articles. However, none of Wiesel's Yiddish articles, such as those published in the *Allgemeiner Journal,* are mentioned. The Wiesel entries are outdone by sixty-three references to the writings of Alfred Werner, including his seven-page article entitled "2,000 Years of German Jewish History." This bibliography needs a revised edition.

Another major bibliographical work is David M. Szonyi's *The Holocaust: An Annotated Bibliography and Resource Guide,* which the publisher, Ktav Publishing House, describes as "the most comprehensive attempt to date to provide lists of resources for those interested in Holocaust education and commemoration." It was published in 1985 in New York. It is in some instances a bit more, and in others a lot less, than its description. It prints, for example, the complete text of the resource material it refers to in some instances. On the other hand, it includes as sections of the book material assembled by others than Mr. Szonyi without avoiding duplications, and it lacks an overall numerical index. Each section, in brief, needs an evaluation. It does, in fact, include the text of the resource material in some instances. In section I-C of chapter 10, two texts are reproduced that are meant for "Yom HaShoah and Day of Remembrance Services, one for Jewish and one for Christian groups" (pp. 354–370). The texts originate with the U.S. Holocaust Memorial Council. Also listed are "three other recommended services." This reviewer passes no positive judgment on any of the five "services."

This comprehensive bibliography includes sections assembled by others than Mr. Szonyi, and the work appears somewhat diffusedly arranged with no overall numerical index. Yet any effort engendered

to consult this work will be rewarding, since its structural arrangement can be overcome. A detailed evaluation of this work is essential
to this study. The work is arranged into sections. Section I-A is divided into twenty-two topics, such as topic 18, verbosely entitled
"Theological, Philosophical, Historical, Psychological and Communal Perspectives on the Holocaust" (pp. 120–129). The concluding topic of the section is called "Bibliographies and Bibliographical
Essays" and lists nine general bibliographies (pp. 141–143).

Section I-B is devoted to a literary bibliography of more than
three hundred works of fiction, including some questionable items
such as Günter Grass, *The Tin Drum* (pp. 145–179). Section I-C lists a
subcategory entitled "Bibliographies of the Holocaust for Young
People." It is a welcome and long list. Some works, such as Elie
Wiesel's *Night*, are also listed in Section I-B. It is hard to comprehend why some of the works listed here, such as Moshe Prager's
Sparks of Glory, Moshe Flinker's *Young Moshe's Diary*, and Luba Drug-
man's *The Death Train*, are not cross-listed. They certainly go beyond
the interest level of just "Young People."

Section II is called "Audio-Visual Materials on the Holocaust"
(pp. 199–222). Although brief, its listing of films includes the pertin-
ent information of the films' distributors. *Sophie's Choice*, with its so
very realistic scenery of the extermination camp, was not found to
be included.

Section III deals with a very important area for programming
by listing musical resources, such as song collections, recordings,
performing scores, musical works, and relevant books and articles.
It does make for greater completeness that works such as Josef
Bor's *The Terezin Requiem*, which is listed in the literature section,
is crosslisted here as well.

A brief section follows which deals with traveling exhibits, while
Section V lists and describes almost forty research institutes and
archives. Section VI shows a quite incomplete list of "Holocaust
Memorials and Landmarks in the U.S. and Canada." For example,
the Brooklyn list mentions one of the most worthwhile research
centers of Holocaust studies, the one headed by Professor Yaffa

Eliach. To be of memorial and landmark status is hardly its function. Only two other synagogues, one Conservative and the other Reform, are listed for Brooklyn, A listing for Holocaust memorials in the Orthodox synagogues of Brooklyn and other cities is sorely needed.

Also included is a listing for survivors' groups (pp. 309–352), and the last chapter is self-explanatory. It is called "Funding for Holocaust Related Research and Programming" and includes the details necessary to reach the various state humanities councils.

In the *Macmillan Atlas of the Holocaust,* Martin Gilbert, a gifted writer on both Churchill and the Holocaust, illustrates his historical bibliographical references in drawings laid out like maps. These "maps" are the mainstay of the work. Are they accurate?

A number of works may effectively be used for displays if the material itself is used in exhibits. Thus it would not infringe upon the restrictions of copyright. One such is Martin Gilbert's *The Macmillan Atlas of the Holocaust,* published by the Macmillan Publishing Co. and the Jewish Publication Society. In essence, it is a good example of pedagogic realia. It is a story, not geographic maps, which is told in drawings laid out like maps. Each "map" is accompanied by a description of the historical events which are illustrated. These visual displays do "tell a lot," although it may be of varying importance, often approximating the truth, and sometimes they are inaccurate in that they fall short of the mark. Map 20, for example, entitled "Destruction of the Synagogues, 9 November 1938," should list also 10 November, the date on which many of Germany's synagogues were destroyed. A more important omission, which also relates to the impact this map is to evoke, are its fifty identifying dots for the names of the cities where this event took place. It is not indicated that hundreds of synagogues went up in smoke, many cities, towns, and villages which are left unrecorded on this map.

The MacMillan company recently published a four volume edition of an *Encyclopedia of the Holocaust,* which runs over 1900 pages. It is described as "the definitive guide to understanding the most important event of the 20th century" (N. Y. Times Book

Review, May 13, 1990, p. 15). Its contributors include the generally accepted authorities who deal with their own specialties. David Kranzler, for example, lists all of the sparse literature available which bears on his concise and factual entry under "Shanghai". Efraim Zuroff lists his three publications at the end of his not-too-kind description of the Vaad Hahatzala.

The encyclopedia, without doubt, will serve as an invaluable tool to introduce the subject of the Holocaust to students of varied levels for further study in depth.

Volume I covers the letters A to D (over 412 pages), including an alphabetical list of the entries (17 pages) and a directory of contributors (13 pages). Israel Gutman is editor in chief. Volume II covers the entries for the letters E to K to page 846, volume III L to R, ending at page 1317, and volume IV S to Z, followed by and Index. This index of 145 pages includes a glossary (pp. 1751–1757) a useful chronology (pp.1759–1782)and a very valuable appendix listing the following items:

1. Major Jewish organizations of the last 50 years.
2. Structure of the *Einsatzgruppen* from June 22, 1941
3. and 4. Nuremberg trial and proceedings
5. British trials
6. Estimated Jewish losses in the Holocaust

All the volumes are well-illustrated with photographic reproductions of portraits, ghettos, concentration and extermination camps with maps and paraphernalia showing the most innocent and the most gruesome reports, anti-semitic propaganda dissemination and resistance monuments.

It is a valiant attempt to categorize and popularize the study of the Holocaust. Not all entries are clear and easily grasped. In the "Joel Brand" entry, Randolph Braham writes that in the "blood for goods" offer, Jews would be permitted to go into any Allied-controlled part of the world except Palestine because of a promise made to the Mufti (Vol. I, pp. 238–240). Yet later Braham mentions"the concern of the British over acquiring responsibility for one million Jews in case of the Nazis kept their part of the bargain"

(Ibid). Would this concern be only because of the Nazis or because of the British acquiescence to the Mufti's wishes?

The study of the Holocaust has become a vast field for scholarly endeavors and one should not fault the encyclopedia for not being exhaustive. I was interested in ascertaining the number of synagogues destroyed in Germany during the actions of "Kristallnacht". There is an entry to be sure, Vol. II, p. 838, which mentions a report of Heydrich to Göring that 267 synagogues were set ablaze or were completely destroyed; he adds that this was only a fraction of the number of synagogues actually destroyed. However, no total figures are given nor is it said that any figure is available or not.[8]

Since Cologne and Leipzig are listed among the five most Jewishly populated cities in Germany after Berlin (Vol. II, p. 560), I searched for an entry to discuss the fate of these communities during the Holocaust. Only their Jewish Cultural societies are discussed.

The only other entry regarding Cologne treats the 'Nacht und Nebel' trials, Vol.III, pp. 10301-31,which did not involve Jews.

In perusing the maps it became evident that more work needs to be done in tracing the route the victims took from identification to concentration and from concentration to extermination. Thousands of Jews, for example, were shipped and concentrated in Izbica and Krasnistov near Lublin prior to their destruction in the Belzec and Maidanek camps. Neither concentration point appears on any of the many maps of the district of Lublin.

The encyclopedia is generally very helpful and informative. The index, pp. 1850-1851, for example lists 70 places which had Judenräte (operating Jewish councils). One of the most moving entries is one written by Israel Gutman, the editor in chief. In his description of Samuel A. Zygelboim a member of the Polish Government in Exile, stationed in London, part of the farewell letter which Zygelboim wrote on May 12, 1943, the day of his suicide, is quoted "Responsibility for the murder of the entire Jewish population of Poland lies primarily with the murderers themselves, but indirectly humanity as a whole is responsible, all the Allied nations and the governments who to date have done nothing to stop the crime from going on" (Vol. IV, pp. 1747-1749).

A review of films is given in *The Holocaust in American Film* by Judith Doneson, (Jewish Publication Society, Philadelphia 1987.)

Not all bibliographies are in printed form. The quite extensive bibliography, "Jewish Resistance Against the Nazis during World War II," is mimeographed and available through its author, J. R. Bennett.[9] Its twenty-six pages contain a total of 255 entries, including 75 from English sources. It is well annotated and carries some personal critcal judgments. These sources given are from books, journals, and bulletins published between 1950 and 1977.

There are a number of other bibliographies on general topics. Some are part of the Yad Vashem and YIVO publications, such as Jacob Robinson's *The Holocaust: The Nuremberg Evidence* (1966). Robinson subsequently published *The Holocaust and After: Sources and Literature in English* (Israel: University Press, 1973), and together with Yehuda Bauer edited *Guide to Unpublished Materials of the Holocaust Period* in three volumes (Jerusalem, 1970–1975).

Specialized bibliographies have also been published. One, sponsored by Yad Vashem and YIVO, is Randolph Braham's *The Hungarian Jewish Catastrophe: A Selected and Annotated Bibliography* (1962). Another one is Robert Singerman's *Anti-Semitic Propaganda,* which is also an annotated bibliography and guide (New York, 1962). This bibliography carries 24,000 entries. Another bibliography, containing abstracts of over 1,000 articles, is called *The Third Reich, 1933–1938.* It is a historical bibliography published as ABC-Clio Research Guide no. 9 (1983).

Another bibliography, entitled *The Holocaust: An Annotated Bibliography,* was compiled by Harry J. Cargas and published by the Catholic Library Association in 1977. The National Holocaust Remembrance Committee of the Canadian Jewish Congress published an annotated bibliography, *The Holocaust,* in 1980, written by Joseph Sharon. This work also contains photographic aids, resource kits, and teachers' guides and classroom libraries.

Even though Lucy S. Dawidowicz, a prominent professor of Jewish history, maintains in her seminal work *The War Against the Jews* (Philadelphia, 1975) that "it would be impracticable and immodest to attempt to present a full bibliography of the Final Solution and the Holocaust" (p. 437), she does provide a list of resource material which includes the sixty-seven volumes of *Guides to German Records Microfilmed at Alexandria, Virginia.* The study of the sources indicated in her bibliography would have to extend beyond the lifetime of an individual researcher. Considerable differences exist between the bibliography given here and that in her recent updated, revised edition.

The recently published study regarding the inability of American Jewry to rescue Jews during World War II, Haskel Lookstein's *Were We Our Brothers' Keepers,* includes an extensive bibliography. It leans heavily upon American journalistic reportage; Dawidowicz quotes much German-language source material. Both bibliographies are substantial and may serve as a further guide.

In many works, besides the bibliographies, copious bibliographical material may be culled from the references which are cited in the notes to each chapter. In Nora Levin's *The Holocaust* (New York, 1968), the notes contain hundreds of bibliographical details.

Some works are almost entirely bibliographical in that the work reproduces or illustrates its bibliographical references. An example is Jack Kugelmass and Jonathan Boyarin's *From a Ruined Garden,* subtitled *The Memorial Books of Polish Jewry* (New York: Schocken Books, 1981). The bibliography consists of one hundered *yisker bikher* in Yiddish. Selections from these memorial books, translated into English, make up the text of this work. Another variety of bibliographies to be studied is one where illustrations of the bibliographical notes make up "the main part" of the work, such as *Macmillan's Atlas.*

The extent to which bibliographical material relating to the Holocaust is also evident in the bibliographies of monographs may be seen, for example, in Konnilyn G. Feig's *Hitler's Death Camps* (New York, 1981). It is perhaps an arbitrary choice. Nevertheless, it is used as an example of a work supplying a wealth of bibliographical data, and even more. It is a work which gives road directions to the major camp sites (pp. 447–450). It lists archives and collections and secondary material in a formal bibliography (pp. 506–534).

This reviewer was impressed by the extensive bibliographies detailed in the notes to each part of the book (pp. 461–501). There is, for example, a list of films on the Holocaust given in a footnote (n. 38 on p. 483), which is quite extensive, although perhaps not entirely complete.

Another area of research to be explored would be the bibliographical studies regarding the leading individuals, including those for whom monographs have been published, such as Molly Abramowitz's *Elie Wiesel: A Bibliography* (Scarecrow Press, 1978).

For bibliographical essays, especially for Orthodox readers, see my article in the Passover 1986 issue of *Amit Women*. General essays on the Holocaust are published without number. A good collection is contained in the *Simon Wiesenthal Center Annual,* four volumes of which have appeared so far.

As a most comprehensive listing of works on Jewish life and scholarship during the Holocaust, one may want to consult Jacob Robinson and Philip Friedman's *Guide to Jewish History under Nazi Impact,* published by YIVO and Yad Vashem with Ktav Publishers in 1974.

The ongoing *Holocaust and Genocide Studies Journal,* under the chief editorship of Yehuda Bauer, made its debut in the spring of 1986.[10] Its proclaimed aims and scope may well sum up the endeavors in Holocaust studies:

> The aim of *Holocaust and Genocide Studies* is to publish the foremost scholarly material reflecting the best in contemporary thought on the Holocaust and the related study of genocide. The journal will contain original material, research and review articles.
>
> By its publication policy, the journal will resolutely endeavour to support all those who combat genocidal practices and maximize human rights worldwide.

NOTES

1. Yad Vashem, Jerusalem, Israel; Yivo, 1048 Fifth Avenue, New York, N.Y.
2. *Congress Weekly* 31, no. 4 (Feb. 24, 1984): 7–13.

3. See Lea Rubinska, *Times of the Holocaust: No Excuse for Apathy.*

4. See the catalogues published by the Centre de Documentation Juive Contemporaine, Paris, France.

5. See the list of titles published by Schocken Judaica.

6. It lists two articles on 723, "Art and Culture After the Holocaust," *Cross Currents,* Fall 1976, and "Conversation with Nelly Sachs," *Jewish Heritage,* Spring 1968.

7. *Night* in subsection 10, p. 386, and *One Generation After* in subsection 15, p. 669.

8. The figures given in the *Encyclopedia Judaica,* vol. 10, p. 1263 "191 synagogues were set on fire and 76 were completely destroyed, ... 171 dwellings were set on fire or destroyed totally" is totally *inadequate.* The entry is authored by Lionel Kochan, who also wrote *Pogrom* (1957), and is based on German reports.

9. English Department, University of Arkansas, Fayetteville, Ark. 72701.

10. Pergamon Press, Fairview Park, Elmsford, N.Y. 10523.

Yom Hashoah Services
and Memorials

Yom Ha-Shoah Service

RABBI DAVID STAVSKY

PSALM 121

שִׁיר לַמַּעֲלוֹת אֶשָּׂא עֵינַי אֶל־הֶהָרִים מֵאַיִן יָבֹא עֶזְרִי: עֶזְרִי מֵעִם יְיָ עֹשֵׂה שָׁמַיִם
וָאָרֶץ: אַל־יִתֵּן לַמּוֹט רַגְלֶךָ אַל־יָנוּם שֹׁמְרֶךָ: הִנֵּה לֹא־יָנוּם וְלֹא יִישָׁן שׁוֹמֵר יִשְׂרָאֵל:
יְיָ שֹׁמְרֶךָ יְיָ צִלְּךָ עַל־יַד יְמִינֶךָ: יוֹמָם הַשֶּׁמֶשׁ לֹא־יַכֶּכָּה וְיָרֵחַ בַּלָּיְלָה: יְיָ יִשְׁמָרְךָ
מִכָּל־רָע יִשְׁמֹר אֶת־נַפְשֶׁךָ: יְיָ יִשְׁמָר־צֵאתְךָ וּבוֹאֶךָ מֵעַתָּה וְעַד־עוֹלָם:

שְׁפֹךְ חֲמָתְךָ אֶל־הַגּוֹיִם, אֲשֶׁר לֹא יְדָעוּךָ וְעַל־מַמְלָכוֹת אֲשֶׁר בְּשִׁמְךָ לֹא קָרָאוּ: כִּי
אָכַל אֶת־יַעֲקֹב, וְאֶת־נָוֵהוּ הֵשַׁמּוּ: שְׁפָךְ־עֲלֵיהֶם זַעְמֶךָ, וַחֲרוֹן אַפְּךָ יַשִּׂיגֵם: תִּרְדֹּף
בְּאַף וְתַשְׁמִידֵם, מִתַּחַת שְׁמֵי יְיָ:

A SONG OF ASCENTS

I will lift up mine eyes unto the mountains:
From whence shall my help come?
My help cometh from the Lord,
Who made heaven and earth.

He will not suffer thy foot to be moved;
He that keepeth thee will not slumber.
Behold, He that keepeth Israel
Doth neither slumber nor sleep.

The Lord is thy keeper; The Lord is thy shade upon thy right hand.
The sun shall not smite thee by day,
Nor the moon by night.

The Lord shall keep thee from all evil;
He shall keep thy soul.

The Lord shall guard thy going out and thy coming in,
From this time forth and forever.

Remember

A Yom haShoah Reader

Rabbi

In memory of those who gave their lives for
the sanctity of the Jewish people . . . and in
living tribute to our fathers and mothers,
brothers and sisters destroyed by the Nazi
onslaught . . . we are each of us obliged to
see ourselves in every generation of survivors
of the Holocaust, to the end of time.

(*Isachar Miron*)

Congregation

We are still haunted by the warning of the
Holocaust: that the incredible can become
credible, that the impossible can become
possible, if we do not act as we should in
time.

(*Vladka Meed*)

Rabbi

To forget constitutes a crime against
memory . . . whoever forgets becomes the
executioner's accomplice.

(*Elie Wiesel*)

Congregation	*Remember: do not forget!* (*Deuteronomy* 9:7)

The innocent and pure were murdered—man, woman and child—with poison gas and in fiery furnaces.

Rabbi

"All around us were screams, death, smoking chimneys making the air black and heavy with soot and the smell of burning bodies."

(*Kitty Hart*)

Congregation

At night, the red sky over Auschwitz could be seen for miles.

(*Lucy Dawidowicz*)

Rabbi

In the face of their oppression, Jews did *not* cringe.

"They prayed in secret; their children learned in secret; they held lectures in Jewish history in secret; and they even conducted a symphony in secret."

(*Kitty Hart*)

Congregation

They lived as if stretching time itself to prolong existence and to deny to Hitler even for another hour, another minute, another second, the fulfillment of his dream of an earth empty of Jews.

(*Abraham H. Foxman*)

Rabbi

They did *not* get down on their knees and beg for mercy. They weren't led like sheep to the slaughter. The Jews fought back!

"The question is not *why* all the Jews did not

fight, but *how* so many of them did. Tor-
mented, beaten, starved—where did they
find the strength, spiritual and physical, to
resist?"

(Elie Wiesel)

Pour out thy wrath upon the nations that know Thee not, and upon
the kingdoms that call not upon Thy name; for they have consumed
Jacob and laid waste his habitation. Pour out Thy rage upon them
and let Thy fury overtake them. Pursue them in anger and destroy
them from under the heavens of the Eternal.

PSALM 23

(*Rabbi*)

מִזְמוֹר לְדָוִד יְיָ רֹעִי לֹא אֶחְסָר. בִּנְאוֹת דֶּשֶׁא יַרְבִּיצֵנִי עַל־מֵי מְנֻחוֹת יְנַהֲלֵנִי. נַפְשִׁי
יְשׁוֹבֵב יַנְחֵנִי בְמַעְגְּלֵי־צֶדֶק לְמַעַן שְׁמוֹ: גַּם כִּי־אֵלֵךְ בְּגֵיא צַלְמָוֶת לֹא־אִירָא רָע כִּי־
אַתָּה עִמָּדִי שִׁבְטְךָ וּמִשְׁעַנְתֶּךָ הֵמָּה יְנַחֲמֻנִי. תַּעֲרֹךְ לְפָנַי שֻׁלְחָן נֶגֶד צֹרְרָי דִּשַּׁנְתָּ
בַשֶּׁמֶן רֹאשִׁי כּוֹסִי רְוָיָה. אַךְ טוֹב וָחֶסֶד יִרְדְּפוּנִי כָּל־יְמֵי חַיָּי וְשַׁבְתִּי בְּבֵית־יְיָ לְאֹרֶךְ
יָמִים.

Mizmor le-David. Adonai ro'i lo ekhsar. Binot desheh yarbizeini, al
mei menuhot yenahaleni. Nafshi yeshovev, yanheni bemaglei zedek
lema'an shemo. Gam ki elekh begei zalmavet, lo ira ra, ki atah
imadi; Shivtekha umishantekha, hemah yenahamuni. Ta'arokh lefanai
shulhan neged zor'rai; dishanta vashemen roshi, kosi revayah. Akh
tov vahesed yirdefuni kol yemei hayai. Veshavti bevet Adonai, le-
orekh yamim.

Congregational Reading

The Lord is my shepherd; I shall not want. He maketh me to lie
down in green pastures; He leadeth me beside the still waters. He
restoreth my soul; He guideth me in straight paths for His name's

sake. Yea, though I walk through the valley of the shadow of death, I will fear no evil, for Thou art with me; Thy rod and Thy staff, they comfort me. Thou preparest a table before me in the presence of mine enemies: Thou hast anointed my head with oil: my cup runneth over. Surely goodness and mercy shall follow me all the days of my life; and I shall dwell in the house of the Lord forever.

(Rabbi and Congregation responsively)

הירש גליק

זאָג ניט קיינמאָל

זאָג ניט קיינמאָל אַז דו גייסט דעם לעצטן וועג,
כאָטש הימלען בלײַענע פֿאַרשטעלן בלויע טעג,
קומען וועט נאָך אונדזער אויסגעבענקטע שעה,
ס'וועט אַ פויק טאָן אונדזער טראָט — מיר זײַנען דא!

פֿון גרינעם פֿאַלמען־לאַנד ביז ווײַטן לאַנד פֿון שניי
מיר קומען אָן מיט אונזער פּײַן, מיט אונזער וויי,
און וואו געפֿאַלן ס'איז אַ שפּריץ פֿון אונדזער בלוט,
שפּראָצן וועט דאָרט אונדזער גבֿורה, אונדזער מוט.

ס'וועט די מאָרגן־זון באַגילדן אונדז דעם הײַנט,
און דער נעכטן וועט פֿאַרשווינדן מיטן פֿײַנט,
נאָר אויב פֿאַרזאַמען וועט די זון און דער קאַיאָר —
ווי אַ פּאַראָל זאָל גיין דאָס ליד פֿון דור צו דור.

דאָס ליד געשריבן איז מיט בלוט און ניט מיט בלײַ,
ס'איז ניט קיין לידל פֿון אַ פויגל אויף דער פֿרײַ,

דאָס האָט אַ פֿאָלק צווישן פֿאַלנדיקע וועגט

דאָס ליד געזונגען מיט נאַגאַנעס אין די הענט.

טאָ זאָג ניט קיינמאָל אַז דו גייסט דעם לעצטן וועג,

כאָטש הימלען בלײַענע פֿאַרשטעלן בלויע טעג, —

קומען וועט נאָך אונדזער אויסגעבענקטע שעה,

ס׳וועט אַ פּויק טאָן אונדזער טראָט: מיר זײַנען דא!

Translated from the Yiddish by Aaron Kramer

Rabbi	Never say that there is only death for you Though leaden skies may be concealing days of blue— Because the hour we have hungered for is near; Beneath our tread the earth shall tremble: We are here!
Congregation	From land of palm-tree to the far-off land of snow We shall be coming with our torment and our woe, And everywhere our blood has sunk into the earth Shall our bravery, our vigor blossom forth!
Rabbi	We'll have the morning sun to set our day aglow, and all our yesterdays shall vanish with the foe, And if the time is long before the sun appears, Then let this song go like a signal through the years.

Congregation   This song was written with our blood and
not with lead;
It's not a song that birds sing overhead,
It was a people, among toppling barricades,
That sang this song of ours with pistols and
grenades.

Rabbi   So never say that there is only death for you.
Leaden skies may be concealing days of
blue—
Yet the hour we have hungered for is near;
Beneath our tread the earth shall tremble:
We are here!

Rabbi

The S.S. Commander of Lublin was a notorious sadistic murderer by the name of Glabochnik. One night to entertain himself, in an ingenious barbaric way, he ordered all the Jews of the city, young and old, men, women and children to an abandoned field on the them until their backs were up against the barbed wire of the field. in hand.

The Jews stood trembling, their hearts quaking with fear. He herded them until their backs were up against the barbed wire of the field.

Then he shouted, "Sing Jews, sing. Sing a happy song, a Hasidic song. Do as I say quickly."

The Jews were baffled, they were frightened, what can they sing?

"Beat them with all your might," he shouted to his S.S. troops. "Push back the Jews." The barbed wire cut into their backs and skins, and they began to fall onto one another. Then someone freed himself and he began to sing.

"Mir vellen zey iberleben, iberleben, iberleben, Avinu, Shebasha-mayim, Avinu Shebashamayim."

"We shall outlive them, outlive them, outlive them, Heavenly Father."

The bruised and bleeding mob of Jews rose and began singing loud-er and louder, and dancing.

Commander Glabochnik at first roared with laughter until he real-ized they weren't accommodating him, they were defeating him. He started to shout, "Stop! Stop singing!" But they refused. They sang the Hasidic melody louder and louder. He panicked and pleaded with them to stop. But the singing and dancing continued.

The Jews were swept by the flood of their emotions, and they sang and they danced. They paid a high price for it. They were brutally beaten for their strange behavior, but their singing and dancing did not stop. And S.S. Commander Globochnik ran back to his barracks in disgust.

(From *Sparks of Glory*)

INTRODUCTION OF GUEST SPEAKER
(*Rabbi*)

GUEST SPEAKER

CANDLELIGHTING SERVICE

ANI MA'AMIN
(*Congregation and Cantor*)

A-ni ma-a-min be-e-mu-nah she-lei-mah
Be-vi'at ha-mashi'ah.
Ve-af al pi she-yit-ma-he-mei-a,
Im kol zeh a-ni ma'amin.

PROCESSIONAL

CANDLELIGHTING SERVICE

Six million died! More than one third of the Jewish population of the world.

The whole world stood by, silent.

In 1942, the country that regarded itself as the most civilized nation in the world, Germany, *die Kulturträger!* Germany, the center of culture, was responsible for the death of six million Jews. Among them were young innocent children, the aged, sick, defenseless and helpless people.

Six million died. We must not forget them. Their death shall not be in vain. This shall never happen again.

In our tradition we light a Yahrzeit candle for the death of our loved ones.

Let us light six candles, one for each million.

First Candle

In memory of helpless infants, children, and teenagers who were cut down like young trees before their time . . . before they had a chance to experience life.

We shall not forget!

Second Candle

In memory of all mothers who died with their children in their arms.

We shall not forget!

Third Candle

In memory of all mothers and fathers who were cruelly separated from their families

We shall not forget!

Fourth Candle

In memory of all scholars, teachers, rabbis who were the first to be seized.

We shall not forget!

Fifth Candle

In memory of the "heroes of the resistance" who fought the Nazis—so few against so many.

We shall not forget!

Sixth Candle

In memory of the martyrs who gave their lives to help their brothers under the Nazis.

We shall not forget!

While the six candles burn in memory of our loved ones, let us rise for the Memorial Prayer.

MEMORIAL PRAYER
(*Rabbi*)

God of Abraham, Isaac, and Jacob:

We remember this day the nameless millions of martyrs of the children of Israel for whom there exists no monument nor final resting place other than in our own inner recesses. With heavy heart, we bear the tragedy of the death of a full third of Your children, our brothers and sisters, offered up by the Nazis on altars of savagery and demonic brutality. There is not the Jewish family over whose home there does not hover a pall of grief at the wanton murder of relatives during the years of the unforgettable Holocaust.

You did bid us to remember from generation to generation the inhumanity of Amalek. Can we ever forget the sadism of the followers of Hitler?

Help us, O Lord, that in remembering the dead, we do not remain in the abyss of hatred, but rise to the mountain of resolve. We must sanctify the names of the *Kedoshim* whose deaths deepend the holiness of Your chosen people. We must dedicate ourselves to the perpetuation of Your saving remnant through greater devotion to Your holy Torah and through dedication to the creation of a holy land in the State of Israel, The land of Your promise.

May our tears of mourning and signs of grief be acceptable to You as we accompany them with consectation to the fulfillment of Your divine mandate for the exaltation of K'lal Yisrael and the ennoblement of all men.

Amen

EL MOLEH RAHAMIN
(*Cantor*)

MOURNER'S KADDISH

יִתְגַּדַּל וְיִתְקַדַּשׁ שְׁמֵהּ רַבָּא.בְּעָלְמָא דִּי בְרָא כִרְעוּתֵהּ.וְיַמְלִיךְ מַלְכוּתֵהּ.בְּחַיֵּיכוֹן וּבְיוֹמֵיכוֹן. וּבְחַיֵּי דְכָל בֵּית יִשְׂרָאֵל. בַּעֲגָלָא וּבִזְמַן קָרִיב. וְאִמְרוּ אָמֵן:

Congregation and mourners respond:

יְהֵא שְׁמֵהּ רַבָּא מְבָרַךְ. לְעָלַם וּלְעָלְמֵי עָלְמַיָּא:

יִתְבָּרַךְ. וְיִשְׁתַּבַּח. וְיִתְפָּאַר. וְיִתְרוֹמַם. וְיִתְנַשֵּׂא. וְיִתְהַדָּר. וְיִתְעַלֶּה. וְיִתְהַלָּל. שְׁמֵהּ דְּקוּדְשָׁא

Congregation and mourners respond:

בְּרִיךְ הוּא.

לְעֵלָּא מִן־כָּל־בִּרְכָתָא. וְשִׁירָתָא. תֻּשְׁבְּחָתָא. וְנֶחֱמָתָא. דַּאֲמִירָן בְּעָלְמָא. וְאִמְרוּ
אָמֵן:

יְהֵא שְׁלָמָא רַבָּא מִן שְׁמַיָּא. וְחַיִּים. עָלֵינוּ וְעַל כָּל יִשְׂרָאֵל. וְאִמְרוּ אָמֵן:
עוֹשֶׂה שָׁלוֹם בִּמְרוֹמָיו. הוּא יַעֲשֶׂה שָׁלוֹם. עָלֵינוּ וְעַל־כָּל־יִשְׂרָאֵל. וְאִמְרוּ אָמֵן:

Congregation and morners respond:

Yisgaddal ve-yiskaddash sh'meih rabbbo, b'ol'mo dee-v'ro ḥir'oo-
seih, v'yamleeḥ mal'hooseih, b'ḥayyueihon uv'yomeihon, uv'ḥayyei
d'ḥol beis Yisroeil, ba-agolo uviz'man koreev, v'im'ru Omein.

Yehei sh'meih rabbo m'voraḥ, l'olam ul'ol'mei ol'mayyo.

Yisboraḥ v'yishtabbaḥ, v'yispoar, v'yisromam, v'yisnassei, v'yis-
haddar, v'yisalleh v'yis-hallal, sh'meih d'koodsho

B'reeḥ Hu,

L'eil'lo min kol bir'ḥoso, v'sheeroso, tooshb'ḥoso, v'neḥemoso, da-
ameeron b'ol'mo, v'im'ru Omein.

Yehei sh'lomo rabbo min sh'mayyo, v'ḥayyem, olei'nu v'al kol
Yisroeil, v'im'ru Omein.

Oseh sholom bim'romov, hu ya-aseh sholom, olei'nu v'al kol Yisroeil, vim'ru Omein.

PRAYER FOR THE STATE OF ISRAEL
(Rabbi)

אָבִינוּ שֶׁבַּשָּׁמַיִם. צוּר יִשְׂרָאֵל וְגוֹאֲלוֹ. בָּרֵךְ אֶת־מְדִינַת יִשְׂרָאֵל רֵאשִׁית צְמִיחַת
גְּאֻלָּתֵנוּ, הָגֵן עָלֶיהָ בְּאֶבְרַת חַסְדֶּךָ וּפְרֹשׂ עָלֶיהָ סֻכַּת שְׁלוֹמֶךָ. וּשְׁלַח אוֹרְךָ וַאֲמִתְּךָ
לְרָאשֶׁיהָ שָׂרֶיהָ וְיוֹעֲצֶיהָ, וְתַקְּנֵם בְּעֵצָה טוֹבָה מִלְּפָנֶיךָ. חַזֵּק אֶת יְדֵי מְגִנֵּי אֶרֶץ
קָדְשֵׁנוּ, וְהַנְחִילֵם אֱלֹהֵינוּ יְשׁוּעָה וַעֲטֶרֶת נִצָּחוֹן תְּעַטְּרֵם. וְנָתַתָּ שָׁלוֹם בָּאָרֶץ
וְשִׂמְחַת עוֹלָם לְיוֹשְׁבֶיהָ, וְנֹאמַר אָמֵן.

Our Father in Heavem, Rock and Redeemer of the people Israel:
Bless the State of Israel, the dawn of our redemption. Shield it with
Your love; spread over it the shelter of Your peace. Guide its leaders
and advisors with Your light and Your truth. Help them with Your
good counsel. Strengthen the hands of those who defend our Holy
Land. Deliver them; crown their efforts with triumph. Bless the land
with peace, and its inhabitants with lasting joy. And let us say:
Amen.

כָּל עוֹד בַּלֵּבָב פְּנִימָה. נֶפֶשׁ יְהוּדִי הוֹמִיָּה.
וּלְפַאֲתֵי מִזְרָח קָדִימָה. עַיִן לְצִיּוֹן צוֹפִיָּה:
עוֹד לֹא אָבְדָה תִקְוָתֵנוּ. הַתִּקְוָה שְׁנוֹת אַלְפַּיִם.
לִהְיוֹת עַם חָפְשִׁי בְּאַרְצֵנוּ. בְּאֶרֶץ צִיּוֹן וִירוּשָׁלָיִם:

Kol od ba-lei-vav pe-ni-ma,
ne-fesh ye-hu-di ho-mi-ya.
U-le-fa-a-tei Miz-raḥ ka-di-ma
a-yin le-tsi-yon tso-fi-ya.

Od lo a-ve-da tik-va-tei-nu,
ha-tik-va she-not al-pa-yim,
li-he-yot am ḥof-shi be-ar-tsei-nu,
be-e-rets tsi-yon vi-ru-sha-la-yim.

Alei Sho'ah

Rabbi Dr. Israel Lerner

קינה על השואה

עֲלֵי שׁוֹאָה וּמְשׁוֹאָה   עֲלֵי הַדּוּךְ וְעַל הַתֹּם

שֶׁלֹּא יָדַעְנוּ כְּמוֹתָהּ,   יְלָדִים חַפִּים מִפֶּשַׁע,

רִשְׁעֵי־עוֹלָם רָצְחוּ וְרָצוּ   שֶׁכֻּלּוֹ כְּלֹא הָיוּ

לִרְאוֹת אוּמָה בְּמוֹתָהּ.   בְּעוֹלָם חָשׁוּךְ מֵרֶשַׁע.

עֲלֵי כָּל קְהִלָּה קְדוֹשָׁה   עֲלֵי הַשֹּׁד וְהַבְּעֵרָה,

שֶׁנִּשְׂרְפָה בְּאֵשׁ צָרֶיהָ,   שֶׁיָּקְדָה חֳדָשִׁים, שָׁנִים, —

עֲצֵי חַיִּים, שֶׁעָלוּ בְּלֶהָבוֹת,   לֹא כְּמַשּׂוּאוֹת בֶּהָרִים —

תּוֹרָה, תּוֹרָה עִם גְּוִילֶיהָ.   בְּשָׂרְפָם קְדוֹשִׁים בַּכִּבְשָׁנִים.

עֲלֵי יְשִׁיבוֹת וּבָתֵּי־מִדְרָשׁוֹת,   עֲלֵי חֵטְא שֶׁל אֲזֶלַת־יָד

הֶחָלַף בְּ"מָלֵא" נִגּוּן גְּמָרָא,   בְּעוֹלָם שֶׁהֶחֱרִישׁ וְדָמַם.

עַל יְשָׁרִים וְגִבּוֹרִים,   נִקְרַשׁ לֵב־אָדָם וְלֹא רָעַד

שֶׁנִּשְׁמָתָם יָצְאָה בְּטָהֳרָה.   בְּעֵת שֶׁשָּׁתַת וְנִגַּר הַדָּם.

עֲלֵי אָבוֹת וְאִמָּהוֹת,   עֲלֵי כָּל הַשְּׁמָדוֹת וְהַהֶרֶג

שֶׁלֹּא זָכוּ לִשְׂמֹחַ בְּנֵיהֶם,   בְּדִבְרֵי יְמֵי עַם־עוֹלָם,

וְעַל בָּנִים וְעַל בָּנוֹת   לֹא נִשְׁכַּח, לֹא נִסְלַח לָהֶם,

שֶׁלֹּא הֵקִימוּ אֶת בָּתֵּיהֶם.   אוֹת־קַיִן לְדִרְאוֹן עוֹלָם.

עַל כָּל הַקִּינוֹת וְהַתְּחִנּוֹת

לְרִבּוֹן הָעוֹלָם תְּפִלָּה מַפְּנִים:

לְעַמְּךָ מֵעַתָּה תֵּן כֹּחַ וְכָבוֹד,

תַּחַת הַ"הֶסְתֵּר" — הָאֵרַת פָּנִים.

יִשְׂרָאֵל מְלַמֵּד (לֶרְנֶר)

On the Holocaust and the tragedy
Unprecedented, we lament and cry.
The wicked murdered and wished to see
An entire people disappear and die.

For every holy community,
Consumed by crematoria fire,
Trees of life wrapped in parchment,
Torah, Torah on a pyre.

For yeshivot and houses of study,
Instead of Gemara melody lure,
The stark sadness of the *maleh*
For holy souls brave and pure.

For the fathers and the mothers,
The daughters and the sons,
Who never experienced joys of weddings,
The homes of beloved ones.

For all the innocent children,
Free from guilt and all sin
In a darkened evil world
Perished as if they had never been.

Of flames burning, burning,
Not as bonfires on a hill,
Months and years soul-searing,
Fires which did our martyrs kill.

For the callousness of heart,
The mean spirit demeaning man,
When there withdrew saving hands
To stanch the blood which ran and ran.

For all the deaths in history inflicted,
For all our suffering and our pain,
We shall not forget nor withdraw
From the enemy the sign of Cain.

From lamentations and sorrow
From our grief we do pine,
Vouchsafe to your people strength and honor,
Master of the World, a heavenly sign!

Israel Melamed (Lerner)